PRAISE FOR THE FIRST EDITION

"[This book] satisfies a long-standing need for a comprehensive guide to the many public gardens that grace New York City . . . Readers will find themselves looking at public gardens with an increased awareness of their intent, design, and value . . . Although compact in size, it fulfills its ambitious title with intelligence and largesse."

—Diane Schaub, Central Park Conservancy

". . . a refuge from the concrete, or added to a bookshelf of other guidebooks . . . it can help New Yorkers find the riches that are theirs in this great city."

—*Urban Outdoors*

"A celebration of New York City horticulture . . . the reader feels a wonderful secret is being shared."

—Brooklyn Botanical Garden

Garden Guide:
New York City

REVISED EDITION

Garden Guide: New York City

REVISED EDITION

Nancy Berner and Susan Lowry

PHOTOGRAPHS BY JOSEPH DE SCIOSE

W. W. Norton & Company

New York • London

Title page: aerial view of Bryant Park
Copyright © 2010, 2002 by Nancy Berner and Susan Lowry
Photographs (unless otherwise noted) copyright © 2010, 2002 by Joseph De Sciose

For information about permission to reproduce selections
from this book, write to Permissions,
W. W. Norton & Company, Inc., 500 Fifth Avenue, New York, NY 10110

For information about special discounts for bulk purchases, please contact
W. W. Norton Special Sales at specialsales@wwnorton.com or 800-233-4830.

Composition and book design by Jonathan Lippincott
Manufacturing by Everbest
Electronic production: Joe Lops
Production Manager: Leeann Graham

Library of Congress Cataloging-in-Publication Data
Berner, Nancy, 1950–
  Garden guide : New York City / Nancy Berner & Susan Lowry ; photographs by
Joseph De Sciose. — Rev. ed.
    p. cm.
  Includes index.
  ISBN 978-0-393-73307-5 (pbk.)
  1. Gardens—New York (State)—New York—Guidebooks. 2. New York (N.Y.)—
Guidebooks. I. Lowry, Susan, 1951– II. De Sciose, Joseph. III. Title.
  SB466.U65N727 2010
  712.09747'1—dc22
                                    2009033125
  ISBN 13: 978-0-393-70530-0

W. W. Norton & Company, Inc., 500 Fifth Avenue, New York, N.Y. 10110
www.wwnorton.com
W. W. Norton & Company Ltd., Castle House, 75/76 Wells St., London W1T 3QT
9 8 7 6 5 4 3 2 1 0

Contents

Acknowledgments   *11*
Authors' Note   *14*
Preface to the Second Edition   *15*

MANHATTAN
Upper Manhattan
Swindler Cove Park   26
Dyckman Farmhouse Museum   31
The Cloisters   33
The Heather Garden   40
Morris-Jumel Mansion   44
Riverside Valley Community Garden   47
Pleasant Village Community Garden and Neighboring
    Gardens   49
Cathedral Church of St. John the Divine   52

Upper West Side
The Lotus Garden   60
The 91st Street Garden   63
West Side Community Garden   65
Arthur Ross Terrace at the American Museum of Natural
    History   70
Shakespeare Garden   73

Upper East Side
The Conservatory Garden   80

Cooper-Hewitt, National Design Museum, Smithsonian
    Institution   87
The Metropolitan Museum of Art   92
Park Avenue Malls   96
The Frick Collection   101
Central Park Wildlife Center   104
Mount Vernon Hotel Museum and Garden   106

Midtown
Rockefeller Center   112
The Museum of Modern Art   116
Samuel Paley Plaza   121
Greenacre Park   123
United Nations Neighborhood Gardens   125
The Ford Foundation   130
Tudor City Greens   132
The Howard A. Rusk Institute of Rehabilitation
    Medicine   135
Gramercy Park   138
General Theological Seminary   141
Herald Square and Greeley Square   144
Bryant Park   147
Clinton Community Garden   154
Balsley Park   157

Downtown
The High Line   162
Vera List Courtyard   170
Jefferson Market Garden   173
Sheridan Square Viewing Garden and Neighboring
    Gardens   175

The Garden at the Church of St. Luke in the Fields   178
Canal Park and Duane Park   180
Washington Market Park   186
Hudson River Park   188
Battery Park City   192
The Gardens at the Battery   202
The Elevated Acre   209
British Memorial Garden at Hanover Square   211
Federal Plaza and City Hall Park   214
M'Finda Kalunga Garden   217
Lower East Side Community Gardens   219
Merchant's House Museum   229

BRONX

The Rainforest Garden at Patterson Houses   238
Bronx County Courthouse Greenroof Garden   241
Taqwa Community Farm   245
Tremont Community Garden   247
Garden of Happiness   250
The New York Botanical Garden   252
The Enchanted Garden   266
Wave Hill   269
Bartow-Pell Mansion Museum   278

BROOKLYN

The Green Dome Garden   288
Brooklyn Heights Promenade   292
Columbia St. Waterfront District Community
    Gardens   295
Red Hook Gardens   300
The Brooklyn Bear's Community Gardens   308

Brooklyn Botanic Garden   311
Hattie Carthan Community Garden   321
Brooklyn Public Library, Saratoga Branch   326
The Floyd Bennett Gardens   329
The Narrows Botanical Gardens   331

QUEENS
Isamu Noguchi Garden Museum   340
Gantry Plaza State Park   343
Queens Botanical Garden   349
Queens County Farm Museum   356
Veterans Memorial Garden   361
Mother Carter Garden   363
Curtis "50 Cent" Jackson Community Garden   365
Merrick Marsden Community Garden   368

STATEN ISLAND
Snug Harbor Cultural Center and Botanical Garden   376
Jacques Marchais Museum of Tibetan Art   388
Stephens-Prier House at Historic Richmond Town   392
Bayview Habitat   394
The Conference House Park   396

Listings by Category   399
Greening Organizations   409
Credits   416
Index   417

Acknowledgments

Both the first edition of our book and this second edition would not have been possible without the generosity of the countless gardeners, both professional and amateur, who tend the city's gardens. Their enthusiasm and dedication were an inspiration to us, and we feel privileged to share their stories and their gardens. First and foremost, our thanks to Lynden B. Miller and Diane Schaub, who are Director and Curator of the Conservatory Garden, respectively. Not only are they responsible for one of the city's crown jewels, but Lynden has shared her knowledge of the city's gardens and their histories with us, and she and Diane have taught us much about what makes a garden great. Lynden's passion and commitment for the public gardens of the city has been an inspiration. We especially thank the Conservatory staff and our fellow Tuesday volunteers, who have cheered on this project from the beginning.

We are grateful to other stewards and designers of gardens who have been particularly helpful, including Thomas Balsley, Nancy Chambers, Billie Cohen, Maureen Hackett, Kathy Holler, Galen Lee, Patricia McCobb, Camilla McFadden, Susan Moody, Dave Murbach, Signe Nielsen, Chris Seita, Mary Riley Smith, Nancy Tim, David Varnell, and Lee Weintraub.

Without the help of the keepers of institutional memory, the history of many of these gardens would be hard to trace, since few have written records. For their considerable assistance, we thank Mary Bloom, Neil Calet, Nick Dowen,

Nancy Fitzpatrick, Steve Gould, Herb Katz, Catha Grace Rambusch, Joanna H. Schoff, Arthur Sheppard, Barbara Stonecipher, and Anne Whidden.

We greatly appreciate the help we received from the staff at New York's four outstanding botanical gardens. Karl F. Lauby at The New York Botanical Garden, Josie Phelps at Brooklyn Botanic Garden, Susan Lacerte and her staff at Queens Botanical Garden, and Frances X. Huber at the Snug Harbor Cultural Center and Botanical Garden have all gone out of their way to be accommodating, answering endless questions and helping us gather information about the gardening communities within their boroughs.

Community gardeners throughout the city welcomed us warmly, sharing information as well as their harvests with us. We deeply appreciate the time they took with us, and thank them for their hospitality. They include Jenny Benitez, Launa Beuhler, Miss Ruth Carter, Yu'en Chen, Jon Crow, Norma Cruz, Juliette Davis, Bill Dodds, Pedro Figureo, Melinda Futrell, Bob Halligan, Sebert Harper, James Johnson, Diana Signe Klein, Claire Merlino, Margaret Moore, Meg Movshon, Anne Spira, Abu Talib, Tony Thoman and all the students at the Enchanted Garden, Eric Thomann, and Karen Washington.

The many greening organizations have been a great resource for us. Especially helpful have been Howard Hemmings of the New York City Housing Authority, Paula Hewitt of Open Road of New York, Lenny Librizzi from Council on the Environment of New York City, Michael O'Connor of Bronx Green-Up, Andy Stone and Paul Coppa of The Trust for Public Land, Margaret Ternes of the Park Avenue Planting Project, Julie Warsowe of Brooklyn GreenBridge, and

Jane Weissman of Battery Park City, as well as Edie Kean, whose extensive knowledge of community gardens and designer's eye were invaluable.

The parks department's history project has uncovered a treasure trove of information about our public spaces, and their work has been invaluable. We thank them for sharing some still unpublished work, and for the informational plaques that are posted on parks all over the city. Scott Sendrow, historian in the Arts and Antiques Department, was enthusiastic in responding to our many requests, and Audrey Davis, in the Queens office of the parks department, especially helped us in that borough.

For this second edition, we would like to thank the following: Elizabeth Butler, Ursula Chance, Ben Diaz, Todd Forrest, Karl F. Lauby, Sally Leone, and Kate Shackford in the Bronx; Susan Fowler, Frances X. Huber, Greg Lord, Brian Morris, and Gertrude Sokolowsky in Staten Island; Tim Heimerle and Susan Lacerte in Queens; Julie Farris, Yonette Fleming, A. J. Loeffler, Ian Marvy, Avigail Milder, Sarah Wayland Smith, Michael Van Valkenburgh, and Amir Yarkoni in Brooklyn; and Dick Connette, Melissa Fisher, Amy Gavaris, Sigrid Gray, Jane Greenlaw, Camilla Hellman, Bob Humber, Kenneth Karpel, Dierdre Larkin, Alexis Lowry, John Rommel, and Ken Smith in Manhattan. We would like to thank our editor at Norton, Andrea Costella, for her invaluable help in preparing this new edition of *Garden Guide*.

Authors' Note

The term *garden* often is used loosely to denote anything from a small planting bed to a sports venue, but we have been guided in our choices for this book by a traditional interpretation: a garden is an enclosed piece of ground dedicated to the cultivation of plants. While some of the gardens we have chosen are not literally enclosed, each has a strong sense of place. Metaphorically, at least, there are walls between the garden and the street. Plant material is always an integral element of the design.

New York is fortunate in the number and variety of its gardens and any selective list is bound to leave out a number of worthy examples. There are over 400 community gardens in New York. Each has its own voice in the choir, and although we have only been able to describe a small fraction of them, we have sought to include as many different voices as possible.

We have tried to describe the gardens as faithfully as possible, but visitors should remember that gardens are organic, living designs. Plants die, grow, or are replaced, making one of the delights of garden visiting the opportunity to note the changes wrought by the seasons and then the years, as one returns again and again.

Preface to the Second Edition

In 2001, when we were working on the first edition of *Garden Guide* and would tell people that we were writing a guidebook to New York City gardens, the reaction was often skepticism, if not disbelief: Where exactly would we find these gardens? Were there really enough to fill a whole book? What a difference eight years can make. Now, New Yorkers of all walks of life have taken notice of their communal landscapes and there is clearly a shared recognition of their importance to our lives. Putting together the words "greening" and "New York" finally makes some sense.

Since 2002, many new gardens have been added to our city—major design ventures like the High Line and the gardens at the Battery, cutting-edge sustainable projects like the new visitors' center at the Queens Botanical Garden and the Bronx County Courthouse greenroof, serious urban farming efforts like the Red Hook Community Farm. This second edition of *Garden Guide* includes ten important new city gardens and many other, smaller ones, none of which existed when the first edition was published. Many of these new gardens are in downtown Manhattan, where we see the influence of the Lower Manhattan Development Corporation, which is charged with directing the city's recovery from 9/11.

As the landscape architect Michael Van Valkenburgh has said, landscape has gone from the caboose to the engine of development. And these new projects are creative and forward-thinking, setting a high standard for the future. The city is reclaiming its shoreline at an unprecedented rate: not just in Manhattan, with Battery Park City and Hudson River Park, but throughout the five boroughs, with projects like Swindler Cove Park, Brooklyn Bridge Park, and the Red Hook gardens, whose view of the harbor is one of the city's best-kept secrets. The parks department has built several small waterfront parks at Hunt's Point in the Bronx on what was previously no man's land and the Bronx River is being brought back to life; the riverfront in Long Island City in Queens also has a large new park.

It is not only in major public projects that we see this resurgence of gardens and green space. Community gardens, many of which were threatened with extinction ten years ago, are thriving thanks to groups like the Trust for Public Land, the New York Restoration Project, and the parks department's GreenThumb program. Many of our community gardens not only beautify their communities and provide much-needed green space to park-starved neighborhoods, but also serve as urban farms, providing fresh food and often educating young people about food production.

This has been a period of great park and garden building in New York. The parks department is committed to their survival—working creatively to put together partnerships that can carve out new parks for the city and also sustain the city's green space for the future. This vision of a green city is supported as well by Mayor Bloomberg's blueprint for the city's next growth phase, PlaNYC. Going forward, we can only hope that the momentum will continue and that our green spaces will thrive and remain a resilient and vital part of the city.

Garden Guide: New York City

REVISED EDITION

The Elevated Acre

MANHATTAN

MANHATTAN

An aerial view of Manhattan reveals a large, rectangular block of green surrounded by a vast stone and steel grid. The green is, of course, Central Park, and this dynamic relationship between the natural and the man-made is one that is repeated throughout Manhattan. The dialogue between the two is central to our appreciation of city gardens, as the intensity and urgency of the streetscape heightens the experience of the garden. We prize the slackening of the city's pressure, and even the smallest of gardens has a large impact. Paley Park is just a sliver of Midtown, but it is enjoyed by thousands on any given day and has influenced generations of urban planners.

As befits the center of one of the greatest metropolises in the world, Manhattan has an extraordinary number of museums, foundations, libraries, and universities, which boast a correspondingly large number of gardens created to enhance their prestige. These institutions provide the money and resources to commission great designers. Where else can the works of Dan Kiley, Robert Zion, and Russell Page be seen within walking distance of the masterpiece of Frederick Law Olmsted and Calvert Vaux?

It is somewhat ironic that a city known for its dense urbanity should also be famous for its parks. Central Park is of course the icon, but recent additions like the High Line ensure that Manhattan is once again at the forefront of innovation and park design.

Manhattan is also the birthplace of the city's community gardening movement, and the cluster of gardens on the Lower East Side, with their compost bins, folk art fences, and decidedly multicultural flavor, could not provide a greater contrast to the lofty tone of the formal gardens of our cultural institutions or the sleek design of our newest parks. These are the opposite ends of the spectrum; in between, there are gardens in every neighborhood, and they are as varied and unexpected as Manhattan itself.

Park Avenue Malls

1 Swindler Cove Park

2 Dyckman Farmhouse Museum

3 The Cloisters

4 The Heather Garden

5 Morris-Jumel Mansion

6 Riverside Valley Community Garden

7 Pleasant Village Community Garden and
       Neighboring Gardens

8 Cathedral Church of St. John the Divine

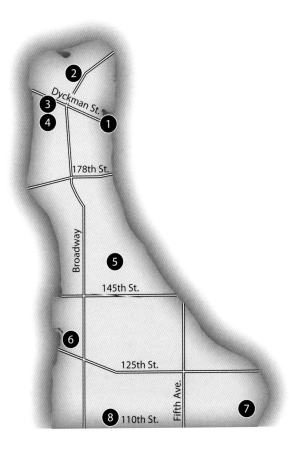

2

Dyckman St.

3

4

1

178th St.

Broadway

5

145th St.

6

125th St.

Fifth Ave.

8 110th St.

7

Swindler Cove Park

Location: Harlem River Drive and Dyckman St. at Tenth Ave.
Hours: 8:00am–8:00pm (summer); 8:00am–4:00pm (winter)
Garden info: (212) 333-2552
Web site: www.nyrp.org
Admission fee: no*
Bus: BxM3
Subway: 1 to Dyckman St.
Facilities: wheelchair accessible, rest rooms
Best seasons: spring, summer, fall

Located on a piece of no-man's-land at the intersection of the
Harlem River Drive and Dyckman Street, Swindler Cove Park
is an ambitious five-acre riverfront park that has transformed
a derelict stretch of waterfront into a showpiece of environmental and civic sensitivity. It is the linchpin in an ambitious plan to green the shore of the Harlem River from Tenth
Avenue and Dyckman all the way south to the historic High
Bridge. Bette Midler's New York Restoration Project (NYRP)
was the driving force in this collaborative initiative between
the New York Department of Transportation, NYRP, and the
NYC Department of Parks & Recreation. NYRP has been
designated as the manager of this park by the parks department and provides ongoing maintenance and care.

A hundred years ago, when this part of Inwood consisted

*For sites that charge admission, we have not listed the exact amounts,
which often change over time. Call or check the garden's Web site for up-
to-date information.

mostly of country estates, this spot was the terminus of the Harlem Speedway, which began several miles south at Macomb's Dam on 155th Street. The speedway was a dirt track where drivers would race their horses and carriages to the delight of spectators. It was an informal racing track for many years, and was officially recognized and rebuilt in 1898. Over the years the dirt track gave way to a paved road and horses gave way to cars; eventually, the racing stopped altogether and Robert Moses replaced it with the Harlem River Drive. After the A train arrived in the 1930s, mid-sized apartment buildings replaced the estates. As recently as the 1950s the waterfront was still vibrant, with many active boat docks and marinas along the shore, but over time businesses and docks were abandoned and the shoreline was left to degrade. When Bette Midler and her team at NYRP began work there in 1993, the shoreline had become an illegal dumping ground and was marred by tons of garbage.

Swindler Cove is adjacent to two other NYRP projects—Sherman Creek Park, a nature habitat used for educational programming with schoolchildren, where a colorful planting of blocks of native perennials has replaced the decrepit waterfront, and the Peter Jay Sharp Boathouse, designed by Robert A. M. Stern Associates, where neighborhood children have an opportunity to learn the sport of rowing. The garden itself is a stylish and thoughtfully planted enclave whose environmental and educational mission is well served by both its location next to PS 5, a large, modern elementary school, and also its careful architectural details and wide-ranging plant palette. Opened in 2003, it is the result of many years of hard work and advocacy on the part of NYRP: the hard work was getting rid of the garbage and cleaning the site, the advocacy

Founded in 1995 by Bette Midler, New York Restoration Project works to restore, clean, and maintain a network of parks and open spaces in a large swath of northern Manhattan. The area it covers stretches from Fort Washington Park, where the divine Miss M. and a group of volunteers first hauled out 20,000 pounds of junk to jump-start her organization, to Fort Tryon and Highbridge Parks. Educational programming is emphasized in each NYRP location. In addition to its work in northern Manhattan, in 1999 NYRP joined with other greening organizations in the city to save 114 community gardens that had been slated for sale, and 55 of those are now part of NYRP's garden trust. NYRP has been able to attract many well-known designers and corporate underwriters to create attractive gardens in underserved neighborhoods. NYRP is also partnering with the city in the Million-TreesNYC project, which aims to plant trees in public and private spaces in all five boroughs throughout the city.

was partnering with the New York Department of Transportation to turn the newly cleaned-up riverfront into an unusual city park, where there are no playgrounds or ball fields but ample opportunity to experience and observe natural systems in idyllic surroundings.

New York–based garden designer Billie Cohen, who did the overall schematic design, conceived the plantings with the height of a child in mind. The beds gradually evolve from traditional horticulture—vegetable and flower gardens near the entrance—progressing through various stages of non-native and native combinations to a natural habitat at the water's edge.

Although Swindler Cove is not easy to find, it is worth persevering. The garden presents a surprisingly complete and pleasingly finished appearance when you get there. The entry gate is flanked by complex garden plantings of perennials and flowering trees; to the left is an oval lawn with picnic tables, and on the right a small garden house, adorned with tiles that delicately depict indigenous flora and fauna, like cattails and bullfrogs. The decorative tiles were specially commissioned for this park in order to comply with an unusual parks department regulation that existed under former parks commissioner Henry Stern: each new park was required to include "animal" art.

In front of the house is a small formal sitting area and herb garden; then, to the left, through a garden arch festooned with grapevines, is the Riley Levin Children's Garden, a vegetable garden with 18 rectangular garden plots on either side of the brick-paved central path leading to a podium. The four corners of each plot are marked with short stone posts, a clever way to stop errant watering hoses from sliding over planted plots and decapitating precious crops. An after-school garden club uses the space, and a few teachers also have plots.

The child-centered design is particularly evident in the butterfly and hummingbird garden just south of the vegetable garden, where the child-size height of the shrubs and the multitude of birds and butterflies create a wonderland for small humans. Other features include Jonathan's Pond, named for a young New York high-school teacher who was

Jonathan's Pond

murdered by a former student (his father, Gerald Levin, and stepmother, Barbara Riley, endowed the park). There are also woodland plants and tidal wetlands, and great care has been taken at every stage to make this an attractive and accessible natural experience; note the eye-catching cattail motif on the fence around the pond.

Wide paths through a woodland lead to a sleek steel bridge that takes you over the wetland and the spartina grass at the river's edge. A small jetty extends into the river, affording visitors a closer look at the boathouse and river traffic. There is even a slender 30-foot sand "beach." At the entrance to the jetty are two "before" pictures that give you a good idea of how large a task it was to transform this waterfront.

Swindler Cove is named for Billy Swindler, a musician and city garden advocate who, while working on a garden project with the students at PS 5, introduced Ms. Midler to the area. He died in 1997.

Dyckman Farmhouse Museum

Location: 4881 Broadway at 204th St.
Hours: Wed.–Sat. 11:00am–4:00pm; Sun. 12:00pm–4:00pm
Garden info: (212) 304-9422
Web site: www.dyckmanfarmhouse.org
Admission fee: no (grounds); yes (house)
Bus: M100, Bx7
Subway: 1, A to 207th St.
Facilities: rest rooms and telephone in museum
Best seasons: spring, summer

This Dutch colonial farmhouse—Manhattan's last—and its surrounding tiny plot of land are all that remain of a huge 450-acre farm and orchard that once stretched all the way to the Harlem River. Today, the quaint little house perched on top of a rock outcropping overlooks the stores and apartment buildings of busy upper Broadway.

In 1784, William Dyckman, a descendant of one of the earliest Dutch settlers, returned to his family's farmland after the Revolution and built this farmhouse with its gambrel roof and double Dutch doors. Eventually the Dyckmans moved on to grander quarters and the structure deteriorated. In 1915 it was rescued by two Dyckman sisters who restored and furnished it with period pieces, among them some family heirlooms. The family donated the house to the city in 1916.

It is thought that the original parterre gardens were located across what is now 204th Street. All that is left of the grounds is a backyard, designed in 1916 in a style that we

now call Colonial Revival by
Alexander McMillan Welch,
who was married to one of
the Dyckman sisters. It is
part neighborhood park and
part historic house restoration. A curious log structure
turns out to be a twentieth-
century interpretation of an
eighteenth-century Hessian
officers' hut, a feature added
in 1916 as an allusion to the
site's dramatic past, when
British and Hessian troops fought Revolutionary War battles
on the family's land. In front of the hut is a Dutch-influenced
parterre laid out in boxwood and gravel, with a star magnolia
in the center. Renovation of the garden was begun in 2006,
and the staff intends to stay as close as they can to the 1916
Colonial Revival design. Behind the parterre is a row of tear-
shaped hornbeams, their formal outline and tight silhouettes
making a good visual break between the garden and the adjacent apartment building. A large crape myrtle in an unusually
intense shade of pink lights up the corner of the garden. Two
huge copper beeches cast the backyard in shade so that what
would have been the back lawn is now covered in ivy.

To the north of the house a sitting area is a popular neighborhood amenity. Volunteers help keep the grounds and
the plantings in good shape. They have planted hundreds
of bulbs and perennials, many of them heirloom varieties,
greatly improving the Broadway side of the garden.

The Cloisters

Location: 99 Margaret Corbin Drive, in Fort Tryon Park
Hours: Tues.–Sun. 9:30am–5:15pm (March–October); 9:30am–4:45pm
    (November–February); closed Mon.
Garden info: (212) 923-3700
Web site: www.metmuseum.org/cloisters
Admission fee: yes
Bus: M4
Subway: A to 190th St.; exit by elevator and walk via Margaret Corbin
    Dr., or take M4 bus for short ride through Fort Tryon Park
Facilities: limited wheelchair accessibility (call in advance for help getting
    up cobblestone hill entrance), rest rooms, gift shop, café (May–
    October), telephones, free parking
Best seasons: all seasons

Perched on a four-acre hilltop in Fort Tryon Park, with striking
views across the Hudson River to the New Jersey Palisades,
the Cloisters, a branch of the Metropolitan Museum of Art,
houses part of the museum's superb collection of medieval art,
including the famous Unicorn Tapestries. Created in the 1930s
on land donated by John D. Rockefeller Jr., the building incorporates architectural fragments collected from across Europe
and evokes the atmosphere of a medieval monastery. Within
the museum are three reconstructed cloisters, each enclosing
gardens and designed to enrich our understanding of medieval
life. Traditionally, cloisters were the heart of a monastic complex where members of a religious community would meditate,
read, copy manuscripts, walk, and wash clothes.

Although the gardens at the Cloisters were first installed in 1938, the horticultural staff continues to research and refine them, and their ongoing efforts to maintain and improve the garden are described in their blog, "The Medieval Garden Enclosed," found on the Cloisters Web site. The basis for our knowledge of medieval plants is Charlemagne's ninth-century list of the 89 plants to be grown in his gardens. Additionally, a prime source of inspiration for these particular gardens is the writing of the Abbot of Reichenau, Walahfrid Strabo (809–849). In his poem "Hortulus," Strabo writes about his own garden, describing not only his plants but also the trials and tribulations of tending them, including the still-familiar problems of dry areas, moles, and shade: "and if you do not/refuse to harden or dirty/your hands in the open air/or to spread whole baskets of dung on the sun-parched soil—/ then, you may rest assured, your/soil will not fail you."*

The Cuxa Cloister Garth Garden

Situated in the heart of the main floor of the museum, Cuxa is the first cloister garden a visitor encounters. As one emerges from the dim galleries into the light of the cloister, the small garden seems to glow as daylight reflects off the sharp green of the lawn and highlights the exuberant carving of the arcades. This space demonstrates the key elements of the medieval garden: it is enclosed, rigorously symmetrical, and organized around a central feature, here a handsome fountain.

*Walahfrid Strabo, "Hortulus," translated by Raef Payne (Pittsburgh: The Hunt Botanical Library, 1966), quoted in *Sweet Herbs and Sundry Flowers: Medieval Gardens and the Gardens of the Cloisters*, by Tania Bayard (Metropolitan Museum, 1985).

The Cuxa Cloister was assembled from the remnants of a Romanesque (eleventh century) Benedictine monastery, Saint-Michel-de-Cuxa, located in the French Pyrenees. The garden is modeled on a garth, an enclosed yard often situated on the south side of a monastery in order to take advantage of the sun. Garths were usually grassed and divided by crossed paths into quadrants around a central fountain. Although there are no records of extensive flower planting in medieval garths, in this garden the inside edges of the paths are densely packed with a mix of flowers that were common in the Middle Ages (columbine, lilies, sage, and hellebores) and some newer plants (candytuft, alyssum, and coreopsis) that have been included to ensure a continuous season of bloom. A pollarded Wyman crab apple in each of the quadrants produces the sour fruit that medieval monasteries once used for making verjuice and cider.

As visitors leave the Cuxa garden, they pass a grouping of potted aromatic plants that fill the cloister arcades during the winter months. Like their modern counterparts, medieval gardeners grew houseplants to extend the gardening season and to provide herbs and fragrance. From Christmas to Easter the Cloisters opens a small indoor garden in the Saint-Guilhem Cloister.

The Bonnefont Cloister Herb Garden

On the lower level of the museum is the Bonnefont Cloister, a tidy working herb garden that, except for the stunning views of the George Washington Bridge in the distance, looks like a page from a medieval manuscript. This garden, designed to display a range of styles, techniques, and plants, is a result of dedicated scholarship combined with a fine aesthetic eye. All of the 250 plants grown here were known in medieval times, and the staff continues to do extensive research to determine the most authentic varieties. Although scholars aren't always sure which plants were cultivated and which were found in the wild, they have identified 400 species that would have been familiar to gardeners in the Middle Ages.

Nineteen beds are laid out around a fifteenth-century Venetian wellhead that still retains the grooves incised by generations of people raising and lowering their buckets. Surrounded by low wattle fencing, each bed is enclosed in brick and raised several inches above grade (typically, medieval gardens featured raised beds for better drainage). Each is devoted to a particular group of plants, including those used for medicine, seasonings, decorations, dye, and magic potions. All the plants are labeled, and because many of the herbs had multiple uses, the same ones often appear in different beds. For instance, fennel, mint, and sage were used not only as seasonings but also as remedies for illness and injury. The same plants that produced the dyes that colored the celebrated tapestries in the indoor galleries are grown here. Throughout, inventive garden supports that evoke medieval techniques have been used, including grapevines bent into hoops, coppiced branches supporting vegetables, and conical wicker baskets serving as growing pots.

In early spring, four gnarled fruiting quince trees grouped around the wellhead and set in beds full of bulbs show off their delicate pink flowers. A mature Cornelian cherry displays its unusual bark. Another attraction is the espaliered pear that is trained up the wall of the Gothic chapel in the northwest corner. The tree was planted in 1940, and its branches are now the thickness of a strong man's arm, extending in even rows up the mellow stone walls of the chapel. On the gentle hill outside the cloister a small orchard flourishes, underplanted with a wildflower meadow whose blooms would have been familiar to medieval monks.

The Trie Cloister Garden

Next to the Bonnefont garden is the Trie Cloister Garden, named for the Carmelite convent in Trie-en-Bigorre in south-western France, the original site of much of the stonework. The garden is a fanciful version of the millefleurs (literally, a thousand flowers) found in late medieval tapestries, in which the ground is carpeted with blooming flowers. The plants in the scattered, naturalistic setting in the Trie draw on what we know of medieval European native woodlands and meadows. Among the varieties that bloom in the garden, foxglove, snow-drops, daffodils, violets, bluebells, pansies, yarrow, pinks, and columbine spring from a tightly woven mat of ground covers such as periwinkle and ajuga. The fountain in the center, from northeastern France, dates from the late fifteenth or early sixteenth century.

Clockwise from left: Biblical Garden at St. John the Divine; and all at the Cloisters—Bonnefont Cloister; espaliered pear; and Cuxa Cloister

The Heather Garden

Location: Margaret Corbin Circle at Fort Washington Ave. and Cabrini
    Blvd.
Hours: daily dawn to dusk
Garden info: (212) 795-1388
Web site: www.nycgovparks.org/parks/forttryonpark
Admission fee: no
Bus: M4 or M98
Subway: A to 190th St.; exit by Margaret Corbin Circle
Facilities: wheelchair accessible, picnic area, New Leaf café, rest rooms
    and telephone available in café, limited parking
Best seasons: spring, summer, fall

The three-acre Heather Garden, which occupies a command-
ing spot at the southern end of Fort Tryon Park, is the largest
heath and heather garden in the eastern United States. Many
New Yorkers have never heard of it, even though it is right
next to the Cloisters and a visit to both can be easily combined. Like the Cloisters, the Heather Garden is the legacy
of John D. Rockefeller Jr., who commissioned it in the 1920s
as part of Fort Tryon Park. He took a personal interest in the
construction of this park, and in the New York Public Library
there are many archival photographs of him as he inspected
and supervised the project.

    The original planting scheme by Frederick Law Olmsted
Jr., son of the co-designer of Central Park and Prospect Park,
balanced the requirements of a formal traditional flower garden with sensitivity to the magnificent view. In the Olmsted

there is a balance between preservation and renewal, but there is an ongoing effort to restore the scale of the Heather Garden plantings, and 4,500 heaths and heathers have been added to the beds. Public garden designer Lynden B. Miller has been hired to focus on consolidating the perennial plantings. Several huge storms, while devastating in the immediate, opened up the tremendous views of the Hudson and the Palisades that the original designers had sought to emphasize but that had become obscured over the years.

The garden has an old-fashioned, romantic feel (note the knotted old apple tree at the entrance to the Linden Terrace), due in no small part to the magnificent yews, some of which date to the period when this was the private Billings estate. Ericaceous plants dominate the display, and the extensive heath and heather plantings, so low to the ground and roughly textured with an intense but muted color palette, give the garden a unique identity. An early spring moment, when the purple heaths and the purple PJM azaleas bloom together, is strident but surprisingly effective in such a large-scale, sweeping garden. Flowering trees, including apples, cherries, hawthorns, and dogwoods, many of them planted when the garden was first built, are now very handsome specimens; they are scattered throughout and add significantly to the spring show. Hundreds of azaleas, both deciduous and evergreen, bloom progressively from April to the end of May. Also in spring, there is a spectacular moment when a multitude of English bluebells bloom with the purple heaths beneath the soft yellow and red brooms. The entire western border turns into a sea of blue, and the broom floats like huge yellow and red clouds above it. Over 200 roses have been added in recent years, and there is a colorful summer perennial display as well.

In the autumn, a time when many gardens are finished, the Heather Garden is worth a special trip. A carpet of heather covers the sloping beds from midsummer to late fall, its soft lavender, pink, and white contrasting with the yellowing tree foliage. A golden glow hovers over the garden, punctuated by the red of the sourwoods and dogwoods and echoed in the colors of the purple asters and red sedums that stretch to the skyline. Several rare franklinia trees in the park bloom only in the fall.

The Heather Garden used to be known as the hidden gem among city parks, but it

The Heather Garden

is hidden no longer. The parks department provides extensive programming, including nature and fitness walks, classes, and family events, as well as numerous garden tours; as a result, the garden and its surrounding park are getting many more visitors. The Heather Garden remains a gem, but now that it has been polished, it shines even more brightly.

Morris-Jumel Mansion

Location: 65 Jumel Terr., between W. 160th and W. 162nd Sts.
Hours: daily 10:00am–4:00pm (grounds); Wed.–Sun. 10:00am–4:00pm
    (mansion)
Garden info: (212) 923-8008
Web site: www.morrisjumel.org
Admission fee: no (grounds); yes (mansion)
Bus: M2, M3, M18, M101
Subway: C to 163rd St.
Facilities: call ahead for wheelchair access; rest rooms, gift shop, and
    telephone in mansion
Best season: spring

The 1.5-acre Roger Morris Park is all that remains of a vast 130-acre estate that once extended from the Hudson to the Harlem Rivers. In the center of the park stands the Morris-Jumel Mansion, the oldest historic house and one of the very few pre-Revolutionary residences in Manhattan. The mansion occupies the second-highest point in Manhattan and once boasted glorious prospects in every direction. Although today some of the views are blocked by large trees and apartment buildings and the grounds are unassuming, the history of the site still casts a spell.

Roger Morris was a British officer who built the Palladian-inspired house as his summer residence in 1765. During the Revolution, he and his American wife were forced to return to England. Mt. Morris, as it was then called, boasted an excellent strategic location, with sight lines stretching far in every direction, and it became George Washington's headquarters for a month during the Battle of Harlem Heights. The mansion changed hands a number of times after the Revolution, and it was acquired in 1810 by a wealthy merchant of French origin, Stephen Jumel, who bought it as a present for his wife, Eliza. Jumel died in 1832, and shortly thereafter Madame Jumel (described in one account as "an adventuress") married Aaron Burr (though she quickly divorced him) at a ceremony that took place in the house. She was considered the wealthiest woman in the city and continued to live there until her death in 1865, making several changes to the building, among them the remodeling of the entrance to include the classic Federal-style doorway. In 1903 the city acquired the property, by then reduced to its present size, and it was opened to the public in 1907.

Convent Garden, at the intersection of W. 151st Street and St. Nicholas Avenue, is just ten blocks away from Morris-Jumel and well worth a visit. When this small triangle was created in 1909, it was designated a public park, yet in the way that urban open spaces are often vulnerable to development, a gas station was later built there. When the station was eventually demolished, the community reestablished a garden on the site; in 1989, Convent became the pilot location for Greenstreets, a city program committed to transforming traffic islands into attractive green spaces.

The entrance to the mansion and surrounding Roger Morris Park is on Jumel Terrace, a cobblestone street lined with imposing nineteenth-century row houses. Across the street, on Sylvan Terrace, the former carriage drive to the mansion, the small clapboard houses with their meticulously restored facades are among the only surviving examples of the wood frame buildings that were also common in Washington Heights in the late nineteenth century. A saucer magnolia stands at the stone gate; along the brick path are several other stately trees, including an American elm and large clumps of lilac and mock orange. In 1935 Robert Moses hired landscape architect Helen Elise Bullard to design a colonial garden for the grounds and, although the 50-by-50-foot octagonal sunken garden has become overgrown, some exceptional Japanese quince remains, and ivy, daylilies, vinca, daisies, and forsythia have spread throughout the beds. Roger Morris Park now has its own conservancy, and ambitious plans are afoot to reinstall the sunken garden in a design that is sympathetic to the original Colonial Revival plan. The garden is at its best in the spring, when the magnolia, lilac, and hundreds of bulbs brighten the grounds. During other seasons, the garden is quieter, a gentle, slightly melancholy reminder of a prosperous past.

Riverside Valley Community Garden

Location: 138th St. and Twelfth Ave.

Hours: daily dawn to dusk

Garden info: (212) 870-3070

Web site: www.riversideparkfund.org

Admission fee: no

Bus: M5

Subway: 1 to 137th St.

Facilities: rest rooms at Riverbank Camel Playground (143rd St. and Riverside Dr.)

Best season: summer (June for the roses)

Working with her husband, Victor, park warden Jenny Benitez reclaimed a sadly neglected swath of Riverside Park, once a forgotten hillside at the bottom of a dead end street. Partly hidden under the elevated Riverside Drive, Riverside Valley had been a choice spot for drugs, crime, and garbage, yet Mr. and Mrs. Benitez have built a flourishing garden here, with raised vegetable plots and a mass of rosebushes that dazzle motorists on the West Side Highway in June. Years of composting have produced abundant vegetables and a wide variety of fruit-bearing trees, including apple, pear, and peach. The garden now stretches from 138th to 150th Streets.

There are about 30 official garden members, but because the area is secluded, members work together on all the plots, and Mrs. Benitez brings in volunteer groups for large tasks. Each year they extend the boundaries of the garden, cleaning up and replanting a new section of the park. This must be one of the best volunteer opportunities in the city; not only do workers share in the harvest, but at the end of the day they also are treated to a home-cooked meal, usually prepared by Mrs. Benitez herself.

Just south of Riverside Valley is the West Harlem Piers Park, which opened in 2009. Extending from St. Clair Place to West 133rd Street, and from Marginal Street to the Hudson River, this narrow, two-acre park provides direct access to the waterfront for many local fisherman and serves as a link between Riverside Park to the south and Riverbank State Park, which is on the rooftop of a large sewage treatment plant just across the West Side Highway from Riverside Valley. Next to the track complex at Riverbank is a well-tended community graden that includes tabletop plots for handicapped gardeners. Open from April to November, the garden can be reached via the 138th Street pedestrian bridge and can be viewed any time over the waist-high fence.

Pleasant Village Community Garden and Neighboring Gardens

Location: 342–353 Pleasant Ave. at 118th St.; 431 E. 114th St. (Family
   Garden); 437–439 E. 114th St. (Rodale Pleasant Park Community
   Garden)
Hours: Pleasant Village: Tues. 4:00–6:00pm, Sat. 9:00am–12:00pm;
   Family Garden: Sat.–Sun. 12:00pm–5:00pm; Rodale Pleasant
   Park Community Garden: Mon.–Fri. 5:00pm–6:00pm, Fri.
   1:00pm–7:00pm
Garden info: (212) 788-8067 (PV); (212) 333-2552 (FG & RPP)
Web site: www.nyrp.org (FG & RPP)
Admission fee: no
Bus: M15
Subway: 6 to 116th St.
Facilities: none
Best season: summer

Within four blocks of each other in this quiet corner of East
Harlem are three exceptional community gardens: one has
a rich history in the neighborhood, the other two have been
given extreme makeovers by New York Restoration Project
(NYRP) and offer traditional community garden pleasures
wrapped up in smartly designed envelopes.

Founded in 1978 on the site of several abandoned tenements, Pleasant Village, a wild luxuriance of vegetables and
flowers, is one of the oldest community gardens in Harlem.
Dominated by a huge mural of ghostly gardeners working

the soil, it includes a real orchard with nearly a dozen bearing fruit trees. Arriving in the middle of summer, a visitor is greeted by a white picket fence with literally hundreds of sunflowers towering over it. A brick path leads from the entrance to a small communal seating area surrounded by shrubs. The gardeners are active year-round with barbecues and community events, and they tend their plots as long as weather permits. Deep into November, they can be found examining their collards, making sure the greens last until Thanksgiving.

Pleasant Village Community Garden

Four blocks away on 114th Street, just around the corner from Pleasant Avenue, are two noteworthy gardens owned by NYRP. Both are across the street from Thomas Jefferson Park, a large city park with a playground and lots of sports activity. When NYRP consulted local residents about what they wanted out of the space, the answer was a quiet place to enjoy the outdoors, protected from the hubbub of the street and the noisy playground in the park. The Family Garden (sponsored by Tiffany & Co. and designed by longtime Tiffany design guru John Loring) takes its cue from Thomas Jefferson. It's an elegant little colonially-inspired mini-park whose central feature is an amusing wrought-iron table-and-chair set underneath a simple pergola. The chair-backs are formed by cutout silhouettes of Thomas Jefferson's head, and lurking in the back of the garden is a life-size silhouette of the Revolutionary hero. Several doors down the block is Rodale Pleasant Park, a large and very active community garden with 17 neat plots and a simple grape arbor at the rear of the lot. It was designed as a working garden by Billie Cohen, who understood the needs of the keen gardeners who had been growing their vegetables here for years. The garden, which runs right through the block, is overlooked by a handsome church on 115th Street and the layout takes full advantage of this attractive background. A communal area at the 114th Street entrance features a circular gathering spot set off by a low drystone wall and a good-sized garden shed partially built of encased hay bales. Tools are powered by solar energy and the garden has one of the biggest rainwater collection systems in the city.

Cathedral Church of St. John the Divine

Location: 1047 Amsterdam Ave. at W. 112th St.
Hours: daily dawn to dusk (grounds)
Garden info: (212) 316-7540
Web site: www.stjohndivine.org
Admission fee: no (grounds); yes (cathedral)
Bus: M4, M60, M11, M104
Subway: 1 to 110th St.
Facilities: wheelchair accessible via the 113th St. ramp
Best seasons: spring, summer

The cathedral and its grounds and auxiliary buildings occupy 11.3 acres on Morningside Heights. Within the grounds, or close, are the Biblical Garden and the expanse of the Pulpit Lawn. First-time visitors may have difficulty finding their way into the gardens, as the entire close is surrounded by a chain-link fence, driveways, and guard huts; it is further screened from the street by the Peace Statue, a large installation that includes a massive sculpture surrounded by paths and planters. Follow the driveway just north of 110th Street and ask the guard for directions.

The cathedral complex, like the cathedral itself, is a work in progress. It was begun in 1892 on the grounds of the Leake and Watts Orphan Asylum, whose pillared remains are still visible just west of the Biblical Garden. The buildings that make up the complex have gone up in fits and starts over the last hundred years as money has become available; they differ in style, but all are of gray stone that imparts a certain visual unity. Like the buildings, the gardens were established at different times and each has its own story and ambiance.

Behind the Peace Statue is the Pulpit Lawn, perhaps best known for its resident peacocks, Phil, Jim and Harry. Surrounded by deep shrub and perennial borders, its centerpiece is a 40-foot-high sandstone pulpit (Howells and Stokes, 1916). Thirty thousand bulbs, donated as a memorial, bloom here in the spring.

Tucked beside the southeastern end of the cathedral, shadowed by the thick walls of the St. James Chapel, lies the 1,600-square-foot Biblical

Pulpit Lawn

Garden. Simply configured as a circle in a square in a circle, enclosed by a stone wall pierced with windows, it contains only those plants mentioned in the Bible. Originally installed in 1972 and renovated several times, the garden was the gift of Sarah Larkin Loening, in gratitude for the comfort and hope she found there during her husband's illness. The most recent renovation, completed in 2001, is the work of the late Keith Corlett, who not only redesigned the garden but also built and installed new structures that are meant to echo the themes and shapes of the cathedral. These include Gothic arches and benches inspired by the magnificent stonework at the entrance to the cathedral, as well as colorful mosaics installed by Corlett himself. The seal of St. John is underfoot as one enters; simple crosses lie at the end of each path. The center of the garden and its focal point is a fountain that rises from a remarkable 12-foot-wide mosaic, a copy of the cathedral's beautiful rose window. Twenty-five thousand tiny chips were used to create the intricate design.

An enormous amount of research has gone into selecting plants that are both mentioned in the Bible and viable in present-day New York City. Like the structures and the mosaics, the planting has been designed to echo and complement the architecture and to increase the drama of the design. Organized so that taller plants are in the outer beds, the plant heights gradually diminish to draw the eye down to the central mosaic and fountain. Low boxwood hedges contain the beds. Junipers and a single cedar of Lebanon have been used for their upright forms, which replicate the cathedral spires. Notice the Judas tree (a redbud), bay laurel, myrtle bush, pine, quince, plum, and tamarisk. Grapevines and climbing roses cover the Gothic arches. There is a surprisingly large selection of perennials given the constraints of the program, including artemisia, sage, anemone, cyclamen, iris, and both the Madonna and martagon lilies. Among the many spring bulbs are an exceptional number of crocuses, making late March and early April good times to visit. Intimate and protected, the Biblical Garden invites contemplation.

There had been a rose garden on the southeastern corner of the close—the Hope Rosary, containing over 75 varieties of roses—but it was supplanted by an apartment complex. Fortunately, cuttings were taken from the roses and there are plans for a new rose garden just to the east of the old location. The old Hope Rosary was one of the largest collections of English roses in the United States and was the work of one donor, Patrick Cullen, a scholar of Renaissance literature.

Another garden in the close, across the drive from the Biblical Garden between the Deanery and the Cathedral House, while not open to the public, can be viewed over the gate. Well maintained, it has a brilliant spring display of azaleas grouped around a handsome carved-stone basin.

1 The Lotus Garden

2 The 91st Street Garden

3 West Side Community Garden

4 Arthur Ross Terrace at the American Museum
    of Natural History

5 Shakespeare Garden

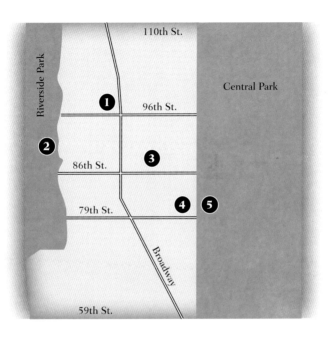

110th St.

Riverside Park

Central Park

❶ 96th St.

❷

86th St. **❸**

79th St. **❹** **❺**

Broadway

59th St.

The Lotus Garden

Location: W. 97th St. between Broadway and West End Ave.

Hours: Sun. 1:00pm–4:00pm (first weekend of April through
   mid-November)

Web site: www.thelotusgarden.org

Admission fee: no

Bus: M96, M104

Subway: 1, 2, 3 to 96th St.

Facilities: none

Best seasons: spring, summer

The Lotus Garden is the only community garden on a rooftop
in New York; how it landed there is an unusual real estate
story with a happy ending. Few people passing by the nondescript garage on 97th Street would even realize that a
community garden thrives above. While most of the other
community gardens in the city can easily be admired through
their fences, here only the tops of the trees and shrubs are
visible from the street. But once through the gate draped in
grapevines and up the stairs, a visitor is totally removed from
the noise and bustle of Broadway and begins to experience
what feels like a private city terrace.

In the 1960s and 1970s, while developers, bankers, and
politicians haggled over the fate of a large vacant lot on the
corner of 96th Street and Broadway, local residents took mat-
ters into their own hands and transformed it into the lively
Broadway Gardens. When a high-rise condominium was
approved for the site, community gardeners went to work to

save what they could of the gardens. Hundreds of plants were dug up and moved to Riverside Park, where they formed the beginnings of the 91st Street Garden (see p. 63). After almost a year of negotiations between developer William Zeckendorf Jr. and community leaders and gardeners, and with help from the Trust for Public Land, a compromise was reached that allowed for a community garden to be included in the condominium plan. Zeckendorf, convinced that it would enhance his property, provided funds for continuing support, and the community succeeded in keeping a portion of green space for the neighborhood.

Since 1980, the Broadway Mall Association has worked with the NYC Department of Parks & Recreation to improve the strips of greenery in the middle of Broadway, and all of the malls were renovated and replanted as of 2000. Some blocks look better than others, depending on the season and the particular year, although all of the planters put on an early spring display, when the pink blooms of the saucer magnolias and the bright yellow narcissus and multicolored tulips brighten the busy commercial street. Notable are the very effective gardens at 135th Street, designed by Lynden B. Miller, and the gardens at the only "double" mall, at 153rd and 155th Streets, adjacent to the Trinity Church cemetery (where John James Audubon is buried), designed by Anne Warner Linville.

Three-and-one-half feet of lightweight organic soil were hoisted onto the condominium's garage rooftop to create the 7,000-square-foot garden. Neighbors now look out over a well-maintained, sophisticated garden, which includes an herb garden, two fishponds, fruit trees, and flowering shrubs. Ferns, rhododendron, a fringe tree, serviceberry, and witch hazels thrive in the native plant section. This is a highly productive garden, with crops including grapes, cherries, peaches, and currants. The light-colored brick of the building reflects so much sunlight that there are many different microclimates, creating a challenge for the 25 gardeners who maintain their own plots but also making it possible to grow plants that benefit from the milder temperatures. In midsummer, a multitude of lilies as well as several varieties of hydrangea—including oakleaf, macrophylla, and variegated—unify the beds.

The 91st Street Garden

Location: Riverside Park at W. 91st St.
Hours: daily dawn to dusk
Web site: www.thegardenpeople.org
Admission fee: no
Bus: M5
Subway: 1, 2 to 86th St.; 1, 2, 3 to 96th St.
Facilities: wheelchair accessible, rest rooms in nearby playground
Best seasons: spring, summer, fall

Visit the 91st Street Garden in late April if you can, at cherry and crab apple blossom time. Clouds of pink and white trees form a soft, fragrant frame for this exceptional community garden in Riverside Park. Located on the esplanade down the hill from the 91st Street entrance, it is laid out in two sections, an octagon and a rectangle, both of which are intensively cultivated. The simple iron fence is only waist-high, so that even when the garden is closed, all the plots are visible. The garden is a particularly pleasant destination for an early evening walk as the sun sets over the Hudson River.

While the octagon is cared for communally, the 150-by-24-foot rectangle consists of 26 gardens that are maintained individually. Each plot has a different personality and, as one garden member says, "everyone does his or her own thing, but it works." With so many different voices, there are hundreds of vignettes to savor over the fence: two honey-scented fothergilla standing sentry at the ends of the rectangle; delicate mounds of epimedium softening the ground under the corky branches of a standard winged euonymous. Given the small spaces, the gardeners wage a perpetual battle to keep plantings in bounds and thus all of the shrubs are tightly pruned, creating a formal structure for the beds. Even so, it's easy to identify the grass lovers, the neatniks, the alpine specialists, the rose aficionados.

The origins of this garden go back to 1977, when a group of neighborhood residents planted bulbs in a vacant lot on Broadway between 96th and 97th Streets. When the bulbs bloomed, the excited residents began to garden in earnest. When the property was slated for development the gardeners soon had to look for new quarters, ultimately approaching the parks department to ask for a bit of land in Riverside Park. Another group remained linked with the condominium project and formed the Lotus Garden (see p. 60). Despite initial controversy over the issue of a private group gardening on public land, a permit was granted (with the stipulation that only flowers, no vegetables, could be planted). In 1981 the newly incorporated Garden People created the octagon and, a year later, the rectangle. The garden is the centerpiece of this section of Riverside Park: the slopes on both sides have been landscaped as well, with large stands of single-petal kerria to the east and a mix of daylilies and rosa rugosa to the west. Walk south along the esplanade in Riverside Park to see the sophisticated woodland planting surrounding the Warsaw Ghetto Memorial Plaza at 83rd Street, which is the work of a devoted Riverside Park Fund volunteer, David Goldstick, who has also planted a wild and exuberant flower border that brightens the park alongside the entrance ramp to the West Side Highway at 79th Street.

West Side Community Garden

Location: between W. 89th and W. 90th Sts. and Columbus and
    Amsterdam Aves.

Hours: daily 8:30am to dusk

Web site: www.westsidecommunitygarden.org

Admission fee: no

Bus: M11, M7

Subway: B, C, 1, 2 to 86th St.

Facilities: partially wheelchair accessible

Best seasons: spring, summer

Tulip season in early May is the high point at the West Side Community Garden. Enter from 89th Street: a small amphitheater is ringed with tiers of planting boxes filled with hundreds of tulips in the clear, bright colors for which they are famous. The yellows, reds, purples, pinks, and oranges dance from the ground plane to eye level, momentarily dazzling the eye and blocking out the rest of the garden and the city beyond.

It is quite a spectacle to find mid-block in the residential neighborhood between Columbus and Amsterdam Avenues, and at first it's difficult to figure out just where this large garden fits in the scheme of things. It doesn't seem to be private, because the gates are wide open and there are no guards. It doesn't look like a public park, nor does it look like a bedded-out apartment building plaza. On the other hand, the walks, iron fencing, arches, and mature plantings are clearly signs of a permanent and established enterprise. What doesn't spring to mind is a community garden, but that is exactly what it is, albeit one that has come a long way from its origins.

In the early 1970s the entire block of Columbus Avenue between 89th and 90th Streets had been razed for a development that failed to materialize. Urban gardeners attracted by the unused land cleared the lot and created a garden that was flourishing by the time the economy turned around and developers were ready to build. Instead of the usual acrimonious standoffs between gardeners and developers, however, a solution was devised with the aid of the local community board and the Trust for Public Land: the developers were allowed to build their buildings and the gardeners were awarded a 17,500-square-foot permanent garden, complete with expensive fence, arbors, pergolas, and walks. Half the cost of the garden was funded by the developers, who also facilitated the design and supervised construction. Opened in

West Side Community Garden

1988, this revised version has gone on to win a number of prestigious design awards and has been designated a bird sanctuary.

The garden extends the entire depth of the block. A gentle walk shaded by birch, dogwood, oak, spruce, and viburnum winds from the northern gate on 90th Street

Behind a sturdy iron fence with a decorative grape pattern, through a wisteria-covered pergola, is a small garden that is all that remains of the old Dome community garden that used to occupy a much larger space across the street. Now part of the Louis D. Brandeis High School property, the garden is open only to students and staff from the school, but passersby can still enjoy the birches and magnolia and the patch of greenery at the corner of 84th Street and Amsterdam Avenue.

to the amphitheater to the south (more tulips are planted here, extending the display). Members cultivate individual vegetable patches in a fenced-off area in the northwestern corner of the garden.

Roughly bisecting the space is a rock garden created with large boulders salvaged from the excavation of the adjacent apartment building. Sensitively planted with more than 80 different species of shrubs, and perennials, including Solomon's seal, hellebores, bergenia, lady's mantle, small bulbs, and ornamental grasses, it strikes a subtle and delicate note.

Clockwise from left: Shakespeare Garden; rustic bench in the Shakespeare Garden; West Side Community Garden

Arthur Ross Terrace at the American Museum of Natural History

Location: American Museum of Natural History, Central Park West at
    W. 79th St.
Hours: daily 10:00am–5:45pm
Garden info: (212) 769-5100
Web site: www.amnh.org
Admission fee: no
Bus: M7, M10, M11, M79
Subway: B, C to 81st St.; 1, 2 to 79th St.
Facilities: wheelchair accessible through the W. 77th St. museum
    entrance; rest rooms, telephones, and food courts in the museum
Best seasons: spring, summer, fall

The formal Arthur Ross Terrace at the American Museum of Natural History is an imaginative addition to the much-acclaimed Rose Center for Earth and Space. Located on top of the museum's parking garage on West 81st Street, it lies between the transparent, futuristic Rose Center and a traditional red brick building that once housed a power plant and now contains museum offices. It is quite dramatically a twenty-first-century garden floating above the refurbished nineteenth-century Theodore Roosevelt Park, designed by landscape architect Judith Heinz, in conjunction with the museum's biodiversity project. The manner and design of the planting of wide swaths of native shrubs and perennials subtly brings the park into the modern age without disturbing the Olmstedian calm of the original.

Appropriately, the garden above abounds with allusions

to the cosmos. Designed by landscape artist Kathryn Gustafson, in conjunction with landscape architects Anderson & Ray and Polshek Partnership Architects, the terrace was conceived as a series of wedges—representing the phases of the moon—that appear to be cast onto the stone and grass of the terrace by the shadow of the Hayden sphere within the Rose Center.

Deceptively simple at first glance, the garden seems to be no more than a clipped lawn and granite plaza, but closer inspection reveals many components. The long, gently sloping panels of lawn flank a central wedge of granite animated by water jets spurting playfully at different intervals. In addition, a wash of water flows across the granite, making it gleam a dark gray. The water on the stone is never higher than the thick sole of a shoe and was designed so that people could walk through the fountains. Three shallow rivulets that are etched into the stone channel the water into a narrow reflecting pool at the foot of the Rose Center; when the water is turned off and the granite is dry, the pathways appear as three white lines, two straight and one slightly curved, which represent meteor trails.

Set into stone are more than 100 tiny sapphire mirrors that reflect the changing sky; fiber-optic lights representing the constellation Orion create the appearance of stars and produce an outdoor light show at night. Wide granite seating steps on the western edge of the terrace opposite the Rose Center are topped by a planting of mature ginkgo trees. The gingko were chosen for their brilliant fall leaves of "solar" yellow, as well as for the fact that they are the only surviving species of a family of trees that originated more than 300 million years ago.

An allée of fine-textured Japanese pagoda trees along the northern edge of the terrace blends into the green of the mature trees in Roosevelt Park beyond. Substantial wooden benches located in alcoves at intervals along the promenade are crafted from the same wood used for the railing around the edge. Planting beds at the eastern end of the promenade feature a "mist" planting: two rows of closely planted beach plum underplanted with blue-flowering perennials such as epimedium Milky Way and nepeta. The white spring blooms of the plum trees form the "mist" on the base of the blue sky of the perennials.

There is a new-millennium feel about the terrace, with its allusions to the cosmos both implicit and explicit, the restrained use of the carefully chosen and unusual plant material, and the graphic clarity of the panels of grass and granite that make up the central space. The cool serenity is balanced by the joy of being allowed to run through the water washing down the granite slope and the visual frisson of the gaily spouting fountains.

Shakespeare Garden

Location: Central Park at W. 79th St. and West Drive

Hours: daily dawn to dusk

Garden info: (212) 310-6600

Web site: www.centralparknyc.org

Admission fee: no

Bus: M10, M79

Subway: B, C to 81st St.

Facilities: not wheelchair accessible; public phone at Swedish Cottage directly below garden

Best seasons: spring, summer

The wild, romantic Shakespeare Garden occupies four acres on the rocky hill leading up to Belvedere Castle, just north of the 79th Street transverse. Usually, reconstructed Elizabethan gardens are variations on traditional knot gardens, where trimmed and shaped boxwood hedges are joined at elaborate central knots; here, refreshingly, the designers opted for a relaxed cottage garden effect, with rustic touches linking the garden to the naturalistic style of the rest of the park.

A Shakespeare garden was not part of Olmsted and Vaux's original plan for Central Park. In 1913, a Victorian-style rock garden, the Garden of the Heart, also not part of the original plan, was established on the site. Three years later, on the 300th anniversary of Shakespeare's death, the Shakespeare Society of New York replaced the rock garden with plants mentioned in his works and a marble bust of the Bard himself, which was later vandalized and never replaced. The demise of the society in 1929 was a blow; the garden continued to deteriorate until 1975, when volunteers calling themselves the Shakespeare Gardeners adopted it. In 1986, the Samuel and May Rudin Foundation donated funds to completely redesign and rebuild it as the garden we know today.

The new designers, Bruce Kelly and David Varnell, consulted a nineteenth-century work, *The Plant Lore and Garden-craft of Shakespeare* by Rev. Henry Ellacombe, to make sure that all the plants they used were mentioned in Shakespeare's oeuvre. They found it necessary, however, to be liberal in the actual implementation, since twentieth-century varieties are often much different from those of the sixteenth century. For instance, the opium poppy referred to in Shakespeare is illegal, so other varieties have been substituted, and although the quince known by Shakespeare was probably a West Asian variety, a hardier Japanese flowering quince more suited to the New York climate has been used. Several different plants represent briers ("O, how full of briers is this

Primroses in the Shakespeare Garden

working-day world," *As You Like It*), including rose and berberis.

The garden really begins at the steps behind the Swedish Cottage, where the Marionette Theatre is in weekend residence. Fieldstone paths with rustic fencing wander up the hill. Eye-catching fences made of sturdy black locust are used throughout to provide structure for the riot of shrubs and perennials that are planted in drifts all over the slope. The paths eventually reach a plateau that serves as the entrance to the Belvedere Castle complex.

Just down the path from the Shakespeare Garden, on the west side of the park between 71st and 74th Streets, is another garden designed by Bruce Kelly—Strawberry Fields, a special planting in memory of John Lennon, who lived at the nearby Dakota apartment house until his death in 1980. Note the many unusual varieties of plants and trees that were sent as gifts to the park from countries all over the world.

The romantic atmosphere is reinforced by the variety of plants sprawling over the hillside—magnolia, yew, holly, boxwood, spiderwort, silphium, primrose, lilies, ferns, and astilbe, to name but a few. Old-fashioned roses climb through fences and spill over pathways. Meticulously pruned crab apples preside over rustic benches in the same style as the fencing, each carefully placed so visitors can stop and rest. Quotations from Shakespeare can be found throughout the garden on little bronze plaques. After the Ramble, the Shakespeare Garden is the second most popular bird-watching spot in the park.

1 The Conservatory Garden

2 Cooper-Hewitt, National Design Museum,
    Smithsonian Institution

3 The Metropolitan Museum of Art

4 Park Avenue Malls

5 The Frick Collection

6 Central Park Wildlife Center

7 Mount Vernon Hotel Museum and Garden

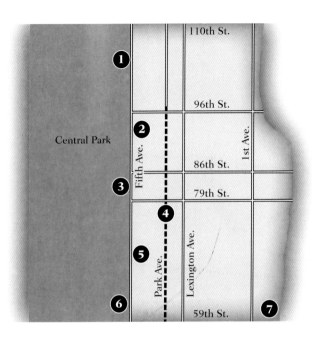

The Conservatory Garden

Location: Central Park at Fifth Ave. and E. 105th St.
Hours: daily 8:00am to dusk
Garden info: (212) 860-1382
Web site: www.centralparknyc.org
Admission fee: no
Bus: M1, M2, M3, M4
Subway: 6 to 103rd St.
Facilities: wheelchair accessible through the North and South gates; rest
    rooms, telephone, free public tours on Saturdays (April–October)
Best seasons: all seasons

For many New Yorkers, the Conservatory Garden is the most beautiful place in Manhattan. A combination of grand gestures and dense, sophisticated planting, it has the manicured and polished look of a great beauty prepared for a ball. In a city that is notoriously tough on itself, these six formal, elegant acres tucked into the northeast corner of Central Park are treated lovingly and respectfully by visitors and remains pristine, clipped, pruned, weeded, and full of vibrant, flourishing plants.

Historically, this corner of Central Park has always been dedicated to horticulture. The name refers to the glasshouses that were built on the site in 1899 and used for growing flowers and shrubs for city parks. Although the conservatories attracted crowds, they were too expensive to maintain during the Depression and parks commissioner Robert Moses had them torn down. In their place he commissioned the Conservatory Garden, one of a number of gardens built at this time by the Work Projects Administration. Gilmore D. Clarke was the consulting landscape architect for the project, executed by the parks department. The team included noted designer Thomas Drees Price and Clarke's future wife, M. Betty Sprout, who designed the plantings and went on to work on a number of important projects, including the 1939 World's Fair. Like the glasshouses that preceded it, the new garden was both extremely popular with the public and expensive to maintain. By the 1960s and 1970s, funds for maintenance had dwindled and the neglected garden became known as one of the most dangerous areas of Central Park.

Not until nearly 50 years after its creation did the garden become what it is today. In the late 1970s, attempts were made to breathe new life into it by the Garden Club of America. In the early 1980s, however, the newly formed Central Park Conservancy enlisted the aid of artist and designer Lynden B. Miller, who redesigned and replanted the planting beds; this hugely successful project at the Garden launched her career as a preeminent public garden designer; she remains the garden's director. In 1987, its future was ensured by an endowment grant and the establishment of the permanent positions of curator and staff gardeners. The garden is in talented hands. Curator Diane Schaub is in charge of the ongoing evolution of the garden, keeping it dynamic and current while respecting its historical roots. Assisted by a dedicated staff and group of volunteers, she is continually refining and improving it so that, at all times of the year, visitors experience the ordered serenity of a garden in its prime.

The Conservatory Garden is that rare achievement, a truly four-season garden. In the winter, snow outlines the hedges

Pergola at the Conservatory Garden

and the twisted shapes of the crab apples, highlighting the garden's elegant bones; in the spring, the garden is unbelievably romantic, with its thousands of flowering bulbs among venerable lilacs and crab apples; in the summer, the perennial borders come into their own; in the fall, when most people assume gardens are finished, the chrysanthemums and the late-blooming annuals put on their spectacular show.

The Central Garden

From the gilded, ornate entrance gates that once belonged to the Vanderbilt mansion at 58th Street and Fifth Avenue, the visitor looks down on the Italian-style Central Garden, a sweeping half-acre of lawn surrounded by clipped yew hedges and flanked by two dramatic crab apple allées. These crab apples were brought down the Hudson River in full bloom in 1937, and each year garden visitors look forward to the pale pink and raspberry display in late April/early May. The rest of the year their gnarled forms and romantic aspect are a favorite of photographers and painters.

Directly across the lawn from the gates, alternating tiers of yew and spirea hedges ascend to an imposing wrought-iron pergola covered in lavender Chinese wisteria. The dark green of the yew subtly contrasts with the light yellow-green of the spirea, creating a pleasing striped effect as the eye travels upward. In early spring, the frothy white flowers of the spirea and the white and yellow narcissus on the slope beyond are among the earliest signals that the garden is beginning to come into bloom. The wooded hill behind the pergola rises another 20 feet, a wild green backdrop to the tailored scene. At the foot of the hedges, a single jet fountain provides a favorite spot for wedding pictures. On June weekends, the garden hosts up to 25 ceremonies a day.

Although Gilmore D. Clarke's name is not a household word, his influence on the city landscape was considerable. As an associate of Robert Moses, Clarke (1892–1982) and his firm Clarke and Rapuano were responsible for the overall design of many important public spaces (including Bryant Park, the United Nations, and the Brooklyn Heights Promenade). It is Clarke's design for "ribbon parks," as Moses described his motor parkways, that is most familiar to us today. He was the landscape architect for the Hutchinson River, Saw Mill River, and Henry Hudson Parkways. These were among the first parkways in the country to eliminate traffic lights and to use overpasses and underpasses instead of intersections. The parkways brought Olmsted's principles of park design to highway construction. Clarke's influence extended to Washington, D.C., where he was Chairman of the National Capital Commission for 13 years and was responsible for the siting of the Pentagon. Clarke was also dean of the College of Architecture at Cornell University from 1938 to 1950.

The North Garden
This part of the garden is inspired by formal French garden

design, although it resembles more the simple Hotel de Ville than the elaborate Versailles. The scrolls of the central decorative flower beds are laid out in germander, surrounded by blue pansies followed by red alternanthera. The focus is the lighthearted Untermyer Fountain of Three Dancing Maidens (sculptor: Walter Schott, circa 1910). Partially surrounding the beds is a spirea hedge—the same spirea that is used in the Central Garden and in a less controlled form in the woodland adjacent to the South Garden.

Encircling the parterre are the sloping beds, with pergolas of climbing Silver Moon roses arching over the wide steps. The beds are planted with 21,000 tulips, a stunning sight in early spring; each year, they are laid out in a different pattern. In the fall, the glowing colors of 2,000 Korean chrysanthemums—not the usual tight pompoms but a single, loose-petaled variety shown in a mix of pale yellows, pinks, and russets—last well into November.

The South Garden

Although each of the Conservatory Garden's three gardens has its virtues and delights, to the gardener, the mixed shrub and herbaceous borders of the South Garden are its true heart. Originally planted in a formal layout with large shrubs and bedded-out flowers, the South Garden is now anything but a typical municipal garden. Its English style is by turns energetic, romantic, and calm, displaying an extensive range of plant material unequaled anywhere else in Manhattan. At its center is the Secret Garden, a small garden room with a fountain depicting Mary and Dickon from Frances Hodgson Burnett's children's classic *The Secret Garden* (1926-1936; sculptor: Bessie Potter Vonnoh).

The ghosts of the great English landscape designers Gertrude Jekyll and Edwin Lutyens can be sensed in the way the complicated geometry of the garden meets the exuberance of the planting. Clipped hedges of Japanese holly and wintergreen barberry and rounded mounds of Japanese red barberry and purple sand cherry bring vertical order against which plants billow and spill out over the wide flagstone paths. Although new annuals and perennials are constantly added, a backbone of mature plantings creates a framework for the yearly displays. Each

Mary and Dickon in the South Garden

perennial bed is anchored with at least one large spring-flowering tree, often a magnolia, though in one bed it is a magnificent multitrunk tree lilac. Beds are further grounded by several imposing oakleaf hydrangeas and well-established clumps of grasses and perennials, including Siberian iris, coneflower, and meadow rue.

The use of red-leafed plants for accent is one signature of Lynden Miller's designs and is particularly effective here as the color carries the eye from bed to bed and serves as a unifying element. Favorites include purple sand cherry, rosa glauca, Japanese barberry, and purple smoke bush;

these are echoed in red-leafed perennials and annuals such as heuchera, fringed loosestrife, coleus, and perilla. Texture, another important factor, is ultimately more important to this design than flower color; thus, many unusually textured plants are interspersed with more familiar ones, such as the spiky thistlelike gray-leaf cardoon that shoots up amid a group of stalwarts such as phlox and boltonia.

Inner beds are planted with a formal display of 30,000 spring bulbs, including different varieties of narcissus, tulips, and minor bulbs—grape hyacinths, anemones, species tulips—followed in summer by an inventive planting of annuals that differs each year and is often an index for what's hot and what's not in the world of horticulture. Salvias, coleus, angelonia, pentas, plumbago, tibouchina, and abutilon, to name but a few, fill the beds from May through September.

The southwestern end of the garden is bounded by a naturalized woodland bank designed in the 1980s by Penelope Maynard. Many shrubs and plants used more formally elsewhere in the garden—spirea, yew, Japanese holly, brunnera, hosta—here are allowed to spread out, providing a transition from the elegant structured garden and the park beyond. In February and March, when most of the gardens in the city are still asleep, the great display of hellebores on the bank and in the beds of the South Garden is worth a special visit. The bank is at its very best in early spring, when drifts of bluebells, native azalea, wild ginger, leucojum, mayapple, brunnera, and epimedium bloom in delicate profusion.

Cooper-Hewitt, National Design Museum, Smithsonian Institution

Location: 2 E. 91st St. at Fifth Ave.

Hours: Monday–Friday 10:00am–5:00pm; Sat. 10:00am–6:00pm; Sun.
noon–6:00pm

Garden info: (212) 849-8400

Web site: www.cooperhewitt.org

Admission fee: yes

Bus: M1, M2, M3, M4

Subway: 4, 5, 6 to 86th St. or 96th St.

Facilities: garden café, rest rooms, telephones; not wheelchair accessible
unless 90th St. gate is open

Best seasons: spring, summer

The Cooper-Hewitt museum occupies the mansion built by industrialist and philanthropist Andrew Carnegie in 1901. He chose this site north of what was then the fashionable part of town so that he could buy enough land for a substantial house and a large garden. Carnegie commissioned the firm of Babb, Cook & Willard to design the stone and brick house, and landscape architect Richard Schermerhorn Jr. to create the stone terrace and garden. Although he died in 1919, his wife, Louise, lived there until her death in 1946. This mansion is the only one of the grand houses built on Fifth Avenue that still occupies its original lot, enabling visitors to admire it as it was meant to be seen, the solid mass of house balanced by a generous expanse of green.

The garden at the Cooper-Hewitt evokes the order of a time now past, with mature oak, maple, and horse chestnut trees underplanted with a mixed shrub and perennial border framing a large lawn. It is in such harmony with the architecture that one might assume it is Mrs. Carnegie's actual garden, carefully preserved. Not so. Until the 1990s, the 230-by-200-foot museum garden was so neglected that, of the original plantings, only the trees remained. It had become a latchkey garden, used as a makeshift playground by neighborhood mothers and toddlers. Two of the mothers—Lynden B. Miller and Mary Riley Smith—were garden designers who, in 1992, found the funding and labor to rehabilitate the grounds. With a crew of volunteers, they replaced the exhausted soil and replanted the shady borders. Looking at the garden today, its beds full of shade-loving plants such as oakleaf hydrangea, variegated dogwood, ferns, lilies, and hosta, one would never suspect the difficulties presented by this windy, exposed site close to the Central Park Reservoir.

Double doors lead from the main reception rooms, now exhibition space, onto a deep terrace planted with a changing group of annuals and perennials. Smith remains the designer of the garden and her artistic eye can be seen everywhere. The choice of plants is often inspired by outdoor exhibitions installed on the lawn, some of which are quite startling when presented against the backdrop of the gentle Edwardian garden. When solar energy was the subject of a show, for instance, the terrace was planted with many different kinds of sunflowers; for an exhibition featuring Latin America, the beds were filled with hot-colored exotic flowers. For years, one of the signatures of the garden has been the four long ropes of wisteria that extend the entire height of the house

Cooper-Hewitt

on either side of the main door to the garden. In the warmer months, the lawn is frequently used for social events and the garden is closed to the public. If a visitor is lucky enough to arrive when there are no parties or installations, the atmosphere of this garden is evocative of the days when Mrs. Carnegie used to send apples from her yard to friends and neighbors.

The Conservatory Garden clockwise from left: an aerial view; North Garden; crab apple allée; Untermeyer fountain; South Garden

The Metropolitan Museum of Art

Location: 1000 Fifth Ave. at E. 82nd St.
Hours: Tues., Wed., Thurs., Sun. 9:30am–5:30pm; Fri.–Sat. 9:30am–
     9:00pm; closed Mon.
Garden info: (212) 535-7710
Web site: www.metmuseum.org
Admission fee: yes
Bus: M1, M2, M3, M4
Subway: 4, 5, 6 to 86th St.
Facilities: wheelchair accessible (wheelchairs available on site), snack bar
     on roof garden, telephones, rest rooms, restaurants; strollers not
     permitted on Sundays
Best seasons: all seasons (Astor Court); spring, summer, fall (Cantor
     Roof Garden)

Within the vast galleries, wings, institutes, temples, and halls
of the Metropolitan Museum of Art, there are two gardens,
both created as exhibition spaces; one, the Astor Court, is
itself a work of art. Not to be overlooked are the four huge
urns filled with extraordinary arrangements of fresh flowers
that grace the main entrance hall of the museum and are
changed every Monday. They are made possible by a gift from
the late Lila Acheson Wallace, a New York philanthropist.

The Astor Court
A meticulous reconstruction of a Ming dynasty scholar's
courtyard, the Astor Court is the centerpiece of the Metropolitan Museum of Art's extensive collection of Chinese

art. In China, the arts of landscape painting, garden making, calligraphy, and poetry were intertwined; proficiency in all was necessary for the practice of any one of them. Landscape painting and garden making were especially closely linked, both aimed at displaying the essence of nature in symbolic form.

The scholar's court was the longtime dream of the late philanthropist Brooke Russell Astor, who spent part of her childhood in China and remembered the serenity of these courtyards. As a trustee of the museum and chair of the Visiting Committee for Asian Art, Astor wanted to bring an example of this facet of Chinese art to the museum. Political differences between China and the United States initially thwarted her hopes, but when the political climate changed, the project went forward, and in 1981 the Chinese scholar's garden became part of the first permanent cultural exchange between the United States and the People's Republic of China.

Chinese and American scholars searched the city of Suzhou, a historic center for both gardens and landscape painting, and chose as a model the courtyard in front of the Late Spring Studio in the Garden of the Master of the Fishing Nets. The required building materials were carefully collected in China; an old imperial kiln was reopened to produce both the roof tiles and the brick. The pillars were made of rare Nan wood, said to be impervious to insects. Traditionally, it has been used only for the most important building projects, such as Chairman Mao's Memorial Hall. A prototype was built in China (it remains there on permanent exhibition), and after American officials inspected it and adjustments were made, 27 Chinese craftsmen came to New York and

Directly across the main entrance to the museum, down in the well in front of 1009 Fifth Avenue, an imposing brick and limestone mansion, is a tiny moat around the basement of the building with an exquisite, classically inspired private garden. Walls covered with elaborately crafted latticework support hydrangeas and roses. A small statue against the western wall is flanked with planters filled with neatly pruned evergreens. The entire garden is set on white gravel. The sensibility is French, and the execution flawless. Designed in 1994 by David Baucher, the garden was installed when the basement, formerly the laundry and service area for the mansion, was turned into professional offices.

spent five months assembling the garden, using traditional techniques.

A moon gate forms the entrance to the courtyard. Over it is inscribed in archaic Chinese script "In Search of Quietude." A small vestibule leads to the garden proper, 59 feet long and 40 feet wide. White plastered walls pierced with windows contrast with the traditional gray roof tiles in two patterns and the gray brick flooring. The lattice windows deserve special attention; their beautiful patterns were copied from a sixteenth-century Chinese monograph. Along the eastern wall, a covered walkway leads to the moon-viewing terrace in front of the scholar's study, with its facade of shuttered doors and windows, which contains some of the Metropolitan's collection of Ming furniture.

Against the western wall stands the small Cold Spring Pavilion, topped by a typical upturned roof. It is flanked by clusters of fantastically shaped rocks pulled from the waters of Lake Tai. For centuries the rocks from this lake have been prized by Chinese garden makers for their weathered and eroded surfaces. A small stream flows out of the rocks to the left of the pavilion. Chinese grasses, bamboo, a banana tree, juniper, and pines spring from cracks between the rocks.

Extensive labels throughout the Astor Court explain how

the elements of the courtyard garden symbolize the principles of Chinese landscape painting and garden making.

The Iris and B. Gerald Cantor Roof Garden

The 10,000-square-foot roof garden on top of the Lila Acheson Wallace Wing overlooks Central Park to the south, west, and north; to the east are the elegant apartment houses along Fifth Avenue. The view is nothing short of spectacular. The garden was created in 1987 to give the museum a place to exhibit sculpture, especially twentieth-century pieces that are often too large for the museum's indoor galleries. The spare minimalism of the architectural elements and the clean horizontal green of the yew hedge set off the sculpture, although it would be nearly impossible for anything to compete with the view. The exhibition on the roof changes every year; often, it is devoted to the work of a single artist, and the opening of the Met's roof is eagerly anticipated each spring. A pergola covered with vines, including clematis, honeysuckle, and wisteria, provides some shade, and there is a small snack bar. The garden is open May to November but closed during inclement weather. Late October is an especially good time to go, when the autumn color in the park is at its peak.

Park Avenue Malls

Location: Park Ave. from 49th St. to 97th St.
Hours: always open
Admission fee: no
Bus: M1, M2, M3, M101, M102, M103
Subway: 4, 5, 6
Best seasons: all seasons

The 20-foot-wide planted median on Park Avenue, running from 49th to 97th Streets is known as the Park Avenue Malls. The malls offer color and interest to drivers and pedestrians all year long, and in their own way are as emblematic of the city as Rockefeller Center or Fifth Avenue. At different times of the year they look festive, or elegant, but their main purpose is to cover the Metro North railroad tunnel, which starts at Grand Central Terminal and pops up above ground after 97th Street. Each of the 47 malls is planted with a mixture of shrubs, flowering trees, and annuals. The spring display includes Kwanzan cherries, crab apples, and hawthorn blooming simultaneously with 100,000 tulips. For the summer, the tulips are replaced with bedding plants such as begonias, impatiens, and petunias. A public art program places art, mostly large-scale sculpture, on different malls several times a year, and artists as divergent as Robert Indiana and Keith Haring have exhibited there. In the winter lighted Christmas trees twinkle cheerfully all along the avenue.

Originally Fourth Avenue, Park Avenue was renamed in 1888 but really came into its own after the completion of Grand Central Terminal in 1913. After this, the city started to cover the open rail yards and tracks north of the new building. The original landscaped malls were 54 feet wide, allowing for a broad path and benches, but they were narrowed to their present size of 20 feet in the 1920s to allow for wider roadways to accommodate more vehicles.

Just off Park Avenue is a little-known garden attached to the Eighth Church of Christ, Scientist (103 E. 77th St., between Lexington and Park Aves.) that manages to create a delicate woodland environment in a very small space. The glossy foliage of a 20-foot-tall hawthorn spills over the steel and bronze entrance gates, hinting at the attractive garden within. Inside, four mature dogwoods set in ivy-filled square beds are the focal point, and in early May their showy flowers form a pink and white canopy above the bluestone plaza. The garden is open Monday–Friday, 9:00am–5:00pm, and is wheelchair accessible.

In the late 1950s the philanthropist Mary Lasker challenged Parks Commissioner Robert Moses to plant flowers along the malls. Moses told her that they would never survive, but Lasker proved him wrong. Filled with flowers during the 1960s, by 1979 only a ten-block length was still being planted by the Carnegie Hill Neighborhood Association. In 1981, the Lasker Foundation's Salute to the Season Fund officially began the present program, to provide funds to keep the malls floriferous and attractive, and today the Park Avenue Malls Planting Project, with contributions from the buildings along the avenue, has taken over the job. The Salute to the Seasons Fund also supported a number of other important plantings, including the cherry trees at the United Nations and on Roosevelt Island, many of the flowering trees along the West Side Highway, and thousands of bulbs in Central Park.

The northern terminus of the malls, the block between 96th and 97th, dismal and untended for many years, has

Clockwise from left: Park Avenue Malls; The Frick Collection; Central Park Wildlife Center

At Madison Avenue and 100th Street, just across from Mount Sinai Hospital, the NYCHA collaborated with the Martha Stewart Foundation and the Council on the Environment of New York City to transform a corner of the grounds at Washington Carver Houses into a welcoming garden for residents of the complex as well as for visitors to the hospital across the street. The George Washington Carver Community Garden for Living includes a mixed woodland planting along Madison Avenue and a border of sun-loving plants around a seating area, with handsome benches donated to the garden by Janus et Cie. The artist Roger Phillips created *Apple Tree*, the sculpture that marks the entrance. At the corner of Madison and 99th Street, look for the carefully tended, vibrant tenant garden titled "Garden Party" that surrounds the official Welcome to Carver Houses sign.

been turned into a small park, its design inspired by the original Park Avenue malls that featured serpentine beds and seating down the center. This park, like all the malls, is really a roof garden, and the trees had to be planted in boxes hung from the ceiling of the tunnel. Lynden B. Miller has created a luxurious planting that protects park visitors from the noise of traffic but also allows them to look north, to see the trains coming up from the tunnel.

The Frick Collection

Location: 1 E. 70th St. between Fifth and Madison Aves.

Hours: Tues.–Sat. 10:00am–6:00pm; Sun. 11:00am–5:00pm

Garden info: (212) 288-0700

Web site: www.frick.org

Admission fee: no (viewing garden); yes (museum)

Bus: M1, M2, M3, M4

Subway: 6 to 68th St.

Facilities: wheelchair accessible, rest rooms and telephones in museum

Best seasons: spring, summer

The only major example in New York City of the work of Russell Page, the outdoor garden at the Frick Collection epitomizes the restrained elegance and satisfying proportions that are the hallmarks of the legendary landscape designer. In 1973, a building adjacent to the museum on 70th Street was torn down to make way for an addition. Bowing to neighborhood opposition, the Frick decided instead to create a garden, and Page was commissioned. This is one of a number of public projects the English designer undertook at the end of his life, hoping to preserve his reputation for posterity. Page was an especially suitable choice for the Frick, which has an impressive architecture pedigree and contains the superb collection of European art amassed by industrialist Henry Clay Frick (1849–1919). Originally designed by Carrère and Hastings, who were also responsible for the design of the New York Public Library, the Frick was renovated by John Russell Pope when it opened as a museum in 1935.

Known for his unerring instinct for tone and proportion, Page enclosed a simple rectangle, creating a formal outdoor room. Raised three feet from grade, the garden can be seen both from the mansion's windows and through the iron railings along the street. The three limestone walls of the room have seventeenth- and eighteenth-century classical detailing; green trellised panels filled with flowering vines such as akebia, clematis, and espaliered quince are set into the walls at regular intervals. Almost a third of the central lawn, the sunniest section, is taken up by a rectangular, limestone-bordered pool (note the blooming water lilies and lotus in the summer), which accomplishes the trick of making the area appear more expansive by being flush with the lawn. Boxwood-edged planting beds run along the walls. The bed on the eastern wall is now filled with hollies (Page wanted white iceberg roses, one of his favorite plants, but these failed to flourish). The bed on the northern wall contains azaleas, hollies and rhododendron. Page had instructed that the beds be filled with a changing group of bulbs and annuals to keep the garden looking fresh.

The classic picture is saved from rigidity and monotony by four flowering trees placed irregularly around the pool, each a different species: a Sargent cherry, a Kentucky coffee tree, a Sugar Tyme crab apple, and a Kentucky yellowwood. Originally planted by Page, the mature yellowwood, with its smooth gray bark, is particularly effective in the winter. Wisteria trained up the north wall completes the picture.

As beautiful as this garden is, it was designed to be seen, not walked through. The exceptional ironwork of the gates to the 70th Street garden, as well as the fence that surrounds the Fifth Avenue garden, is by the famed ironworker Samuel

Yellin. Visitors cannot enter the garden except on the rare occasions when it is used for a museum function. Museum visitors, of course, can see it through the large windows on the east side of the building that perfectly frame the site, and any passerby can peer through the elaborate gate on 70th Street and observe what Page meant when he wrote, "I have always tried to shape gardens each as a harmony."

In addition to the garden on 70th Street there is a light-filled garden court just inside the front doors of the museum. This indoor garden is especially attractive in the winter months when the flowering plants and lush tropicals grouped around a central fountain are particularly appreciated. There is always something blooming, especially in the dead of winter. Along the Fifth Avenue facade of the building are three of the most beautiful magnolias in New York City—two saucer magnolias and a star magnolia by the flagpole—part of a well-kept planting designed in the 1930s by Frederick Law Olmsted Jr. They literally stop traffic when they are in bloom in mid-April. Another high point for passersby on Fifth Avenue is when the pink Queen Elizabeth roses bloom in the front garden in June.

Central Park Wildlife Center

Location: Central Park at E. 64th St. and Fifth Ave.

Hours: weekdays 10:00am–5:00pm; weekends and holidays
    10:30am–5:30pm (April–October); daily 10:00am–4:30pm
    (November–March)

Garden info: (212) 439-6500

Web site: www.centralparkzoo.com

Admission fee: yes

Bus: M1, M2, M3, M5, M30, Q32

Subway: N, R, or W to Fifth Ave.; 6 to 68th St.

Facilities: cafeteria, telephones, rest rooms; wheelchair accessible

Best seasons: spring, summer, fall

The Central Park Wildlife Center is home not only to 1,400 animals and more than 130 different species but also to gardens that both complement the exhibits and create their own sense of place. Located just off Fifth Avenue behind the large, red-brick Arsenal that serves as park headquarters, the zoo attracts nearly one million visitors a year.

Although not part of Olmsted and Vaux's original plan for Central Park, a makeshift menagerie existed on the site beginning in the mid-1800s, housing a varied collection of animals, including stray raccoons and foxes and exotic specimens sent as gifts to the city. Over the years, however, the grounds became dilapidated and the cages so rusted that it was said that keepers had to carry guns for protection. Under the reign of parks commissioner Robert Moses in the 1930s, Aymar Embury designed the first reconstruction of the space, placing sturdy brick zoo buildings around a central sea lion pool area. Although the new zoo was a huge improvement, the philosophy of zoo design changed over the next decades, prompting the Central Park Conservancy to undertake a major renovation in 1985. Cages have given way to naturalistic environments for the animals and the grounds are unified with tall, wisteria-covered arcades in the design created by Kevin Roche John Dinkeloo and Associates and completed in 1988.

The octagonal sea lion pool, with the constant movement and sound of its inhabitants, sets the tone for the surrounding perennial gardens. The plantings are deliberately informal and mix a wide range of choices: there are shady woodland beds, planted with dogwood and ferns; 22 different varieties of roses, most of them "antique" varieties; and exotic plants that are marginally hardy in the city but require little watering during the growing season, including Japanese fiber banana, windmill palm, needle palm, and yucca. Along the paths throughout the grounds are shrubs and perennials that would particularly appeal to birds: a large beauty berry, with its tiny purple berries, stands in a shady grove of white pines, and clumps of high-bush blueberries line the path near the red panda.

Mount Vernon Hotel Museum and Garden

Location: 421 E. 61st St. between First and York Aves.
Hours: Tues.–Sun. 11:00am–4:00pm (closed in August)
Garden info: (212) 838-6878
Web site: www.mvhm.org
Admission fee: yes
Bus: M15, M31, M57
Subway: 4, 5, 6, N, R to 59th St.
Facilities: rest rooms, telephone in museum
Best season: summer

Now hemmed in by an undistinguished office building and a storage facility, the 200-year-old Mount Vernon Hotel is a rare reminder of Manhattan's colonial past. The present museum was the carriage house on a 23-acre country retreat that briefly belonged to Abigail Adams Smith, the daughter of President John Adams, whose family named the property Mount Vernon in honor of George Washington's home in Virginia. Over the years, the carriage house was used as a school and a private residence, as well as a fashionable day resort, hence the name *hotel*. In 1924, the Colonial Dames of America took over the carriage house and small garden, which were all that remained of the original estate. They restored the house and opened it as a historic museum in 1939.

The garden's serene atmosphere is remarkably undisturbed by its modern surroundings. Although nothing remains of the early plantings, a plan of the original estate shows extensive gardens and orchards, and at one time a gentlemen's racetrack was located immediately behind the house. In 1972, the Colonial Dames asked noted New York City garden designer Alice Ireys to create a garden that would evoke life in the late eighteenth century, using materials and plants appropriate to that time. This is the garden we see today.

The main garden space is entered from the rear of the building or by walking through a small brick parterre garden on the eastern side. The brick, laid in overlapping circles creating a bargello-like design, has become uneven with time, which adds to the period atmosphere. In the main garden, the eye is immediately drawn to ivy trained in huge open diamond patterns against the gray wooden back fence and to a mature row of plane trees, carefully pleached so the fullness of the leaves is concentrated just above the fence. These are very effective distractions from the ten-story yellow brick storage building that looms over the property. A small gazebo occupies the northeast corner of the garden.

The restrained plant palette reinforces the tidy domestic atmosphere of the space. Brick paths wind around trim beds of ivy. There is a small circular herb garden planted with old-fashioned plants. Simple benches and abundantly planted pots complete the composition.

There is a secret to this garden: steps set into the hill on the western side lead to a small, sunny terrace built into an impressive natural schist outcropping, an unexpected link with the authentic landscape. A small terrace shaded by mature lilac and rose of Sharon is a perfect location for contemplating the history of Manhattan: before you is the eighteenth-century facade of the building, its backdrop the busy twentieth-century Queensboro Bridge.

1 Rockefeller Center

2 The Museum of Modern Art

3 Samuel Paley Plaza

4 Greenacre Park

5 United Nations Neighborhood Gardens

6 The Ford Foundation

7 Tudor City Greens

8 The Howard A. Rusk Institute of Rehabilitation Medicine

9 Gramercy Park

10 General Theological Seminary

11 Herald Square and Greeley Square

12 Bryant Park

13 Clinton Community Garden

14 Balsley Park

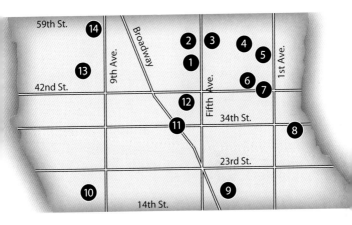

59th St.

Broadway

9th Ave.

Fifth Ave.

1st Ave.

42nd St.

34th St.

23rd St.

14th St.

Rockefeller Center

Location: W. 48th to W. 51st Sts. between Fifth Ave. and Rockefeller
   Plaza
Hours: always open
Web site: www.rockefellercenter.com
Admission fee: no
Bus: M1, M2, M3, M4, M5, M6, M7, M27, M50
Subway: 1 to 50th St.: B, D, F, or V to 47–50 Sts./Rockefeller Center;
   N, R, or W to 49th St.; 6 to 51st St.
Facilities: wheelchair accessible; restaurants inside Rockefeller Center
   buildings
Best seasons: all seasons

At any time of year, one of the great pleasures of the city is walking along Fifth Avenue and looking at the extravagant window displays. One of the most elegant displays, matching the diamonds at Tiffany's and the haute couture at Saks Fifth Avenue, is offered by the Channel Gardens at Rockefeller Center. A staggering 25,000 visitors pass by or through the center each day and are treated to an ever-changing showcase of horticultural pyrotechnics that was directed for many years by the highly talented Dave Murbach. Officially called the Promenade, the Channel Gardens acquired its name because of its position in the long, narrow space between the British Empire Building (620 Fifth Avenue) and the Maison Fran-caise (610 Fifth Avenue). The granite planters slope down from Fifth Avenue on either side of a series of canals, per-fectly framing the gilded statue of Prometheus across the open lower plaza. Originally, the gardens were intended to draw pedestrians to the lower-level shops and restaurants (and, more recently, to the ice-skating rink) but they are now very much a destination of their own.

Rockefeller Center stands on the site of the Elgin Botanical Garden, the first public botanical garden in the country. Established in 1801 by David Hosack, a Columbia College medical and botany professor, it occupied eight acres in what is now midtown but was then the country. In 1810 Hosack sold it to the state. Four years later the state turned it over to Columbia University, which eventually leased the land to Rockefeller Center, which later acquired it.

The inventive displays, which change several times a year, run the gamut from palm trees and cacti to topiary evergreens. The gardens might showcase a particular plant one month or be organized around a theme or idea, such as the restorative garden installed one fall, but above all, the gardens manage to entertain, playing off the serious architecture around them and alleviating the dense midtown experience. Most beloved of all is the winter display, with its angels trumpeting the way to the famous Rockefeller Center Christmas tree. After each display is finished, much of the specimen plant material is donated to a range of greening organizations including the Central Park Zoo, the LongHouse Reserve, and the Horticultural Society of New York, which uses them in their Rikers Island prison garden project. In addition to the horticultural pyrotechnics, the Channel Gardens have been the site of some spectacular public art installations including the giant *Puppy* by Jeff Koons and the huge *Sky Mirror* by Anish Kapoor, both funded by the Public Art Fund. The series of canals are decorated with bronze fountains in the forms of tritons and nereids riding dolphins, designed by Rene Paul Chambellan, an architectural sculptor responsible for much of the decoration at Rockefeller Center in the 1930s.

Less well known than the Channel Gardens are the four gardens located on top of the low-rise buildings facing Fifth Avenue that can be viewed from thousands of neighboring offices. When the plan for Rockefeller Center was first presented to the public in 1931, it provoked a torrent of criticism. In partial response to the negative reaction, one of the consulting architects, Raymond Hood, proposed an elaborate series of roof gardens connected by skybridges. John R. Todd, whose firm was managing the development, needed some persuading but came around when it became clear that a garden view would enhance the value of the overlooking offices. Eventually, between 1933 and 1936, four gardens (but not the skybridges) were built on top of the buildings on Fifth Avenue and two more were built on the third- and eleventh-floor setbacks of the RCA building. During the first years of Rockefeller Center's existence the roof gardens were open to the public, but they no longer are. For those who have no reason to visit one of the offices overlooking the gardens, there is an excellent view from the seventh-floor café of Saks Fifth Avenue, across the street.

The formal, geometric roof gardens are credited to the British landscape architect Ralph Hancock. The gardens are meant to be read from above: they have a satisfying clarity with clean, bold shapes and large blocks of contrasting colors. They share the same elements: clipped yew hedges surrounding a perfectly manicured lawn, cone-shaped clipped yews at the corners, stone planters, and an aquamarine pool. The lawns are gently saddle-shaped, which makes them look slightly wider when seen from above and also improves drainage. They are planted with brightly colored bulbs in the spring and equally eye-catching annuals in the summer, most often pink wax begonias and pink geraniums. Although they were renovated in 1987 and some of the plant material was changed, the look of the gardens is true to the original plan. Describing this innovative urban design, Raymond Hood wrote, "The city architect can no more ignore the roofs that continually spread out below him than the country architect can afford to neglect the planting around the house." The Rockefeller Center rooftops are a legacy of that enlightened philosophy.

The Museum of Modern Art

Location: 11 W. 53rd St. between Fifth Ave. and Ave. of the Americas
Hours: Wed.–Mon. 10:30am–5:30pm; closed Tue.; Fri.
      10:30am–8:00pm
Garden info: (212) 708-9400
Web site: www.moma.org
Admission fee: yes
Bus: M1, M2, M3 M4, M5
Subway: E, V to Fifth Ave./53rd St.; B, D, F, V to 47th–50th Sts.
Facilities: wheelchair accessible, restaurants, café, rest rooms,
      telephones
Best seasons: all seasons

One of the earliest modernist gardens and still one of the most highly regarded, the sculpture garden at the Museum of Modern Art is celebrated by critics and users alike as a place where architecture, sculpture, and nature meet in perfect harmony.

Philip Johnson, former curator of architecture and design at the museum, designed the garden as part of a renovation of the museum in 1953. It replaced one that Johnson has described as "a collection of trees in which we served food." Johnson's garden—named for one of the museum's original founders, Abby Aldrich Rockefeller, whose former home was on this site—was an elegant Mies van der Rohe–influenced outdoor room filled with sculpture. Johnson worked with the landscape architect James Fanning in 1953 and, when the garden was refurbished in 1964, with the landscape architect

Robert Zion, whose Paley Park would be built down the street in 1966. The garden was modified again in the 1984 museum expansion when the south terrace was incorporated into the building. After another expansion and renovation, the museum reopened in 2004 and the south terrace was once again joined with the garden, and the east and west terraces were enlarged and partially covered with dramatic porticos, bookending the original Johnson garden that was completely replanted to its original specifications, with new plant material in scale with the original design (the famous weeping beeches, which had grown too large for the site, were moved to the New York Botanical Garden).

Throughout its renovations, the basic shape of the garden has remained constant, although the inevitable growth of trees and plants and the addition and subtraction of sculpture alter the balance periodically.

The garden is a play of rectangles intersecting and sometimes overlapping, with a change of orientation usually indicating a change of level. The materials—rectangular slabs of gray unpolished Vermont marble for the ground plane and smooth gray rectangular panels for the walls—reinforce the geometry of the space. Two canals are set off-center; note how the paving used as bridges over the canals is set at right angles to the paving on the ground plane. The layout of beds and watercourses encourages the visitor to circle around the space rather than cut though it.

Trees are grouped in rectangular planted beds and provide both verticality and, in the summer, opacity. The graceful outlines of the trees—birch and weeping European beech—underplanted with ivy and pieris, soften the paving. Little-leaf elms have been planted on the inside and outside

Clockwise from left: Rockefeller Center; Abby Aldrich Rockefeller Sculpture Garden at MoMA; Samuel Paley Plaza

of the 54th Street wall; their mottled bark is subtly decorative against the gray concrete, and their canopy with its small leaves offers a delicate visual transition between the garden and the landmarked streetscape of 54th Street. Two beds of annuals are usually planted in blocks of color.

The garden is an active part of the museum's display space. While some of the sculptures might seem like permanent installations, it is often the site of current exhibitions. It has seen racing cars, Japanese teahouses, and performance art, and its walls have been used as an outdoor film screen; but whatever the activity going on here, the clear sense of identity of this icon of modernism is undiminished.

Samuel Paley Plaza

Location: 3–5 E. 53rd St. between Fifth and Madison Aves.

Hours: Mon.–Sat. 8:00am–7:45pm; closed January

Admission fee: no

Bus: M1, M2, M3, M4, M5

Subway: E, V to Fifth Ave./53rd St.

Facilities: concession stand

Best season: summer

Opened to the public in 1967, this is one of the original vest-pocket parks in the city and still an icon among landscape architects and urban planners. Robert Zion, the park's designer in consultation with architect Albert Preston Moore, had been an early advocate of using the empty lots between buildings to create small "parklets," or urban oases. With the commission by William S. Paley, longtime chairman of CBS, for a park to donate to the city in honor of his father, Zion was able to put his ideas into action.

His brilliantly clean design manages to use very few elements to create a space completely urban yet removed from the cacophony and confusion of the street. Paley Park, as it is called, is a simple box, and once the visitor has walked up the three steps from the street, the sense of enclosure is complete. The rear wall is a freestanding curtain of water that dominates the space, both as a white sound that drowns out city noise and as a sight to draw the eye away from the street. Twelve honey locusts planted in rows of three provide a canopy. (Honey locusts are ideal for this kind of city planting

The city's—perhaps the country's—first vest-pocket park was created at 65 West 128th Street in 1965, two years before Paley Park opened in Midtown. Rev. Linnette C. Williamson, whose small church was next door on 128th Street, was the motivating spirit, and her work is continued by the nonprofit Rev. Linnette C. Williamson Memorial Park Association, one of the few inner-city, urban land trusts in the country.

as they leaf out late and lose their leaves early, providing sun in the cooler spring and autumn months and shade in the summer.) The brick walls are covered with ivy, creating vertical lawns; simple granite sets are used as paving, another key to the park's classic modern elegance. The choice of loose tables and chairs, designed by Harry Bertoia, gives people the opportunity to arrange their own seating and makes the park particularly inviting.

This is not the first enterprise on this tiny 42-by-100-foot plot to achieve renown; it was once the site of the legendary Stork Club, which opened in 1934 and for almost 30 years set the standard for a fashionable New York nightclub.

Greenacre Park

Location: 217 E. 51st St. between Second and Third Aves.

Hours: 8:00am–8:00pm (spring and summer); 8:00am–6:00pm (fall and
early spring)

Garden info: (212) 838-0528

Admission fee: no

Bus: M15, M27, M50, M101, M102, M103

Subway: 6 to 51st St.

Facilities: wheelchair accessible, snack bar, rest rooms

Best seasons: summer, fall

Hideo Sasaki, often called the most influential landscape
architect of his generation, designed this park in 1971. One
of many vest-pocket parks inspired by the success of Paley
Park, Greenacre is somewhat larger than its precursor (110
feet deep by 63 feet wide) and much more complex. Within
its relatively small space, the park is divided into four discreet
sections over three levels: a small entrance plaza, a raised
central court, a pergola running along the western wall, and a
lower garden at the foot of the waterfall.

Dominating Greenacre is the dramatic 25-foot-high water
sculpture/waterfall along the back wall; 2,500 gallons of
water a minute crash over large granite blocks into a small
pool. The sound of water effectively blocks out all the hubbub of midtown Manhattan. Water also trickles down a granite block sculpture at the front of the garden, falling into a
pool that empties into a canal that runs next to the eastern
wall and to the water feature at the rear. The eastern wall is

Amster Yard is a beautifully planted, quiet, L-shaped courtyard complex on the north side of 49th Street just east of Third Avenue. Consisting of a square paved courtyard, with a central planting featuring a large hornbeam, and an adjacent shady rectangular gravel garden, which seems double its size due to a mirrored arch at its far end, this elegant courtyard was originally developed after World War II and was home to a number of famous decorators and artists. It is now surrounded by the offices and library of the Cervantes Institute, which was responsible for the renovation.

made up of granite blocks set in gentle relief.

The central court is paved in a warm shade of russet brick, with loose tables and chairs scattered underneath the carefully aligned honey locusts. An assertive steel pergola affords visitors a pleasant place to sit on all but the most inclement days (it provides shade in the summer months, and heating elements inside the clear acrylic vaults provide warmth in colder weather). The lush plantings include a star magnolia on the west side of the main waterfall, Hinoki cypress, and a handsome Japanese maple; shrubs include azalea, rhododendron, bamboo, viburnum, and mahonia. Planters scattered around the park are inventively planted with seasonal material; in the spring, pots of pink hydrangea complement the blooming azalea in the garden beds.

At the gate to Greenacre Park a small sign informs visitors that they are entering "a private park for public enjoyment." Judging from the lunchtime crowd, it is evident that the public enjoys this park very much, thanks to the continuing care of the Greenacre Foundation, which employs a staff of three plus a horticulturist to keep it in tip-top condition. You will rarely see a collection of broadleaved evergreens this well maintained. To add to the amenities of the park, there is a small café that serves smoothies and coffee tucked into the southwest corner.

United Nations
Neighborhood Gardens

Location: E. 47th St. between First and Second Aves.

Hours: under each garden entry

Admission fee: no (except Japan Society)

Bus: M15, M27, M50

Subway: 6 to 51st St./Lexington Ave.

Facilities: none (rest rooms and telephone at Japan Society)

Best seasons: spring, summer

Walking eastward along 47th Street from Second Avenue, you are as likely to hear Japanese or Swahili spoken by passersby as you are to hear English. This is the heart of Turtle Bay, around the corner from the headquarters of the United Nations, which extends from 42nd Street to 48th Street along First Avenue.

Although the buildings of the UN are now an integral part of the New York skyline, it once seemed more likely that it would be based in San Francisco or Boston. The dream became a New York reality in the late 1940s, when a group of politicians put together a deal between the philanthropist John D. Rockefeller Jr. and real-estate magnate William Zeckendorf. Seventeen acres of land that once held slaughterhouses, cattle pens, and tenements were donated for the new, idealistic enterprise. The dramatic buildings were designed by a committee of international architects led by the American Wallace K. Harrison and including the renowned

French architect Le Corbusier, whose scheme was the basis for the final plan. The parks department, under the direction of Robert Moses and his landscape architect, Gilmore D. Clarke, folded the new project into the existing grid of the city, redirecting traffic to a tunnel underneath First Avenue and establishing seven acres of landscaped grounds in a part of the city that had very few previously existing green spaces.

One of the many minor casualties of 9/11 has been public access to the UN grounds. The magnificent group of 200 Kwanzan cherries underplanted with daffodils was one of the marvels of a Manhattan spring, and the rose garden, which featured All-American rose selections, was among the most extensive in the city. These grounds are only available to UN personnel now, although it is possible that when the renovation of the General Assembly buildings is finished in 2013 the authorities will reconsider the policy. As it is, as part of their greening strategy, the UN is planning to add 150 trees to their grounds and also to the Turtle Bay neighborhood.

Fortunately for garden lovers, in the shadow of the UN are a number of other small gardens and plazas, each very different in style and inspiration but located within a stone's throw of each other.

Dag Hammarskjold Plaza & Katherine Hepburn Garden

Location: entrance on 47th Street, just west of First Ave.

Hours: daily dawn to 11:00pm

Named for the Nobel Prize–winning secretary general of the UN who died in a plane crash in the Congo in 1961, Dag Hammarskjold Plaza runs along the south side of 47th Street between First and Second Avenues, an area that was once the staging ground for raucous demonstrations aimed at the

UN. In 1997 the parks department renovated this one-and-a-half-acre park, installing six imposing steel pavilions each housing a fountain, linked by steel pergolas (designed by George Vellonakis). Look for the brown turtle on the edge of the second fountain from the western end.

Although it is not immediately obvious, a gate facing First Avenue gives access to the Katharine Hepburn Garden, which is a narrow sliver of densely planted woodland. Threaded through the white birch and shade-loving shrubs and ground covers, the stepping-stone path bears close attention: some stones are etched with images from Hepburn's most famous movies, others are engraved with quotes that effectively express her bracing personality. You almost hear the famous voice uttering the first quote, "I can remember walking as a child, it was not customary to say you were fatigued. It was customary to complete the goal of the expedition." A well-organized community group (www.hammarskjoldplaza.org) helps maintain the park and gardens.

Japan Society

Location: 333 E. 47th St.
Hours: Mon.–Fri. 11:00am–6:00pm (Mon.–Fri.); weekends
       11:00am–5:00pm
Garden info: (212) 832-1155
Web site: www.japansociety.org

Opened in 1971, the Japan Society was the first place in New York to showcase contemporary Japanese design. The spare, modern building by Junzo Yoshimura in collaboration with George Shimamoto included a large reflecting pool on the ground floor surrounded by planters filled with bamboo. The garden we see today was part of a 1997 renovation by the architectural firm of Beyer Blinder Belle, working with the landscape architect Robert Zion, designer of Paley Park. The new design included the expansion and remodeling of the original reflecting pool and the addition of a two-story atrium and three new gardens on two floors. The aim of the designers and the Japan Society was not to re-create a Japanese garden but rather to offer an American interpretation of one, with its refined sensibility and restrained plant palette.

The garden complex, now reduced to two linked gardens on two floors, animates the building. As is customary in Japanese garden design, water, stones, and plants are the key elements, meant to present an idealized vision of the rhythms and flow of nature. Water is the driving force here, from the moment a visitor enters the building and first hears the sound of the waterfall, which is so loud that at times it needs to be turned off during conferences.

Mary's Garden

Location: Holy Family Church, 315 E. 47th St.
Hours: Mon.–Fri. 6:30am–8:00pm; Sat. 11:00am–3:00pm; Sun.
    7:30am–1:30pm
Garden info: (212) 753-3401

Like hippies and worry beads, Mary's Garden is a product of the Sixties, a self-styled "peace garden" tucked between Holy Family Church and church buildings that once housed a papal library of peace documents. Much care is lavished on this garden, which is planted with varieties not usually seen in city gardens, such as rodgersia and epimediums. An open-work steel fence covered with wisteria and trumpet vine demarcates the garden proper. An arched bridge over a pool filled with water lilies and iris connects the two sections of the garden. The eastern planting beds feature several dogwood, underplanted with rhododendrons, azaleas, hosta, cimicifuga, and spring bulbs and a statue commemorating the victims of 9/11. The rear plaza is a little brighter and displays hydrangea, monkshood, roses, and liriope, as well as an unusual forest pansy redbud in the far corner. The focal point of the entire garden, on a pedestal surrounded by a rose arbor, is a statue of the Virgin made by the same Italian studio that created the figure of the risen Christ and two other statues in the sanctuary next door.

Scattered throughout the city are many "privately owned public spaces." Since the 1960s, office and residential tower buildings have received zoning variances in exchange for the creation of public plazas, atriums, and parks. Many, though hardly all, of these spaces are successful, but among the best is the elegant garden behind the Trump World Tower at the corner of 47th Street and First Avenue, designed by M. Paul Friedberg, and the lush waterfall garden designed by Thomas Balsley for 100 United Nations Plaza at 48th Street and First Avenue, which can be reached through the Trump driveway.

The Ford Foundation

Location: 320 E. 43rd St. between First and Second Aves.
Hours: Mon.–Fri. 8:00am–4:00pm
Garden info: (212) 573-5000
Admission fee: no
Bus: M15, M27, M42, M50, M104
Subway: 4, 5, 6, S to 42nd St./Grand Central
Facilities: none
Best season: winter

When the Ford Foundation headquarters were built in 1967, the design for a C-shaped building that incorporated a major atrium garden was a novel idea in the United States. Characterized by Ada Louise Huxtable in the *New York Times* as "one of the most romantic environments ever devised by corporate man," it was quickly hailed as one of the city's finest works of architecture and has influenced office design ever since. Instead of facing the street like most conventional buildings, the offices look out over the garden court, a third of an acre and 160 feet high, that is bathed in the natural light provided by a huge glass wall and by a skylight 12 stories above. Humid smells of growing plants and the patter of running water effectively provide a strikingly different environment from that of the surrounding city.

The garden design by Dan Kiley, a distinguished landscape architect known for his pioneering modernism, called for a temperate garden of indigenous plant material. Kiley filled the cavernous space with lush terraces threaded with walkways. Of the 17 full-grown trees, 999 shrubs, 148 vines, and 21,954 groundcover plants that were installed the first year, many have since been replaced with more tropical selections, but every effort has been made to stay true to the intent of Kiley's design.

The eight huge original Southern magnolias, which lived for 18 years, have been replaced with podocarpus and Norfolk pine. Mature ficus trees line the stairs. Several varieties of ivy and wandering Jew have been successful introductions, forming a thick and colorful ground cover. The original bougainvillea is still blooming, joined by gardenias and powderpuff trees. Recently, camellias and sweet-smelling jasmine have been added to the mix, along with seasonal flowers. Near the 42nd Street entrance, the three levels of the garden step down to a small square pool holding one bonsai in a specially designed planter. Rainwater gathered and stored in cisterns on the roof is recycled to water the garden and fill the pool, and visitors are encouraged to throw coins into the pool. These are collected and then given to Unicef.

The garden court has no benches, and casual visitors are welcome but not encouraged to linger. Go in winter, when the camellias, jasmine, and gardenias are in bloom and the warm, moist air is particularly appealing.

Tudor City Greens

Location: between E. 41st St. and E. 43rd St. between First and Second
    Aves.
Hours: daily dawn to dusk
Admission fee: no
Bus: M15, M27, M42, M50, M104
Subway: 4, 5, 6, S to 42nd St./Grand Central
Facilities: wheelchair accessible
Best seasons: spring, summer

When Tudor City was built (1925–1928), these two small
parks were created to orient the buildings away from the sight
and smell of the slaughterhouse district to the east and to
provide a landscaped forecourt for the large-scale apartment
complex. Fully grown trees were transplanted to the site,
which was surrounded by an iron fence; a small golf course
was designed for the south garden, complete with water
hazard and sand trap. Despite the intentions of the original
developers, when Tudor City was sold in 1972 the new owners made plans to build two apartment towers in the open
space. Tudor City residents resisted, and the Tudor City
Association began a long fight to save its precious parks.

    The battle dragged on through the courts until 1980,
when the developers arrived early one morning with bulldoz-
ers, ready to raze the parks. The head of the Tudor City Association got on his bullhorn and summoned the residents to
the rescue. Descending from their towers, they linked arms
and formed a human chain around the parks until an injunc-

tion against the bulldozing could be obtained. Eventually, the parks were given to the Trust for Public Land, which got the development rights rescinded and used an endowment to create the Tudor City Greens, a nonprofit corporation charged with administering and maintaining the parks. In 1988 Tudor City was declared a city landmark. A memorial in the north park to John Ferguson McKean of bullhorn fame, the founder of the Tudor City Association, spells out the residents' feelings about their parks: "Together as a community we shall strive to preserve these oases of greenery."

During the 14 years of conflict between the developers and the Tudor City Association, the parks themselves were neglected, and when Tudor City Greens took over there was much work to be done. To begin with, the infrastructure was renovated. The paths were repaired and, in some places, redirected, benches added, and the iron fences restored. The original trees, mostly maples and London plane trees, had grown huge, and the gardens were in deepest shade, so careful pruning was done to let in more light. Understory trees and shrubs have been added to establish a midlevel for the garden; variegated dogwood, amelanchier, witch hazel, and redbud have joined hollies, yew, rhododendron, and oakleaf hydrangea. Deep borders have been planted with shade-loving perennials, including hosta, hellebores, myrtle, and a spring bulb display.

Today these two parks remain one of the chief attractions of Tudor City, preserving rare open space and serving as a locus for community-based activities such as an annual Easter egg hunt, Halloween party, Christmas caroling, and menorah lighting. Although the parks are private, the public is welcome; there isn't a free bench at lunchtime in the spring, summer, or fall. An extra bonus is the unusually clear crosstown view from the bridge between the two sections of the park, making it possible to see right across 42nd Street westward across the Hudson River to New Jersey and, turning around, eastward across the East River to Gantry State Park in Queens.

The Howard A. Rusk Institute of Rehabilitation Medicine

Location: 400 E. 34th St. between First Ave. and FDR Drive
Hours: Mon.–Fri. 8:00am–6:00pm; weekends and holidays
     noon–6:00pm
Garden info: (212) 263-6058
Web site: www.med.nyu.edu/glassgardens
Admission fee: no
Bus: M15, M16, M34
Subway: 6 to 33rd St.
Facilities: wheelchair accessible, rest rooms, telephones
Best seasons: all seasons

Walking along the paths of the greenhouse at the Rusk Institute, listening to the laughter of the children in the PlayGarden, admiring the plant groupings in the perennial borders, one can easily forget that these gardens all were created with a serious purpose in mind, which was to actively support rehabilitation services. In fact, the pleasant, peaceful space serves as a model for horticultural therapy programs throughout the country, and its director, Nancy Chambers, is a pioneer in the field. This is the first facility of its kind designed to be totally accessible to people in wheelchairs, and it hosts more than 100,000 visitors—mostly patients and their families—each year. Rusk sponsors a variety of workshops and classes throughout the year, and an active group of volunteers helps with gardening tasks and works

Inside the Conservatory at Rusk

with patients on seeding, planting, and potting.

In the Glass Garden, immediately to the right of the main lobby, tropical plants and comfortable lawn chairs surround a large goldfish pond; beyond are low tables filled with carefully labeled pots of ordinary houseplants as well as more specialized orchids and bromeliads. Bird-cages of lovebirds, parakeets, and finches hang everywhere and contribute to the hum of the greenhouse. Just outside, in the shadow of the institute building, is a perennial garden, opened in 1991. Although a neighboring construction project has occupied at least half the garden, plans are to reestablish the perennial beds as soon as it is done. Meandering brick paths, wide enough for a wheelchair user and a companion, lead the visitor through a woodland setting filled with a great variety of plants, each accompanied by an identifying note. Some of the plants are chosen for their interesting habit and form; some for their texture; others for their scent; still others, such as the ubiquitous impatiens, for their bright colors. There is nothing institutional about this garden; it is an inviting space clearly cherished by patients, visitors, and staff.

The latest addition is the Children's PlayGarden, which opened in 1998. Landscape architects Sonja Johansson and Donna Walcavage were assisted in the design by a team of physical, occupational, and horticultural therapy staff and teachers from the pediatric unit at the institute. The resulting lively space manages to be truly fun for children while providing them with opportunities to engage in physical, cognitive, and sensory activities. The pastel colors enhance the whimsical quality of the playground. In addition to the usual equipment adapted to children with disabilities, there are playful surprises: a grassy hill for rolling, a large hammock, frog sprayers, and a waterfall that children can activate with the turn of a dinosaur handle. A prism sculpture over the sandbox, designed by Robert Perless, catches light and flings rainbows all around. A wide variety of perennials, trees, and shrubs edge the garden.

The Glass Garden was donated to the Rusk Institute in 1958, the first of many horticultural gifts to the city from Enid A. Haupt, who donated the perennial garden 30 years later. Heiress to a publishing fortune that included *TV Guide* and *Seventeen* magazine, Haupt was one of the foremost horticultural philanthropists in the country. Besides the gardens at Rusk, her major gifts in New York City include the restoration of the Victorian glasshouse at the New York Botanical Garden and the maintenance of the gardens at the Cloisters.

Gramercy Park

Location: between E. 20th and E. 21st Sts. and Park and Third Aves.

Hours: always open only as a viewing garden

Admission fee: no (viewing garden; only residents have keys)

Bus: M1, M2, M3, M101, M102, M103

Subway: 6 to 23rd St.

Facilities: wheelchair accessible

Best season: spring

Although Gramercy Park is open only to residents and members of the Gramercy Park Trust, any passerby can catch tantalizing views through the wrought-iron fence surrounding this picturesque square where the walks and plantings are largely unchanged from those of the nineteenth century.

In 1831, a forward-thinking developer named Samuel Ruggles acquired Gramercy Farm from a descendant of Peter Stuyvesant, who had purchased the property from the Dutch East India Company. Realizing that the grid plan for development contained no provisions for public green space in the rapidly expanding city, Ruggles proposed to develop this parcel of 66 lots around an exclusive park; the increase in value of the bordering lots would make up for the tax revenue lost by the park. His plan accepted, Ruggles began the arduous job of preparing the lots according to city regulations. A small creek ran through the swampy land; a million loads of earth were required to fill and grade the area. In 1834, although the lots were still empty, Ruggles put up a handsome iron fence with two fancy gates that surrounds the park to this day.

Responsibility for the park was given to the Gramercy Park Trust. The mandate to the trustees was to "lay out ornamental grounds and walks and plant and place therein trees, shrubbery, and appropriate decorations." Although the first house was not built until 1843, in 1838 the trust hired a gardener and started the work of design and planting, and by 1839 the park was planted with 50 kinds of trees and shrubs, including horse chestnut, elm, willow, linden, maple, and catalpa.

The park layout is simple: a gravel path circulates in an oval, separating the space into perimeter woodland beds and four grassy inner quadrants. A statue of the acclaimed actor Edwin Booth as a brooding Hamlet occupies the central open space, surrounded by a rose garden that replaced a privet and euonymus hedge. Each of the grassed quadrants is edged in boxwood and the perimeter beds are filled with groundcovers and woodland plants. Venerable upper-story shade trees line the walks, and a wide range of understory trees and shrubs, many labeled, have been chosen to provide at least two seasons of interest—including dogwood, stewartia, sorrel, black gum, viburnum, disanthus, rhododendron, clethra, witch hazel, and deciduous and evergreen azalea.

The Gramercy Park Trust continues to administer the park, preserving its unique appeal. Although the layout remains what it was in the nineteenth century, the plant material has been constantly renewed. (The tenderly preserved stump of an English elm seems to be all that is left of the 1838 installation.) A landscape renovation plan commissioned in 1992 produced a series of recommendations for the park's maintenance and renewal, while staying faithful to the original charge of the trust.

The lively architecture surrounding the square is an integral part of its appeal. Many of the original townhouses have been replaced by apartment buildings, but there are enough left so that the original character of the park remains. Number 15, now the National Arts Club, was built for former presidential contender and New York governor Samuel J. Tilden by Calvert Vaux. In 1888, Stanford White remodeled the Players Club at Number 16 for its founder, Edwin Booth. Booth was one of Gramercy Park's most illustrious inhabitants, and when he died the Players commissioned Edmond T. Quinn to sculpt the memorial statue that still dominates the surroundings. Quinn also created a memorial to Samuel Ruggles, installed in the park in 1919. In the western quadrants are two noteworthy art nouveau iron urns with elaborately curved handles. Other statuary and memorials are scattered throughout the park.

General Theological Seminary

Location: 175 Ninth Ave. between W. 20th and W. 21st Sts. (entrance on W. 21st St. halfway down the block between Ninth and Tenth Aves.

Hours: Mon.–Fri. 11:00am–3:00pm; Sat. 11:00am–3:00pm; closed Sun. and school holidays

Garden info: (212) 243-5150

Web site: www.gts.edu

Admission fee: no

Bus: M11

Subway: 1 to 18th St.; C, E to 23rd St.

Facilities: wheelchair accessible; rest rooms and telephones inside seminary

Best seasons: spring, summer

For those who seek tranquility, there are very few places more serene than the three-and-one-half-acre grounds of the General Theological Seminary. The generous lawn is shaded by large trees and surrounded by stone and brick collegiate-style buildings. A contemporary residential and administrative building designed by Polshek Partnership Architects on the Ninth Avenue side of the campus replaces an undistinguished 1950s administration building and adds a twenty-first-century note to an otherwise old-fashioned enclave. A quiet, restorative tone seems to remove the campus, both physically and spiritually, from the city and street.

General Theological is the oldest Episcopal seminary in the country. Established in 1817, it found a permanent home ten years later on land donated by Clement Clarke Moore, professor of biblical languages at the seminary and author of "A Visit from St. Nicholas" (more popularly known as "The Night before Christmas"). The site of the seminary, Chelsea Square, was originally Moore's orchard. The westernmost end of the land was the outer tidal limit of the Hudson River and was unusable until the area was filled and bulwarked. In fact, life for the seminarians in the early days was almost intolerable because of the terrible dampness of the buildings and grounds.

The present campus, or close, as it is called, is the result of the vision, will, and resources of one man, Eugene Augustus Hoffman, dean of the seminary from 1879 until 1902. When he took over, the campus consisted of just two damp stone buildings. Hoffman commissioned architect Charles Coolidge Haight to execute his "Grand Design," as it was known in his lifetime, which called for a campus based on the English model of quads, with the buildings oriented inward to the close, so that, in Hoffman's words, "the function of the grounds as a private park is interfered with as little as possible." The seminary was one of the first American institutions to use this English model for a campus and is landmarked as the oldest such campus in the city. The close is divided into two quadrangles by the Chapel of the Good Shepherd, and early photographs show the buildings surrounded by grass with no paths or borders and very few trees. Haight's red-brick and sandstone buildings are in the English Gothic Revival style he popularized.

The most remarkable aspect of the close is the large lawn, which is both a curse and a blessing. For visitors and students, the expansive swath of brilliant green is a visual treat; for the horticultural staff, keeping it healthy is an ongoing challenge, given the amount of shade and the fact that there are no pesticides or chemicals of any kind used in the garden. The 60 deciduous trees—including mature specimens of London plane, American elm, oak, birch, linden, and gingko—add to the idyllic campus atmosphere. As in other sheltered city spaces, plants that are usually at home much farther south are at home here, like a 15-foot crape myrtle and several camellias. The lawn is bordered by pleasant mixed shrub and perennial beds that feature an extensive bulb display in the spring. There is also a small children's playground on the eastern edge of the garden where raised organic vegetable beds have been established. The Chelsea Square Conservancy raises funds for garden projects and supports the maintenance of the garden, which is a large undertaking.

Although the grounds belong to the seminary, the general public is, if not welcomed, at least allowed in. Hours are fairly restricted, the entrance on 21st Street is very discreet, and visitors must leave a photo ID with an attendant in order to get into the close. As a result, the grounds are never crowded and the calm suitable to a seminary is maintained.

On the Tenth Avenue side of the seminary the nineteenth-century buildings have been updated and renovated to create the Desmond Tutu Conference Center. The old service yard has been turned into an attractive, contemporary entrance garden with crisp plantings and a trough water feature parallel to the building and bisected by the main path. Quennell Rothschild and Partners designed the new garden and, although it couldn't be more different from the sleepy sensibility of the seminary close, it does share with it a contemplative mood.

Herald Square and Greeley Square

Location: Broadway at W. 34th Street (HS); Broadway at W. 33rd
        Street (GS)
Hours: daily dawn to dusk
Admission fee: no
Bus: M5, M6, M7, M16, M34
Subway: B, D, F, Q, N, R to 34th St.
Facilities: wheelchair accessible, restrooms
Best seasons: spring, summer, fall

Traversed by millions of pedestrians a year, the bow-tie-shaped intersection where Broadway crosses Sixth Avenue at 34th Street lies above one of the busiest subway stations in the city and is home to Macy's, "the world's largest department store." This would seem to be the most unlikely place in the world to find two small but luxuriously planted gardens, and, indeed Herald Square and Greeley Square used to be little more than traffic islands. Now, however, a visitor entering the gates beholds blooming hydrangeas, elegant Japanese maples, handsome conifers, and pots overflowing with annuals; café tables and chairs are all about.

The twin gardens are almost mirror images of each other. An iron fence encloses the triangles, but the generously proportioned entrance gates allow the visitor to see out of the park from any point. Narrow granite planters line the inside of the fence and are densely packed with flowers and shrubs. Plants cascade over the edges of the planters. The planting schemes are alike in both parks. Visitors might notice a similarity between the plantings here and in Bryant Park. Whereas in Bryant Park purple sand cherry is used as a red-foliaged accent plant, here red-leaved Japanese maples provide the punctuation. The fine texture and delicate habit of the maples are well suited to this kind of small space.

With almost 750,000 visitors to Herald Square and a million visitors to Greeley, the need for security and sanitation in these busy parks is addressed head on: security guards patrol and a special crew sweeps, picks up garbage, and wipes the tables. Notice that there are no benches; all the seating is provided by loose café chairs. In 1992, the 34th Street Partnership was established to improve the quality of life in this business and shopping district. Fixing up Herald and Greeley Squares was one of its original initiatives. Formed by the same team that ran the Bryant Park Restoration Corporation, the partnership used the expertise garnered from that hugely successful renovation to create parks that would succeed on both practical and aesthetic levels. Having learned from the experience at Bryant Park, they installed luxurious restrooms in July 2009.

The renovation of these two small areas was so extensive that all that remains of the originals is the statuary that anchored each park, reminders of the New York City newspaper industry that once thrived in the neighborhood. Be sure to notice the impressive columns guarding the entrance gates to each park. At Herald Square, they are crowned by a pair of owls, a reference to *Minerva, the Bellringers, and Owl* (Antonin Jean Carles, 1895), a dramatically sculpted bell and clock that now stands in the park but originally crowned the McKim, Mead and White–designed palazzo headquarters of the New York Herald just to the north. The sculpture consists of two heroic figures, Stuff and Gruff (sometimes called Gog and Magog), striking the bell, overlooked by a bronze Minerva and her owl. When the Herald moved uptown in the 1920s, the building was demolished, but in 1940 the city installed Minerva's statue in the newly built Herald Square as a memorial to the publishers. At Horace Greeley Square each pier supports an eagle, the symbol on the masthead of the New York Tribune, which was edited by Greeley for many years. A statue of Greeley (Alexander Doyle, 1890) stands in the square as well.

Bryant Park

Location: 6th Ave. between W. 40th and W. 42nd Sts.

Hours: daily 7:00am–11:00pm (May–September); 7:00am–8:00pm
(October); 7:00am–10:00pm (November–February); 7:00am–
7:00pm (March); 7:00am–10:00pm (April)

Garden info: (212) 768-4242

Web site: www.bryantpark.org

Admission fee: no

Bus: M1, M2, M3, M4, M5, M6, M7, M42, M104

Subway: F, B, V, D to 42nd St./Bryant Park; 7 to Fifth Avenue

Facilities: wheelchair accessible, concession stands, telephones, rest
rooms

Best seasons: spring, summer, fall

As recently as the 1980s, Bryant Park was a disreputable
and dilapidated place better known for its thieves and drug
dealers than for its landscape design. Today it is filled with
visitors—5 million a year of them—-sitting on the café chairs
scattered throughout its grounds and enjoying the deep
flower borders that surround the great lawn. The transformation of Bryant Park—at 9.6 acres the only large green space
in midtown Manhattan—is one of the most successful urban
renewal projects in the city, and one of the best documented.
It came about through an innovative public/private partnership that has become a model for other projects and a key to
the revitalization of midtown.

The park has a colorful history. During the Revolutionary War the area was the scene of a battle between George

Washington's troops and the British. From 1822 to 1825 it was a paupers' burial ground. In the 1840s the Croton Reservoir was built on the site of the present library and the land behind the reservoir was designated Reservoir Park. Some years later, the city used the park for one of the nineteenth century's most famous buildings, the Crystal Palace, a huge glass and steel structure built for the first World's Fair in 1853. It burned down in 12 minutes in 1856. Troops were drilled here during the Civil War, and in 1884 the park was named for William Cullen Bryant, editor, poet, and civic leader.

In 1911, when the Croton Reservoir was torn down and replaced with the Beaux-Arts New York Public Library, Bryant Park was redesigned in the Victorian style. Twenty years later, the park had fallen into disrepair and a competition was held to refurbish it. The winner of the competition was the designer Lusby Simpson of Queens, whose plan for a French-inspired park with a large *tapis vert* surrounded by walks and

Bryant Park

allées of London plane trees was implemented in 1934 as one of the many WPA projects undertaken by the redoubtable parks commissioner Robert Moses. Gilmore Clarke, who also designed the Conservatory Garden in Central Park, was responsible for the great lawn. The design, which entailed raising the park on a plinth four feet above the street and surrounding it with balustrades and hedges, was roundly criticized when it was completed. Lewis Mumford, the distinguished architecture critic, wrote in the *New Yorker,* "Now that the architect has had his fun, let's throw the design into the wastebasket and start again."

Three blocks west of Bryant Park, across from the Port Authority bus terminal, is the dramatic 52-story headquarters building of the New York Times, designed by Renzo Piano. The heart of this LEED-certified green building is a serene 70-square-foot viewing garden that can be seen from the lobby of the building at 620 Eighth Avenue. The garden, designed by Hank White and Cornelia Hahn Oberlander in collaboration with the architect, consists of seven large paper birch (they were already 25 years old when they were planted) set in an undulating landscape of little hills and valleys that are never more than three feet above and below grade. The garden was originally planted with moss, but even after the extensive climactic tests the designer performed to ensure that the conditions would be right for moss, it had to be replaced by ferns and wild grasses. Lobby open 7:00am–7:00pm Monday to Friday.

But when the time came to try again, there was no thought of scrapping the design, because the park had been landmarked in 1974. It had once again sunk into disrepute, becoming an infamous hangout for drug dealers, the site of several murders, and a magnet for countless petty criminals. When the trustees of the library decided to mount a capital campaign, it was clear that Bryant Park needed to be cleaned up first. And so, 1990 saw the establishment of the Bryant Park Restoration Corporation, a privately funded enterprise run as a business and charged with the job of rescuing the park.

Security was the main concern. The original Lusby Simpson design had cut the park off from the street, creating a dangerous, secluded island in the middle of the busy neighborhood. The corporation turned to distinguished urban sociologist William H. Whyte to map out a direction for the renovation. Whyte's observation that people feel safe only when connected to the street and when they have some control over their environment was the guiding principle in the retrofitting of the park. The $8.9 million project was designed by Laurie Olin of Hanna/Olin, landscape architects. The hedge came down, entrances were widened, and steps were made more gradual, all to improve sight lines and establish links with the street. Whyte's recommendation that loose seating as well as fixed benches be provided resulted in the café chairs we see today.

Once the bones of the new park were in place, landscape designer Lynden B. Miller created two mixed shrub and perennial borders, each 12 feet deep and 300 feet long, to parallel the great lawn. The generous depth of the beds allows the play of layer upon layer of plant material and texture. The northern border is filled with sun-loving plants; the southern, shady side boasts substantial woodland plantings of oakleaf hydrangea, cherry laurel, hosta, and ferns. These borders are what give the park its special resonance. Each year, the garden staff plants 25,000 bulbs here and in front of the library; in the summer, 20,000 annuals add to the display, and large, handsome pots are filled with flowers in the summer and evergreens in the winter. The park is a busy place, especially in summer when the lunch-hour crowd fills the café chairs and spills over to picnic on the lawn.

The trick for Bryant Park, which is heavily programmed, is to preserve the balance between active and passive uses of the park. Highlights of the summer program include a hugely popular summer film festival, a carousel, a free open-air library, birding tours, yoga classes, and an after-work music program. In the "down" months for parks, November through February, the Bryant Park Partnership has introduced "The Pond," a skating rink that is open for public skating (it's the only free public skating rink in Manhattan), and a Christmas market. The line between event space and park can be very thin, but Bryant Park receives no public money, and so they need to continue to raise funds to keep up the park.

One of the features most commented on about Bryant Park are the restrooms, the nicest public restrooms in the city bar none. They feature fresh flowers, classical music and even scented oils, and are renovated on a regular basis.

Clockwise from left: Bryant Park; lunchtime crowd at Bryant Park; Herald Square

Clinton Community Garden

Location: 436 W. 48th St. between Ninth and Tenth Aves.

Hours: gate is kept locked; garden may be viewed through the fence at any time or entered when a gardener is present

Web site: www.clintoncommunitygarden.org

Admission fee: no

Bus: M11, M50

Subway: C, E to 50th St.

Facilities: wheelchair accessible

Best seasons: spring, summer, fall

Whether you approach from the east or west, it seems unlikely that anything promising will appear on this long, nondescript block in the heart of the Clinton neighborhood. Clinton was originally the notorious Hell's Kitchen made famous by *West Side Story,* and though generations of city governments have made it safer, scenic it is not. The first positive sign is a rose-covered fence in the middle of the block. Within the garden gate, the world is transformed. The flower-filled enclave is full of personality, with a good balance between public communal space and private plots. Climbing roses, peonies, iris, columbine, and aster line the paths and pack the beds, and though there are extensive lawns as well as large shade trees, and a native plant garden, it is the flowers that steal the show.

Founded in 1978 on an unusually large (15,000 square foot) lot that had been vacant for decades, the garden was the scene of some of the earliest and liveliest battles of the community garden movement. In 1981, the city decided to sell the land, which was being leased to the garden members for a dollar a year under Operation GreenThumb. By then the garden was already well-established, and a broad coalition of residents, merchants, and open-space groups joined together in the Committee to Save the Clinton Community Garden. The matter dragged on until 1984, when a major fund-raising initiative, the Square-Inch Campaign, was launched. Supporters could buy one square inch of the garden for a five-dollar donation. Artist Mallory Abramson painted a mural of an inchworm on the eastern wall of the garden. Mayor Ed Koch bought the first inch and the campaign went on to raise $70,000. In November 1984, Clinton became the first community garden in the city to be transferred to the parks department and given permanent status.

Pictures from that tumultuous time in the garden's history show lawns and vegetable plots planted around a geodesic dome. Today, the garden is much more sophisticated. Cleverly designed brick paths lead through the space dividing it into different lawns, each of which is bordered by flowers. There are benches tucked into nooks and crannies providing lots of seating. To the left of the entrance is a delicate Japanese maple standing in a small rock garden banded by low wattle fencing. Beyond the rock garden is a pergola. At the western end of the garden there is a small native plant garden featuring more than 100 species and active beehives that produce between 80 and 100 pounds of honey a year. A rustic pergola covered in honeysuckle and flanked by a huge native American cranberry bush is a focal point. Here the plants are carefully labeled, thanks to a grant from the Greenacre Foundation. This native garden is one of a number of designated plant sanctuaries on the East Coast dedicated to endangered

Clinton Community Garden

indigenous medicinal plants. Running along the back and eastern perimeter of the garden and separated from the communal area by a fence are individual plots, which display a wide range of styles and skills.

The garden is now a neighborhood institution much used by area residents. It is one of the few community gardens with a lawn open to the public dawn to dusk, 365 days of the year. Volunteer gardeners tend the 17 flower beds in the public area. An active bird-watching group has spotted more than 57 different species. Keys are sold for $10 to anyone who lives in the garden's catchment area—34th Street to 59th Street, from Eighth Avenue to the Hudson River. This policy has been going on for many years and there are thousands of keys in the community. There is a city park down the street for active recreation, so Clinton is the perfect place for visitors looking for quiet and contemplation. The mixture of open grass, shade trees, flower beds, and benches give it a warmth and homeyness that is hard to find in larger, more impersonal municipal gardens.

Balsley Park

Location: Ninth Ave. at W. 56th St.

Hours: daily dawn to dusk

Admission fee: no

Bus: M11, M31, M57

Subway: 1, 2, A, B, C, D to 59th St./Columbus Circle; N, R, Q to 57th
    St./Seventh Ave.

Facilities: wheelchair accessible, concession stand

Best season: summer

It's fun, it's graphic, it's fresh. Balsley Park is one of the city's developer-funded public spaces, and definitely one of the most upbeat. Formerly an eyesore known as Sheffield Plaza, it has been transformed into a lively corner park with one gentle hillock of emerald turf, which makes more of an impact here than an acre of lawn in a leafy suburb.

Like many other public spaces in New York City, Sheffield Plaza was built as a kind of trade-off, with the city granting developers a zoning variance in return for the creation of a park or plaza for general use. Although such trade-offs have resulted in some popular public spaces (the IBM bamboo courtyard comes to mind), they have often failed. Sheffield Plaza was one of the failures. Created in conjunction with the Sheffield apartments on West 57th Street, it was an ambitious project featuring an amphitheater, a waterfall, and many planters. Over time the waterfall broke, the amphitheater was used as a giant trash can, and the planters were filled with concrete to discourage rats. A weekend greenmarket provided the only bright spot.

The developer tried again, this time enlisting the help of Thomas Balsley Associates, the firm responsible for Gantry Plaza State Park. Understanding that the first rule of thumb in creating a safe and inviting public space is to have people use it well, Balsley invited a small café to establish itself in a corner of the park. He then created a transverse route through the park to encourage people to leave the city grid. Finally, in a moment of pure inspiration, he shaped the grassy mound in the center of the park. This small, smooth hummock adds an interesting contour and visual zing that only greensward can provide. Pale green in early spring, then deep green throughout the summer and fall, the grass serves as a connection with nature in the concrete urban landscape. It is inviting enough to attract sunbathers on pleasant days.

The park is surrounded by a retractable fence of upright tubes and closed at night as a security precaution. The greens of the fence, corrugated-metal backdrop, and hillock brighten the atmosphere along humdrum Ninth Avenue. Although the grass must be replaced regularly, that seems a worthwhile price to pay for such a visual and tactile treat.

Aerial view of the High Line

1 The High Line

2 Vera List Courtyard

3 Jefferson Market Garden

4 Sheridan Square Viewing Garden and
   Neighboring Gardens

5 The Garden at the Church of St. Luke
   in the Fields

6 Canal Park and Duane Park

7 Washington Market Park

8 Hudson River Park

9 Battery Park City

10 The Gardens at the Battery

11 The Elevated Acre

12 British Memorial Garden at Hanover Square

13 Federal Plaza and City Hall Park

14 M'Finda Kalunga Garden

15 Lower East Side Community Gardens

16 Merchant's House Museum

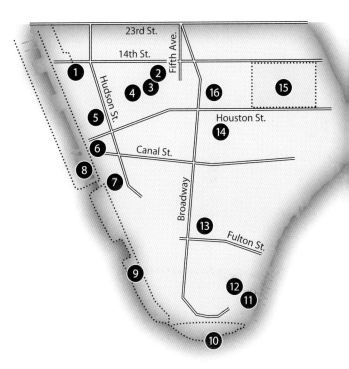

23rd St.

14th St.

Fifth Ave.

Hudson St.

Houston St.

Canal St.

Broadway

Fulton St.

The High Line

Location: section 1: Gansevoort St. to West 20th Street (entrances are
    at Gansevoort and Washington Sts.; 14th St., 16th St., 18th St.,
    and 20th St., along Tenth Ave.)
Hours: daily 7:00am–10:00pm (changes listed on Web site)
Garden info: (212) 206-9922
Web site: www.thehighline.org
Admission fee: no
Bus: M11, M23
Subway: A, C, E to 23rd St. or 14th St.; 1, 2, 3 to 23rd St., 18th St. or
    14th St.
Best seasons: all seasons

Walking the High Line, a twenty-first-century promenade
suspended 30 feet above the city, has all the poetry and thrill
of the street but none of the noise and hustle. As it threads its
way through the changing landscape of the far West Side—at
times gritty, at times sleekly contemporary—this linear garden on a ribbon of park land has transformed an abandoned
elevated railway from a romantic ruin to a subtle living memorial to the industrial past. It has also earned New York international accolades for visionary urban landscape design, and
might well serve as a catalyst for widespread urban renewal
along its path.

From the 1840s to 1929 the rail lines provisioning the
city's factories and warehouses ran down the West Side
between Tenth and Eleventh Avenues. The confluence of
train and street traffic was so dangerous that Tenth Avenue

was nicknamed Death Alley, and riders, dubbed West Side Cowboys, would gallop in front of the trains, waving red flags to alert traffic to impending peril. In 1929 the massive West Side Improvement Project addressed the dangers of the West Side rail lines, and provided money for an elevated rail line running

from Spring Street to 34th Street. Trains would run not over the roadway but through the buildings they served, delivering goods directly to warehouses and factories. It worked for a while, but by the 1950s, rail traffic had decreased, and the southern portion of the line, from Spring Street to Gansevoort, was demolished in the 1960s.

As the neighborhood changed, the demands on the train line continued to decrease. The last train ran on the High Line in 1980 and the line was finally abandoned. Inaccessible (mostly) to the law-abiding public, the High Line was left fallow; over time, plants seeded themselves along the train bed and an eerily beautiful, natural landscape established itself, scarcely noticed by the city 30 feet below.

The track had its champions over the years, including an eccentric train buff named Peter Obletz, who saved it from demolition but never realized his dream to have it reestablished as a working train track. Local property owners wanted it demolished but, as is often the case in New York, no one was willing to pay for the demolition. It was two young area residents, Joshua David and Robert Hammond, entranced by

The High Line

the romance and beauty of the industrial site, who first conceived the notion of turning the 1.45-mile-long abandoned rail line into an elevated park, much like the hugely successful Promenade Plantée in Paris. Unlike that park, which put traditional gardens on a similarly abandoned rail line in central Paris, the New Yorkers envisioned a park on the cutting edge of contemporary landscape design.

In 1999, David and Hammond founded the nonprofit organization Friends of the High Line and went full-steam ahead raising money and raising awareness of the possibilities of the site. This proved to be the right idea at the right time. In remarkably little time, the idea of the elevated park won major support from an impressive array of prominent New Yorkers and politicians, partly because Friends of the High Line proved that the new project would be economically advantageous to the city. In 2003, "Designing the High

Line," an international competition for proposals for the new park, attracted 720 teams from 36 countries. The winning proposal, from two New York firms, James Corner Field Operations and Diller Scofidio + Renfro, was published as a book a full year before the first section of the park opened.

As part of the initial push to galvanize public support for the High Line, the photographer Joel Sternfeld was given access to the site for a year. Sternfeld produced an evocative series of photographs of the desolate but oddly compelling landscape that caught the imagination of an ever-widening circle of supporters. The dilemma for the Friends of the High Line and their supporters was that, in the words of Joshua David, "the landscape existed because nobody could go up there," and turning the High Line into a park meant losing the elements that made it so magical.

The winning design seeks to preserve many of the qualities that make the High Line unique, but also to create a park that many can enjoy. Field Operations focused on a handful of elements that were essential to keep: the otherworldliness of the experience of walking along at a 30 foot remove from the streetscape; the random variation in the vegetation as the different conditions along the length of the span encourage diverse plant communities; the discovery of uncommon views and aspects of the city; and the importance of retaining the industrial beauty of the structure itself. In addressing these issues, the design team developed a guiding principle: "Keep it simple, keep it wild, keep it quiet, keep it slow." Most of the access points are broad stairways that allow people to appreciate the sturdy structure as they slowly leave the street and transition to the world above.

Throughout the park, existing railings have been preserved

The High Line

and the industrial roots are ever-present. The designers came up with a brilliant framework, creating a unique paving system to be used the entire length of the park: concrete planks are set together with special seams that allow rainwater to fall between them and be collected for irrigation. There are four different modules, and some sections are tapered and extend like fingers into the vegetation. The designers think of this relationship between the hard, mineral materials and the softer plant, or vegetal, materials as being "combed" together: the surface can be entirely mineral or entirely vegetal, but most often is somewhere in between. As opposed to a conventional paving system where the path/bed relationship is clearly defined, and the path leads directly to somewhere, here there is no absolute path, and the gradation of the vegetal/mineral relationship encourages meandering and discovering.

The Dutch plantsman Piet Oudolf was an inspired choice to design the plantings. His signature, naturalistic style, in which time and movement inform the design, is singularly apt to this setting. The plants are mulched with gravel, and the old rail lines are preserved in as many places as possible, so the image is of plants coming up almost at random from a rail bed. In addition to Oudolf's grasses and prairie plants, the kinds of trees and shrubs chosen are ones that look like they might have made it here naturally, or look as if they might be remnants of the old High Line landscape. The emphasis is not on perfect specimens, but on trees that look "used" and toughened by time—a slightly stunted pine tree rather than a fresh young specimen, for example. Cultural conditions on the High Line are highly specific and difficult—it's dry, it's windy, and the soil is very shallow—so presumably nature will do a lot of the roughening up itself.

From the very beginning, the High Line, which runs through the Chelsea Gallery district, has attracted strong support from the arts community, and public art is an integral part of the project. There is an official curator and director of arts programs on the staff, and all of the plans call for the park to be anchored at the south end by some kind of cultural facility. The High Line has partnered with a number of arts institutions to produce a variety of performance and also site-specific works.

The High Line includes several "events" or episodes to vary the pace of a visit. Where the Line turns across Ninth Avenue at 10th Street, designers have built a viewing amphi-theatre of wood, and the side rail has been replaced by a wall of glass so that visitors can sit on the stair seats and have a long view up the avenue at the traffic. There is site-specific furniture, such as the chaises that can shift position, recalling the box cars that once moved along the rails. There are also features that we might think of as traditional park or garden amenities—a meadow, a water feature, a place to sunbathe, a forest overlook. But this is truly a park like no other, a trans-formative intervention into the urban landscape, offering us a unique way of experiencing the city and a new approach to creating a landscape.

The Vera List Courtyard

Location: New School University, 66 West 12th St. between Fifth and
    Sixth Aves.
Hours: Mon.–Fri. 8:00am–11:00pm; Sat. 9:00am–6:00pm; closed Sun.
Garden info: (212) 229-5600
Web site: www.newschool.edu
Admission fee: no (note: sign in with guard to see the garden)
Bus: M2, M3, M5, M6
Subway: 1, 2, 3 to 14th St.; 4, 5, 6 to Union Square
Facilities: handicapped accessible, telephones, rest rooms
Best seasons: all seasons

This small space is an intriguing collaboration between well-
known sculptor Martin Puryear, whose work can also be seen
in the gardens at Battery Park City, and contemporary landscape architect Michael Van Valkenburgh. With its swirly,
flowing lines and sculptural furniture, the courtyard is an
installation piece that blurs the boundaries between art and
architecture.

This $2.6 million project took ten years to complete. The
brief to the designers was fairly daunting, since the courtyard,
the only open space within the school, had to serve dual functions—as a ceremonial space for lectures and social events
and also as a place where students and faculty could gather
between classes. In addition, it was to be the only green space
on campus and a work of artistic merit—quite a bit to ask of
a 60-by-150-foot courtyard.

The courtyard is a centering point for the university, joining the two main buildings and blending into the lobbies. The materials (concrete, steel, stone) and the graphic quality of the design—the curving ramp answered by the arc of the amphitheatre and divided by the strong straight lines of the walkway—are very much in the modern idiom and are an interesting contrast to the elegant brick facades of the adjoining Greenwich Village townhouses. From the 12th Street lobby, seven wide steps lead down from the glass double doors to a bluestone

courtyard. A curving path that doubles as a wheelchair-accessible ramp descends gently around a large mound through a thicket of 60 small red maples to a circular bench designed by Puryear. Inspired by a Degas painting, the unusual donut shape of the bench allows for both conversation and privacy. Another Puryear bench, identical in form but made of stone, sits nearby; a wooden one is located in the lobby. On the other side of the courtyard, a small amphitheatre is backed by a stand of black bamboo. Stands of pygmy bamboo and ivy further soften the space.

The building of this artful and creative space was a major test of First Amendment rights. In 1990 the school applied to the National Endowment for the Arts for a grant to fund the initial planning of the courtyard. The NEA awarded the

Vera List Courtyard

grant but required the university to sign an anti-obscenity condition based on the Helms Amendment. The New School refused to sign and challenged the requirement in court, asserting that the condition violated both the First and Fifth Amendments to the Constitution. As a result of the suit, the NEA was forced to drop the anti-obscenity condition for all grant recipients.

Jefferson Market Garden

Location: Greenwich Ave. between Sixth Ave. and W. 10th St.

Hours: daily; open afternoons (May to October)

Web site: www.jeffersonmarketgarden.org

Admission fee: no

Bus: M2, M3, M5, M8, M20

Subway: 1 to Sheridan Sq.; A, B, C, D, E, F, V to West 4th St.

Facilities: rest rooms and telephones inside library

Best seasons: spring, summer

Shadowed by the extravagant, colorful architecture of the Jefferson Market Library, this is one of the most attractive green spaces in Greenwich Village. The red-brick American Gothic library, with its distinctive clock tower, is a Greenwich Village landmark. Designed as a courthouse by Frederic Clarke Withers and Calvert Vaux, it created quite a stir when it opened in 1877. Several years after it was built, architects rated the courthouse the fifth most beautiful building in the country. In 1931, the Women's House of Detention was added next door on the site of the old market. By 1946, however, the city's court system had changed, and in 1959, after several failed attempts to find a use for the space, the city was poised to sell the distinguished old courthouse. (This was six years before the establishment of the Landmarks Preservation Commission, which now identifies and protects landmarks throughout the city.) Village activists lobbied fiercely to save the building from potential destruction and were eventually successful in persuading the city that it was worth preserving. In 1967 it opened as a branch of the New York Public Library, a function it continues to serve today. Its reuse marked an important milestone in the history of the historic preservation movement in the city and an early and successful example of the adaptive reuse of a historic building.

Meanwhile, neighborhood opposition to the Women's House of Detention grew for a variety of reasons both philosophical (the appropriateness of having a jail in a partly residential area) and practical (the sometimes raucous inmates would hang out the windows to chat with friends, relations, and passersby). Eventually, the jail was closed and, in 1974, demolished, leaving one-third of an acre of open space next to the library. Again, Village activists went to work and succeeded in having the land transferred to the parks department. More than two decades later, the space, Jefferson Market Garden, is thriving. Pamela Berdan, the designer of several public and private projects in the Village, used Olmsted and Vaux's Greensward Plan for Central Park as inspiration. A brick path meanders around a central lawn bordered with deep beds filled with spring-flowering shrubs and trees. The original plan called for ten magnolias, two yellowwoods, seven thornless locusts, and ten crab apples, as well as abundant roses, pyracantha, and holly. Volunteers planted thousands of bulbs. Today, many of those original plantings are still visible, complemented by new material that is part of an ambitious renovation. After a great burst of color in early spring when the magnolias and bulbs bloom, a mix of variegated plants lightens the shade of the trees, which have been pruned over time by an expert hand.

The Sheridan Square Viewing Garden and Neighboring Gardens

Location: intersection of W. 4th St., Barrow St., and Washington Place

Hours: always open as viewing gardens

Admission fee: no

Bus: M20

Subway: 1 to Christopher St.

Facilities: none

Best seasons: spring, summer

The little sliver of Sheridan Square in Greenwich Village is a bit of eye candy for those who happen upon it. A tightly planted triangular viewing garden, it was once a traffic island filled with illegally parked vehicles. In 1982, an enterprising group of Villagers, tired of delivery vans and tour buses idling for hours on the spot, transformed the spot into the garden we see today. The Sheridan Square Triangle Association has maintained the garden ever since.

Pamela Berdan, a designer and horticulturalist who worked on many Greenwich Village spaces, including Jefferson Market, designed the viewing garden. At the time it was to be planted, Berdan was elderly though formidable. On the way to the groundbreaking ceremony, she was struck by a car and severely injured. Undeterred, she continued to direct the planting from her hospital bed and, when finally able to get to the site, insisted on replanting where she felt the installation fell short.

The garden remains faithful to Ms. Berdan's vision. A mound toward the center of the triangle, crowned by a handsome magnolia, creates an interesting topography to what would otherwise be a flat space. Most of the plantings are small-scaled and quite intricate, truly a garden of little gems rather than large sweeping moments.

In fact, much of the charm of Greenwich Village lies in its small scale, and there are a number of diminutive gardens near Sheridan Square where derelict or poorly designed parks and lots have been transformed into lushly planted enclaves. Their size—each is a small fraction of an acre—reinforces the intimacy of the Village and provides welcome greenery. Especially notable are four little parks all visible within a block or two of Father Demos Square, at the intersection of Sixth Avenue and Carmine and Bleecker Streets. This square (really a triangle), which was built much later than the other little garden parks, is a typical European-style piazza with a large central fountain, lots of paving, and a perimeter planting of Japanese zelkova trees. It serves as a centering point to this part of Sixth Avenue, and the other parks function as leafy satellites around it, as if all the attributes of a large park were broken up into Greenwich Village–size bits.

Minetta Green (Sixth Avenue and Minetta Street) and Minetta Triangle (Sixth Avenue and Minetta Lane) were named for Minetta Brook, a small stream that originated near Gramercy Square and flowed through and under Greenwich Village until it reached the Hudson (note the images of trout etched into the stone at their entrances, a reference to the fish that formerly swam in Minetta Brook). The brook has been completely built over since colonial times, although some residents complain of occasional basement flooding. Water from the brook bubbles up through a pipe commemorating the ancient stream in the lobby of the apartment building at 2 Fifth Avenue. The Golden Swan (Sixth Avenue and West 3rd Street) is named for a popular bar, the Golden Swan Café, which stood on this site at the turn of the century. Sir Winston Churchill Park (Sixth Avenue and Downing Street), whose focal point is a handsome armillary, was given its name in honor of the British prime minister (not that he ever lived in the Village, but he did live at 10 Downing Street in London).

All four of these parks were renovated in 1998 and 1999 in a similar style by George Vellonakis, a landscape architect with the parks department. Existing trees were retained, asphalt was pulled up and bluestone paths were laid, winding through beds closely planted with shade-loving shrubs. Particular care was taken with materials: the iron fences are more elaborate than standard park fences; the brick wall pierced with octagonal windows at Sir Winston Churchill Park is quite elegant.

The parks are liberally endowed with benches, and the shrubbery does a good job of insulating the seating areas from traffic noise. The plant palette is as wide as can be considering the conditions. There is an emphasis on plants that thrive in a bit of shade—leatherleaf viburnums, oakleaf hydrangeas, dogwoods, some dawn redwoods, and, wherever there is enough sun (frequently at the park entrances), roses. The parks look their best in the early spring, before the canopy has completely unfolded.

The Garden at the Church of St. Luke in the Fields

Location: 487 Hudson St. between Barrow and Christopher Sts.;
     entrance on Barrow St.
Hours: Mon.–Sat. 8:00am–6:00pm; Sun. 8:00am–5:00pm; closed major
     holidays
Admission fee: no
Bus: M201
Subway: 1, 2 to Christopher St.
Facilities: wheelchair accessible
Best seasons: spring, summer

An observant pedestrian walking along Hudson Street just north of Barrow Street might notice the leafy canopy visible above the high brick wall and, like Mary in Frances Hodgson Burnett's classic, wonder if a secret garden lies on the other side. There is a garden there and, although it isn't exactly secret, it can be hard to find the entrance. Situated to the side of the Episcopal church of St. Luke in the Fields, built in 1821, and the neighboring Federal row houses, the garden is entered from around the corner, just west on Barrow Street. Look carefully for the allée of cherry trees that leads alongside a parking lot to the simple gate.

Thanks to a protected southern exposure, several species that aren't ordinarily found this far north flourish here. The Barrow Street Garden, the largest of the series of garden rooms, on the corner of Barrow and Hudson, is laid out in a square bisected with diagonal walks lined with overflowing shrubs and perennials. The venerable crab apple tree at the center, surrounded by abelia, provides welcome shade for several benches. In early summer, the waxy flowers of a southern magnolia sweetly scent the air. Although busy Hudson Street is just over the wall, birdsong nonetheless can be heard above the traffic. The garden lies on the migratory routes of birds and butterflies, and bird-watchers have spotted more than 95 different species here. On the western end, a shrub bed protected by a heat-retaining brick wall seems more like a garden in Virginia than one in New York City, and includes both a good-sized camellia and a full-grown crape myrtle.

The South Lawn is the most picturesque part of the garden complex. An expanse of grass surrounded on three sides by flower and shrub beds, it is bounded on the north by the rosy brick of the sacristy building and on the east by the romantic wall fragment of the Parish Meeting House, which burned down in 1981. The small rectory garden, which is open to the public only occasionally, boasts several unusual historic plants; a franklinia tree, originally discovered in Georgia by the early American botanist John Bartram, but not found in the wild since 1790, shows off its fragrant white flowers in late summer and its bright foliage in the autumn, and the large Roxburgh rose, first discovered in China in the 1800s, which is notable for its shredding bark.

Canal Park and Duane Park

Location: Canal, West, and, Washington Sts. (Canal Park); Hudson and
     Duane Sts. (Duane Park)
Hours: daily dawn to dusk
Admission fee: no
Bus: M20
Subway: 1 to Canal (CP); 1 to Franklin (DP)
Facilities: wheelchair accessible
Best seasons: spring, summer

These two small parks within walking distance of each other
in Tribeca have a similar history: both were renovated exten-
sively in the 1880s by the same legendary design team of Calvert Vaux and Samuel Parsons Jr., and both were revived a
hundred years later as a result of strong community pressure.

Citizen activists can often have a very big impact in New
York City. When Tribeca residents learned in the 1990s
that the state planned to remove a nondescript traffic island
between Washington Street, Canal Street, and the West
Side Highway to make way for another lane of traffic on
Canal Street, they prepared for a fight with the city over the
increased traffic. As they began their research, they discovered that the little triangle had once been a park, first established in 1871, and for several years the city's flower market
had taken place on the sidewalks surrounding it. The park
was upgraded in 1888 when Vaux and Parsons, working for
the parks department, redesigned it in their signature elegant

style. They retained the original wrought-iron fence, which
had itself been recycled from
City Hall Park, but installed
lighting, benches, fine plantings, and its major feature—a
wide, curving walkway leading to the busy riverfront. In
1921, when the nearby Hol-
land Tunnel was being built,
the parks department "lent"
the land to the Department
of Transportation for the
duration of the construction.
Somehow, they never got it
back. Armed with this information, some residents sued
to turn the triangle—by then
being used as a storage facility—back into a park, and in
1998 they won.

Just south of Duane Park is the Bogardus
Triangle, at the intersection of Hudson
Street, West Broadway, and Reade
Street. It was created when the Department of Transportation reconfigured
West Broadway in the mid-1980s, the
heyday of urban renewal. Left with an
awkward plot of land, the DOT and
Tribeca Community Association joined
forces to create a viewing garden. The
triangle was named for James Bogardus, a pioneering inventor and builder
who in the 1840s constructed the first
cast-iron buildings in the city, many in
Tribeca and Soho. The garden sits on
a pale gray granite plinth raised about
18 inches above the street. Stuffed with
old favorites, the triangle resembles
a giant planter by midsummer, with
plants spilling out and over the fence.
Bogardus Triangle also hosts an impressive number of birds, which manage to
make themselves heard above the din
of traffic.

Gracious in defeat, the city decided to use the original
Vaux and Parsons design as the basis for their plans for the
new park. At two-thirds of an acre almost twice the size of
the earlier park, Canal Park uses the original concept but both
expands and streamlines it into a richly detailed, well-executed
project. There is a handsome iron railing, granite bollards and
hoof benches, a good-sized lawn, lush plantings including a
wide variety of mature trees, and an expansive and graceful
curving pathway. The big difference is that while the path-

Cavala Park, five blocks east of Canal Park at the triangle formed by Varick, Canal, and Laight Streets, is a stylish public space on land that was most recently being used as a parking lot. Now, thanks to a donation from the Tribeca Film Festival (just across the street), which was interested in cleaning up the park to create an attractive space for its patrons, the park is a neighborhood amenity, with benches, a small lawn, and a large sculptural fountain designed by noted artist Elyn Zimmerman. Although the surrounding traffic is intense, the sound of the water (a reminder of the canal that once ran where Canal Street now is) almost drowns it out, and the sensitively planted perimeter borders (designed by Gail Wittwer Laird of the parks department) that include an unusual grouping of fragrant dwarf Korean lilacs, Annabelle hydrangea, roses, and witch hazel under the canopy of willow oaks, create a colorful screen with three-season interest.

way of the 1888 park led to a bustling waterfront, this one leads straight to the West Side Highway.

Vaux and Parsons were also the designers of Duane Park, another historically interesting small park just a few blocks away. This park was the first piece of land that the city acquired specifically for use as a public park; the parcel was bought from Trinity Church in 1797 for five dollars. Its long and complicated design history is fully explained on the plaque at the entrance. Originally the park was an open commons; later, trees and shrubs were added and an iron fence enclosed it. Vaux and Parsons redesigned it as part of an initiative in 1887 to improve public access to the city's parks. Their plan featured three paths curving in from the surrounding street. In 1940 the park underwent another transformation when it acquired a more formal Beaux-Arts style and was laid out around a central flagpole inscribed with the site's history.

The most recent reconfiguration of the park was in 1999, when it was returned to the more pastoral spirit of the 1887 design by a neighborhood group called Friends of Duane Park. The landscape architect Signe Nielsen, a Duane Street resident, created a sinuous path that winds through deep, curving beds of mostly shade-loving plants. Even though the large sycamores create more shade than sun, a fairly extensive plant palette has been used, and the relaxed habit of many of the woodland plants adds informality to the design. Shrubs and perennials were selected to block the sight and sound of cars, as the park is essentially a traffic island. Seating areas are delineated by cobblestone salvaged from the previous park. The flagpole from the old park has been replaced by a smaller one at the eastern end that incorporates pieces of the original.

Battery Park City clockwise from left: Wagner Park; Teardrop Park; South Cove; Irish Hunger Memorial

Washington Market Park

Location: Greenwich St. at Chambers St.
Hours: daily dawn to dusk
Admission fee: no
Bus: M20, M22
Subway: 1, 2 to Chambers St.
Facilities: wheelchair accessible, bathrooms
Best season: summer

Washington Market, once the city's largest wholesale market, formerly dominated the neighborhood now called Tribeca. When it was moved to Hunts Point in the 1960s the city demolished many of the market's buildings to make room for several large-scale civic projects, including the five-block-long Manhattan Community College. The land this small park occupies was originally slated to be a terraced plaza for the college but by that time—the 1970s—Tribeca was becoming a fashionable address, and, as one of the designers put it, little children were bursting out of newly renovated lofts. Community leaders decided that a park was needed, and after the usual complicated political dance among the city, the developers, and the community, Washington Market Park was born in 1983.

An innovative design by the firm of Weintraub and di Domenico called for the land to be gently bermed, creating a more naturalistic setting for a central greensward. The park was planted with an unusually wide selection of trees, some not strictly thought of as "city trees." To the surprise and pleasure of the designers, most of these have thrived, and the park boasts a handsome stand of dawn redwood, a grove of cherry, beech, and willow trees, a blue Atlas cedar, and several dogwoods and crab apples. A fanciful gazebo, trimmed in gingerbread and crowned with a pale blue roof, dominates the park. A compact playground sits at the northern entrance and a shrub border separates the playground and the entrance area from the flower-filled community garden. The park succeeds in being both greener and more adventurous than most city parks and has an almost suburban atmosphere, with mothers watching their small children and teenagers playing Frisbee on the lawn.

The community garden consists of twenty-five to thirty small plots separated by square slate stepping stones and a paved seating area. The paving and benches tie the garden into the design of the rest of the park, but the profusion of bloom in this section brings to mind a cottage garden. By midsummer, the flowers and herbs (especially mint) that explode from the beds, interspersed here and there with the odd zucchini and tomato patch, lend this well-designed space a welcome dose of spontaneity.

Hudson River Park

Location: Battery Place to W. 59th St., west of the West Side Highway
Hours: dawn to 1:00am; play areas close at dusk (unless otherwise
    posted)
Garden info: (212) 627-2020
Web site: www.hudsonriverpark.org; www.fohrp.org
Admission fee: no
Bus: M20, M21, M8, M11, M23, M34, M42, M50
Subway: 1, 2, 3, A, C, E
Facilities: rest rooms, bike path, snack bars, boat and bike rentals
Best seasons: spring, summer, fall

Imagine a magician pulling a park out of a hat: it would be impossibly long and thin, with all of the usual park amenities stretched to fit onto the narrow strip of green. Voilà Hudson River Park, which extends five miles along the Hudson River, offering park-starved west-side residents the access to nature and the river that they had sorely lacked for the generations that the west side waterfront was all about shipping and commerce.

If you were to look at a mid-nineteenth-century map of this part of the city, you would see piers lining the shoreline; the city was "belted around by wharves as Indian isles by coral reefs," Herman Melville observed. Sailing ships, ocean liners, and freighters served the fast-growing needs of New York, and they all had to be serviced by wheeled conveyances in order to get their goods to market. The west side became a hubbub of commercial activity, and drivers, let alone pedestrians, took their lives into their hands trying to navigate the streets. In the early twentieth century, after the West Side Improvement plan, the city built an elevated highway that separated wheeled traffic from the train tracks, which solved much of the problem but also cut the city off from the river (see High Line entry, p. 162). Commercial life shifted and changed, the means of transportation evolved, and the wharves and warehouses that had once been so vital grew quiet. One by one, they were taken down and used for scrap. The West Side Highway continued as one of the city's main north-south conduits, carrying cars and trucks up and down the west side. Then, in 1973, a 60-foot section of the West Side Highway collapsed at Gansevoort Street, forcing the city to pay attention. Neighborhood activists went to work to advocate for more green space and less development. After years of arguing and controversy about what should be done, the West Side Task Force recommended that a six-lane road be built at grade where the old elevated highway had been— more a boulevard than a highway—with plenty of access for active and passive uses of the waterfront. In 1998, the Hudson River Park Act was signed, and officials broke ground for the construction of Hudson River Park.

The park, 80 percent completed as of 2009, is the sum of many parts: a five-mile bike path, 13 piers, playgrounds, soccer fields, batting cages, boat launches, tennis courts, and more. Four hundred of its 550 acres are designated as the Hudson River Park Estuarine Sanctuary, where various water activities are encouraged, including boating, fishing, and even swimming. When the park was being designed, the community was consulted about their needs, so each neighborhood has its own particular focus. Commercial ventures are allowed, so there are kiosks selling snacks and bike and boat rentals, but every dollar made goes back to the park, helping to support future construction and ongoing maintenance and operations.

The design guidelines for the park's master plan identified certain elements that the entire park would have in common—primarily paving, lighting, and railing—and certain principles that needed to be respected: the river as a natural resource, the cultural and human history of the waterfront, and the connection to the west-side neighborhoods. Natural resource protection would be an essential focus.

Perhaps because of its narrow shape, and the fact that traffic is often whizzing by close to the esplanade, the park seems like a very busy place, where everything is moving quickly. But in fact there are also several areas—referred to as uplands—that are set aside for passive enjoyment, where verdant plantings cushion park users from the noise and movement. The most extensive areas are Segment 2/3 in Lower Manhattan and Tribeca, designed by Sasaki Associates, with Mathews Nielsen Landscape Architects (look for the blue and green speckled tiles in the paving that indicate this segment), and Section 5 in Chelsea, designed by Michael Van Valkenburgh Associates.

From Laight to Watts Streets in Tribeca, an undulating elevated boardwalk extends over a series of hills through a landscape of grasses, with large, rough stones forming the edging by the promenade, perfect for seating. Bermed planting beds north of Watts further buffer the wide lawn areas, where large-scale plantings of spirea, daylilies, sedum, coneflower, and roses provide color throughout the spring and summer and witch hazel and red cedars provide interest in the fall and winter. The ghostly outlines of Pier 32, now a pile field, is a reminder of the active wharves that were once here. Construction is underway on the two piers that will include lawns and an estuary garden as well as basketball courts and a miniature golf course.

Just north of Chelsea Piers Sports & Entertainment Complex (reconstructed in 1996 and now hugely successful), extending from 22nd to 26th Streets, Michael Van Valkenburgh Associates has transformed three old marine piers into nine-acre Chelsea Cove Park. Because of their location at a bend in the river, the piers have superb views both north and south, and that would be reason enough to visit. But the landscape architects, in partnership with Lynden B. Miller, have also distinguished this unusually wide section of the park from other, more linear sections by using berms and island beds to create a sense of enclosure. A grove of trees separates it from the highway and a broad lawn allows visitors to get close to the water. The entrance gardens designed by Ms. Miller serve as a strong punctuation point for the park; there are big sweeps of plants in bold colors to stand up to the light reflected off the river. Further, she has created four-season interest by planting a variety of evergreens, Knock Out roses, and trees and shrubs with interesting bark.

Battery Park City

Location: along the Hudson River from Chambers St. to the Battery
Hours: always open
Garden info: (212) 267-9700
Web site: www.bpcparks.org
Admission fee: no
Bus: M9
Subway: 1, 2, A, C to Chambers St.; N, R to Rector St.; 4, 5 to Bowling
   Green
Facilities: wheelchair accessible, café in Wagner Park, telephones and
   rest rooms throughout the park
Best seasons: all seasons

This is the place to go to feel the wind in your face. Take a walk along the 1.2-mile riverfront and look out over the Hudson River at the Statue of Liberty and Ellis Island, the boats and ferries chugging back and forth. The numerous gardens at Battery Park City, strung like beads on a string along the Hudson River, vary enormously both in mood and in style, but the river is the constant, and its defining presence creates cohesion where there could have been stylistic chaos. This park is a New York success story, built with a combination of public and private funds over a period of 20 years. It survived the attack on the adjacent World Trade Center towers relatively unscathed. Since the devastation of 9/11, this lush green fringe to the island of Manhattan seems to have grown more beautiful and precious. Two days after the attack, a team of 70 employees (the entire maintenance, horticultural, and programming staff of the park) was in the gardens sweeping up the ash and debris, at times six inches deep. Two weeks later, by the time the first residents were returning to their apartments, the gardens were blooming once again.

The idea for Battery Park City was first proposed in the 1960s, as a way of solving two problems—the decay of the waterfront on the western edge of Manhattan and the disposal of tons of landfill created by huge construction projects such as the World Trade Center. The landfill was used to build a series of new communities along the derelict waterfront; most of the actual park is built on a platform that extends over the Hudson River. The master plan was completed in 1979, and artists and landscape architects were integrated into the design process from the beginning. For those interested in urban design and landscape architecture, this is a mini-primer of late-twentieth-century design; one of the many pleasures of walking through Battery Park City is seeing the work of well-known landscape architects and distinguished artists and designers side by side. The same care has been lavished on the outdoor spaces as on the indoor ones. The entire project is punctuated with well-maintained plantings, gardens, and parks, each with its own special ambiance, that provide both focal points for individual developments and a shared public space that makes Battery Park City so distinctive.

The horticultural staff of Battery Park City are recognized leaders in environmentally sound methods of landscape maintenance, including integrated pest management. Battery Park City avoids, whenever practical, applying poisons of any kind, including herbicides, pesticides, fungicides or chemical fertilizers. This philosophy is carried through to all aspects of managing the parks, including the use of electric rather than gas-powered vehicles.

Rockefeller Park

Rockefeller Park is the northernmost point of the park system. Completed in 1992, the eight-acre park is dedicated to active recreational pursuits. The meadows, playing fields, and basketball, handball, and volleyball courts are tied to the landscape by boldly planted berms designed by Oehme, van Sweden, the Washington, D.C., design firm that pioneered the use of grasses and mass plantings of individual species. Their style is particularly felicitous here, with its emphasis on the gradual evolution of the garden silhouette throughout the season. The grasses sway and dance in the wind off the river, animating the edges of the park. Oehme, van Sweden also designed the adjacent small lily pool. Do not miss Tom Otterness's playful installation, *The Real World*, a wacky collection of bronze figures, both imaginary and recognizable, that has become one of Battery Park's most beloved artworks.

Teardrop Park

The aptly named Teardrop Park is tucked away to the east of Rockefeller Park (between Warren and Murray Streets, just east of River Terrace) and is almost completely hidden by the four large apartment blocks that surround it. The firm of Michael Van Valkenburgh Associates, influenced by Frederick Law Olmsted's design for Central Park and further inspired by the landscape of the Catskills, created this four-acre park that opened in 2004.

The plan is at once intensively designed and strongly naturalistic. To the north, a raised bowl-shaped lawn is tipped to catch every last ray of scarce sunlight and fringed, like Central Park's Great Lawn, with shrubs and trees. The park also boasts a small wetland, a children's playground with a slide and water play area, a rock climbing area and, bisecting the park, a spectacular rock wall that turns into an ice sculpture in the winter. The 27-foot-by-168-foot wall, built of Albany county bluestone, is the dominant feature in the park and it is pierced—again, as an homage to the rock work in Central Park—with a tunnel that allows visitors to pass through the wall to the other side of the site. Eighty-five percent of the unusually dense plantings are native to New York State. The combination of massive stone and native plants laid out in a noticeably naturalistic manner really does succeed as an evocation of a glen in the Catskills filled with places for children to explore, which was one of the goals of the Battery Park City Authority for this park. As in all Battery Park City parks, artists were deeply involved with the design. Here, Anne Hamilton and Michael Mercil created a series of rock installations that thread through the site.

The pace of building at Battery Park City seems never-ending: five years after Teardrop opened, Teardrop Park South, a small extension of the main park across Murray Street, appeared. Tucked into the center of a large U-shaped complex that opens to the north, the site is seriously sun-deficient: the buildings, which include a branch of the New York Public library and Poet's House, block all sunlight. Tall buildings casting deep shade are a familiar New York problem, but designers may have come up with an ingenious solution to a common woe: use a mirror to reflect light into the problem area.

Three south-facing heliostats are installed on the roof of the Verdesian apartment building across Murray Street from the park. The heliostats, eight feet in diameter, are essentially large, disk-shaped mirrors that reflect the sun into the park. They are programmed to track the sun and to move during the day to vary the angle and position of the light so that it reaches all points in the park. The light is further refracted when it hits the flowing water from the large fountain, a major element of the space that is made from massive square-cut stone whose heft and shape recall the rock wall just to the north. This is the first time this technique has been used for exterior lighting in the United States.

Although Teardrop South is surrounded on three sides by tall buildings, there is an opening through the southern section of the complex that allows passage to the Irish Hunger Memorial just to the south.

Irish Hunger Memorial

The Irish Hunger Memorial, located at Vesey Street and North End Avenue, consists of a scrap of meadow—meant to evoke a fallow Irish potato field—stone walls, and a fieldstone cottage imported in its entirety from County Mayo. Starting at grade level and rising to a height of 25 feet, the meadow, planted with flora indigenous to the north Connacht wetlands, is presented like an object on a limestone plinth. Its absolute absence of comprehensible context—it faces the Embassy Suites Hotel and the shores of Hoboken—succeeds in focusing the curious visitor on the linked subjects of the memorial: the great Irish famine of 1845–1852, in which one million people died and another million were forced to emigrate, and the problem of hunger in contemporary society. The minuscule size of the meadow, a quarter of an acre, underscores the poignancy of the subject: a quarter of an acre is the largest amount of land a farmer could own and still receive aid during the famine.

There are two ways to enter the memorial: from the east, a path leads up from the sidewalk on Vesey Street taking you through the meadow to a spot overlooking the Hudson River (and New Jersey); from the west, or Hudson side, a tunnel leads through the base of the plinth, past the museum exhibits and then to the cottage, which then gives out to the meadow. The plinth and tunnel are faced with banded layers of Kilkenny limestone and frosted glass. In the tunnel, quotations from contemporary commentary about the famine are interspersed with references to present-day hunger that are projected onto the glass.

Completed in 2002, the memorial was conceived by a design team led by artist Brian Tolle, which included the architectural firm 1100 Architects and the landscape architect Gail Wittwer-Laird. Gardeners at Battery Park City have learned to nurture the meadow, which contains stones from each one of Ireland's 32 counties nestled between the grasses and wildflowers, and it has evolved into its own miniature ecosystem. In June, when the briar rose covers the stone walls of the cottage, the wildflowers are blooming and the grass smells sweet, the tragedy of being exiled from this Eden seems very real.

North Cove Harbor

Further south is North Cove Harbor, once surrounded by the commercial hub of the World Financial Center and its plaza. Parts of the World Financial Center, including the soaring glass Winter Garden, were severely damaged by the collapse of the World Trade Center, but the plaza and the artwork were spared. The paved plaza looking out over the marina is the focus of this part of the park. Two dramatic stainless steel pylons by the artist Martin Puryear frame the sitelines of the Winter Garden. Scott Burton's stone furniture is reassuringly solid, and the quotes from the works of Walt Whitman and Frank O'Hara, installed by the artist Siah Armajani, remain on the balustrade overlooking the harbor. To the south of the plaza, M. Paul Friedberg, one of the first landscape architects to apply modernist principles to the urban landscape, designed a small formal garden. Although the garden's layout is quite traditional, the clean lines, unfussy detailing, and restrained plant palette reflect Friedberg's contemporary sensibility and complement the hard-edged plaza. What appears from afar to be a bosque of paper birches turns out to be individual islands of birch edged with Japanese holly and underplanted with blocks of vivid annuals. Next to this is a smooth oval lawn surrounded by cherry trees and sturdy wooden benches. Not technically a part of Battery Park City, this garden is the responsibility of the World Financial Center. After 9/11, the entrance became an impromptu shrine to those lost at the World Trade Center. Just west is the quiet and austere police memorial "dedicated to the memory of those members of the police department who lost their lives in service to the people of the City of New York." The small, private space, designed by Stuart Crawford, features a gentle fountain pouring water into a shallow pool, with the names of the dead recorded on a polished granite wall.

Hudson River Esplanade

The Hudson River Esplanade, extending from North Cove to South Cove, was designed by Cooper, Eckstut Associates (co-authors of the Battery Park City master plan) and Hanna/Olin. Similar to the very successful esplanade at Carl Schurz Park on the East River, it features allées of shade trees—silver linden, sweet gum, and Japanese scholar tree—and rows of benches facing the river. The esplanade is backed by deep borders of shade-loving shrubs, small trees, and perennials, including oakleaf hydrangea, climbing hydrangea, yew, viburnum, dogwood, hosta, astilbe, and a spring bulb display. Because the plantings, especially the trees, are relatively mature (the esplanade was begun in 1983) and the details and site furnishings quite traditional (the World's Fair wood-and-cast-iron benches and "B-pole" park lights), the esplanade has a patina of age and permanence.

Rector Park

Halfway down the esplanade is Rector Gate, a fanciful archway by artist R. M. Fischer that forms the entrance to Rector Park, designed by Innocenti-Webel with Vollmer Associates. One of the first of the parks to open, in 1985, it is composed of two formal viewing gardens modeled on Gramercy Park. Partially surrounded by wrought iron railings, both the east and the west gardens feature central lawns surrounded by formal bluestone paths and benches. The western garden has a rectangular lawn; at each end low boxwood hedges enclose planting beds. In the spring, these are filled with a single variety of tulip. The oval lawn in the eastern garden is graced by three Korean dogwoods. The park is surrounded by relatively low apartment blocks and the scale of the park to the buildings is nicely balanced.

South Cove

The formal esplanade terminates at South Cove, perhaps the most interesting installation within Battery Park City and certainly the most poetic. South Cove is meant to evoke the Hudson River's eighteenth- and nineteenth-century history. It is the work of the environmental artist Mary Miss, the architect Stanton Eckstut, and the landscape architect Susan Child, and here the collaboration between the different disciplines is the most complete. The artistic statement is made by the landscape itself. A broad path winds through a long wooded berm, which appears to be an allusion to the natural shoreline, sensitively planted with shadblow, oak, and locust and underplanted with shrubs and small bulbs. In the fall, the grove turns golden yellow as the leaves of the honey locusts and shadbush take on their autumn color. Huge boulders tumble down to the esplanade, mimicking the natural coastline. In the bay in front, wooden pilings, looking like the remains of the decayed waterfront, stand or lean in the water. Atmospheric blue lights hang along the esplanade. The landscape ends at a jetty that curves out over the water; a short bridge connects it to a low island that is frequently flooded or buffeted by the river. Overlooking it all is a metal tower that looks suspiciously like the crown of the Statue of Liberty and from which, fittingly, the statue itself can be seen.

From South Cove, a small esplanade leads past the Museum of Jewish Heritage, where, on the second-floor roof terrace, the artist Andy Goldsworthy has installed his first public commission in New York, called the Garden of

Stones. Goldsworthy inserted dwarf chinkapin oak saplings into the hollowed-out cores of 18 massive glacial boulders. The saplings were chosen for their toughness and despite the difficult conditions they will continue to grow over time, their trunks fusing into the stone—a perfect metaphor for surviving despite adversity.

Wagner Park

South of the museum, through a haunting grove of weeping willows, is the last of Battery Park City's jewels, the three-acre Wagner Park, a collaboration among the landscape architect Laurie Olin, the architects Jorge Silvetti and Rodolfo Machado, and the garden designer Lynden B. Miller. Wide lawns face out to views of New York Harbor and the Statue of Liberty. The gardens feature raised granite planters and planting beds, their shapes inspired by cubist paintings, set in an expanse of concrete and paving. The plantings themselves, designed by Miller, are an ebullient mix of shrubs and flowers; the plant combinations are inventive, by turns invigorating and restful. One of the gardens features "hot" colors, with vivid reds and yellows provided not only by flowers such as helenium, cuphea, euphorbia, and helianthus, but also by foliage: a gold-leafed chamaecyparis positively glows as it plays off a stand of the vermilion dahlia Bishop of Llandaff. The other garden is "cool"; here the predominant colors are the blues and pinks of artemisia, leadwort, phlox Bright Eyes, blue spruce, butterfly bush, purple coneflower, roses, nepeta, and lavender. Taken together, these gardens provide a sensual explosion of color and shape, a fitting finale to the gardens at Battery Park City.

The Gardens at the Battery

Location: 1 New York Plaza
Hours: daily dawn to dusk
Garden info: (212) 344-3491
Web site: www.thebattery.org
Bus: M1, M6, M15 to South Ferry
Subway: 4, 5 to Bowling Green; R, W to Whitehall St.; 1 to South Ferry
Best seasons: all seasons

Set like a prow on the southern tip of Manhattan, the Battery—25 acres of gardens, memorials and historic buildings—is the site of a particularly exciting display of public horticulture. The Battery gardens, completed in 2005, and now the largest public perennial gardens in the United States, have helped to improve this formerly tawdry and depressing park beyond all recognition.

The Battery wasn't always tawdry and depressing. This is a storied location: in 1623, the Dutch landed here at the tip of the island and established New Amsterdam. Soon they built Fort Amsterdam, which became the center of government of the new colony. The British and the Dutch traded Fort Amsterdam back and forth, renaming it each time it changed hands (the name "the Battery" comes from the gun emplacements that were established on this strategic parcel of land). The British finally took over in 1691, renaming the stronghold Fort George, and it remained the administrative center of New York until 1776. During the Revolutionary War the British occupied the Battery and fort, but after the war (1790), Fort George was razed and the rubble used to extend the area of the Battery for a public promenade. A circular fortification called the West Battery was erected on an artificial island just 300 feet off shore, and was connected to the mainland by a causeway. After the war of 1812, it was renamed Castle Clinton after New York Mayor DeWitt Clinton. By 1824 the Battery's military life was over and the acreage and fort were taken over by the City of New York.

The fort was remodeled and renamed Castle Garden, and for 30 years, it was one of the premier entertainment venues in the city. P. T. Barnum presented the Swedish Nightingale, Jenny Lind, here in her first American concert in 1850. Soon after this famous concert the Battery was further extended and Castle Clinton repurposed and made part of the mainland. It was leased to the New York State Commission of Emigration, and from 1855 to 1896, in the years before Ellis Island was established, more than 8 million immigrants were welcomed and processed here.

From 1896 to 1941, Clinton Garden, as remodeled by McKim, Mead and White, became the site of the New York Aquarium. This beloved institution was closed in 1941 and moved to make way for Robert Moses's proposed Brooklyn to Battery Bridge. The idea of a bridge caused a firestorm of criticism, and Moses suffered one of his rare defeats. The bridge was never built and was replaced by the Brooklyn Battery Tunnel. Although Moses persisted in his plans to demolish Castle Clinton, which he called "a red wart," he finally lost the long and bitter battle, and Castle Clinton was declared a National Monument in 1946.

The Battery was closed for ten years during the construction of the Brooklyn Battery Tunnel and was redesigned by the parks department in a standard style with a bosque of plane trees and a central mall extending the sight line of Broadway almost to the water. It reopened in 1951, although Castle Clinton languished until 1986 when, restored to its simple fortlike appearance, it became the ticketing hall for the Statue of Liberty and Ellis Island. At that time the city produced a master plan for the site, but construction was slow to start. For years commuters and tourists were chased by buskers and hawkers as they traversed the dusty bosque and patchy lawns or sat on the decaying boardwalk between ferry terminals. Finally, in 1994, the Battery Conservancy, a public-private partnership under the leadership of Warrie Price, was formed to oversee the complete redevelopment of the Battery. The transformation has been going full tilt ever since.

Major infrastructure improvements were made, and a large amount of clean-up was done. The first project undertaken by the Conservancy was the redesign and installation of the sea wall. Olin Partners (designers of Wagner Park, next door) were the project architects and artist Wopo Lolup created *The River That Flows Two Ways*, 37 panels inserted into the railings that depict the human and ecological history of the Battery An important element in the new plan was the hiring of Dutch garden designer Piet Oudolf to design new gardens and create a master plan. Oudolf's ideas have had a major aesthetic impact on the site, setting it apart from other parks and landscapes in the city and to a certain extent charting new territory in local landscape and horticultural design. Oudolf's singular style of swaths of loose perennials and grasses flowing into one another, with its emphasis on the beauty of the plant over time and its preference for the quieter, more natural species over the showy fashionable variety, has given the Battery its own very distinct aesthetic, in a way that the hardscape never did.

The gardens along the promenade were his first installation, completed in 2003. They are called the Gardens of Remembrance in tribute to those who died on 9/11, as well as the thousands who escaped that day on the ferries departing from the Battery. The gardens line the Battery Wave, a 1,500-foot granite serpentine bench decorated at each of its 23 piers with a spiral based on the golden mean. Oudolf's plantings in the narrow beds that extend from one end of the Battery to the other pick up on the freedom of movement implied by the wave and the spiral. If other plant designers look at their work as a series of beautiful pictures, Oudolf is more interested in the evolution of the composition over time. There are no stiff plants in an Oudolf landscape; it all sways in the breeze. Because of his emphasis on the entire life cycle of the plant, there is no deadheading, or pulling out of spent plants. Oudolf's design, with its own particular approach to maintenance, is made possible by a talented and dedicated horticultural staff led by Sigrid Gray. Emerging flowers, peak blooms, and seed heads all exist together in the composition. The species are often looser in habit and softer in tone than their hybrid relations, so groups of plants seem to fade into each other, evoking a natural condition, in direct contrast to the boardwalks, the towers of Wall Street and the New York harbor that form the context.

The team that designed the Gardens of Remembrance and the Promenade—Saratoga Associates and Piet Oudolf—teamed up again for the Bosque. An existing group of 140 plane trees was limbed up to bring light into the grove, Bel-

Clockwise from left: Bosque Gardens at The Battery; The Elevated Acre; perennials and grasses at The Battery

gian block paving was replaced with gravel, and Oudolf created amoeba-shaped island beds around the trees and filled them with large numbers of perennials of varying heights.

Installed in 2005, the planting in the Bosque took three years to mature to the sensuous, softly colorful landscape the designer intended. Full of movement and light, the perennials have created a compelling matrix of plants that have completely changed the nature of the space. The perennials have established a midstory, exponentially increasing the visual complexity and changing it from a formal, traditional park to something warmer and more natural.

There are about 230 different species in the 57,000 square feet of plantings at the Battery. They are chosen for four-season interest and are only cut down once a year, in March. The gardeners grow some annuals from seeds collected on site, but by and large rely on perennials, and divide clumps and pull seedlings to keep the gardens in shape. Fallen leaves and the chaff from cutting down the plants in the early spring are dug into the beds, and most of the species are drought tolerant. Every spring, the Battery gardeners pot up divisions and sell them at a plant sale to raise money for the Conservancy—the line forms early, so mark your calendars for next year.

The Elevated Acre

Location: 55 Water St.

Hours: daily 8:00am–10:00pm

Garden info: (212) 747-9120

Web site: www.55water.com

Admission fee: no

Bus: M15L

Subway: F to Broadway-Nassau

Best seasons: all

There is a great surprise in store for visitors to the Elevated Acre. The steep two-story approach from Water Street, which has been made to look slightly less forbidding by being broken up with four separate escalators, gives nothing away. You can't see the top from the bottom, and all the contemporary geometry in the world can't eliminate a certain sterility that clings to the city's largest office building. When you emerge from a short passage at the top of the staircase, spread before you is one of those pictures that make you love, love, love New York. A stylized landscape (it's called *Dune*) gently rises to a view of the Brooklyn Bridge and skyline, compact and sturdy, framed by gently waving trees. Walk to the top of the landscape and reach the long boardwalk and the whole panorama of a busy harbor spreads out below.

Designed by Ken Smith Landscape Architect and Rogers Marvel Architects and opened in 2005, this redo of the dispiriting plaza at 55 Water Street is the result of a competition sponsored by the Municipal Art Society and the building's owner, Retirement Systems of Alabama. The one-acre site consists of this "dune landscape," an elegant ipe-wood boardwalk that leads up to a tall glass-paneled cube, and a large artificial turf field. The modernist cube, called the Beacon of Progress, glows at night and recalls the Titanic Memorial Light that stood for many years on this block atop the Seaman's Church Institute. Below the cube, the artificial turf field welcomes organized events but always functions as a good place to just hang out. Already the Elevated Acre is becoming part of the cultural landscape, hosting a series of very popular movie screenings in the summer during the River to River festival. Neighborhood day-care centers bring classes up for outdoor exercise. You can even see the occasional yoga class in the summer.

The landscape, which is the first thing you see when you get to the top of the stairs or escalators, brilliantly evokes that combination of openness and random vegetation that characterizes dunes. The textured concrete panels are laid on the horizontal and subtly expand the view. The planting islands, which are slightly bermed, are geometric shapes and are reminiscent of the island beds in Philip Johnson's garden at the Museum of Modern Art, as is the rectangular grid. They are filled with shrubs and grasses and small trees. There is plenty of seating; in the summer, loose tables and chairs are put out at lunchtime and are quickly filled.

British Memorial Garden at Hanover Square

Location: Pearl, Stone, and Liberty Sts.

Hours: always open

Web site: www.britishmemorialgarden.org

Admission fee: no

Bus: M9, M15

Subway: 2, 3 to Wall St.; 4, 5 to Bowling Green; N, R to Whitehall St./
   South Ferry

Best seasons: all seasons

In an area of town characterized by angles and hard edges, here is a garden that is all flutters and flowing lines: the curving benches, intricately carved paving, and voluptuously shaped topiary seem positively feminine and almost luxurious juxtaposed to Wall Street's sober and solid buildings.

The British Garden started out as a memorial to the 67 citizens of the United Kingdom who died in the World Trade Center attacks, and became a celebration of friendship between Great Britain and the United States and a gathering place for groups associated with ties to both countries. It is described by its founding committee as a "gift from the people of Britain and its Anglo-American friends to the people and city of New York."

It is the brainchild of Englishwoman Camilla G. Hellman, who had been living in New York at the time of the World Trade Center attack. Searching for a way to remember the victims of the attack and heal the city, Hellman conceived of the idea for that most British of memorials—a garden, an enclosed and welcoming place. The site chosen for the memorial seems particularly appropriate. Originally a waterfront dock, when landfill pushed back the shoreline the area was named Hanover Square in 1714 to mark the ascension of King George I to the English throne. The British Memorial Garden Trust, which was formed in 2002, sponsored two design competitions—one for a major art installation and one for a garden design. Anish Kapoor won the competition for the sculpture. The winners of the garden competition were noted British garden designers Isabel and Julian Bannerman, who are consultants to Highgrove, Prince Charles's estate in Gloucestershire, England, among numerous other award-winning projects. The brief was quite complex—create a definitively English-style garden with a twenty-first-century edge and provide enormous amounts of seating in a site that is dark and windy.

In the design that emerged, many of the details are deeply symbolic, and the materials wherever possible hail from the United Kingdom. The stonework unifies the park and is especially noteworthy. Two sets of benches facing each other scroll down the plaza; the stone benches, made from Portland stone brought over from Northern Ireland, are backed by box-edged beds featuring flowers and giant topiaries clipped into bulbous, fanciful forms. Embedded in the stone paving, which all comes from Scotland, is an outline of the British Isles made from a ribbon of intricately carved blocks of stone with the names of the 95 British counties carved into them. Simon Verity, the British master stonecarver who worked on the stone portals of St. John the Divine, did the carving throughout the park; he also carved 67 of the finials on the memorial railing that commemorate the British dead in the attacks. The rill, a water feature that runs through the center of the park, is of Welsh slate. At one end of the park are a series of 14 iron bollards just like those found in the city of London; each bollard will display the shield of a leading Anglo-American society.

The British Garden opened to the public in 2007, though construction continued through 2009, when it was more officially opened with great fanfare and a royal visit from Prince Henry of Wales, who planted a magnolia Elizabeth in the park for the occasion. Although it has become a popular venue for celebrations focusing on Anglo-American relations and cultural events, it is also listed on the National Register as a Living Memorial, with the fitting motto "Reflect, remember, rebuild."

Federal Plaza and City Hall Park

Location: Jacob K. Javits Federal Building, Worth and Lafayette Sts.
    (Federal Plaza); Broadway, Park Row, and Chambers St. (City
    Hall)
Hours: always open (FP); daily dawn to dusk (CH)
Admission fee: no
Bus: M1, M15, M22
Subway: 4, 5, 6 to City Hall
Facilities: wheelchair accessible
Best seasons: all

These two downtown parks within a stone's throw of each
other clearly demonstrate the enormous range of garden and
park design that exists in the city. City Hall Park is a well-executed version of a traditional New York City park composed
of elements that are familiar to all. At the other end of the
design spectrum is Federal Plaza, the witty and playful contemporary landscape designed by architect Martha Schwartz,
which takes the familiar elements of an urban public space—
benches, water fountains, wire trash cans—and colors them
up, twirling them around six-foot-high green mounds to create a lively public garden space in the heart of downtown.

    Martha Schwartz's design for Federal Plaza was a happy
solution for a once-troubled plaza, the site of an epic conflict that centered around *Tilted Arc*, a 75-ton pre-rusted
steel sculpture by Richard Serra. Installed here in 1981, it
provoked a public outcry, most notably from the occupants
of the adjacent Jacob K. Javits Federal Building. Opposition

to the sculpture was so vehement that it was removed in 1989.

In 1992, when the plaza was torn up in order to waterproof the underground garage, the General Services Administration took advantage of the disruption to plan a renovation, completed five years later. Schwartz's design is loosely based on a French garden, in which parterres surround topiary, the carefully clipped plants creating patterns on the ground. The garden here features double rows of park benches (the parterres) curling around large green mounds (the topiary), which exude a cooling spray mist on hot days. Color is used with a sure hand: the trash cans are vivid orange, the water fountains bright blue, the benches a clear acid green. The curly motif, carried through to the hand railings on the steps, pleasingly echoes the form of the benches. The colors and the movement in the design animate the sober landscape of government buildings.

While City Hall Park doesn't exactly animate the area around City Hall, it does give it a comfortable and appropri-

New York seems to have a surfeit of monuments and fountains (there are two dozen in City Hall Park alone) but they get moved around among city facilities. The present fountain is a good case of the city playing musical chairs with its monuments. The fountain that forms the centerpiece of the 1999 design was created for City Hall Park in 1871 by Jacob Wray Mould, a co-designer of Bethesda Fountain in Central Park. It replaced a fountain of 1842 that was powered by water from the old Croton Reservoir. Famously, the Croton fountain had a water jet that leapt 50 feet into the air. In the 1920s, the 1871 Mould fountain was removed and sent to Crotona Park in the Bronx to make way for an installation called *Civic Virtue*, which depicted a male figure stepping on two prone females. Controversial from the beginning, the statue was sent to Queens by Mayor Fiorello LaGuardia in the 1940s, to be replaced by the Delacorte fountain. In the 1999 renovation, the Delacorte fountain was sent to Bronx Borough hall and the Mould fountain triumphantly returned to its original home.

ate context. The land around City Hall is full of history and has been a public gathering place since it was a rebel outpost in Colonial times, and its present incarnation, a renovation that took place in 1999, created a verdant traditional park that matches the nineteenth-century building, and would not have upset Boss Tweed if he had chanced upon it. The new design created a central walkway, added more grass and trees, and installed a fountain as a focal point to the large, 8.8-acre park. The park trees are stately and impressive, and the gardens around the fountain, which consist of beds of perennials backed by mixed shrubs and conifers, are luxuriant and very colorful in the summer, forming a perfect backdrop for benches that are always occupied during good weather.

At the south side of the entrance to the Brooklyn Bridge, right across from City Hall Park, is a small grove of trees, enclosed by a black iron parks department fence with a small plaque indicating that this is one of five Living Memorial Groves in the city. Planted here are five trees that survived the World Trade Center disaster and were transplanted as a living memorial. The trunks are scarred, but the trees are doing well. An elm has joined them, a gift from survivors of the 1995 Oklahoma City bombing.

M'Finda Kalunga Garden

Location: 30 Delancey St., within Sara D. Roosevelt Park
Hours: Wed.–Thurs. 5:00pm–7:00pm; Sat. 2:00pm–4:00pm; Sun.
    12:00pm–4:00pm (April–October)
Garden info: (212) 479-0880
Web site: www.mkgarden.org
Admission fee: no
Bus: M103
Subway: D to Grand St.
Best seasons: spring, summer

Named for an African burying ground that was once located nearby (M'finda Kalunga means "garden at the edge of the other side of the world" in the Kikongo language), this large and very appealing community garden has beautified the area and, perhaps more importantly, has succeeded in its mission of ridding Sara D. Roosevelt Park of the drug dealers who had colonized it in the 1970s and 80s. It was the effort to take back the park that propelled the founders to start the community garden.

Serpentine walks twist among free-form plots, and there is lots of shade from the stately trees that date to the creation of the park in 1934, when Sara D. Roosevelt Park, named after the President's mother, was called the most progressive playground and park in New York City. Some of the larger plots are edged with good-sized London plane tree branches that had been felled by wind or pruned for safety. Their graceful curves and gently mottled bark make for a unique and idiosyncratic edging, greatly adding to the sense of place and identity of this garden. Paths lead under iron or wooden arches sporting vines. Thousands of bulbs, many of them from the New Yorkers for Parks Daffodil Project, brighten the garden in the early spring. A giant compost operation is an inspiration to less ambitious programs.

A small group of gardeners do most of the work, led by Bob Humber, one of the original members of the community, whose initial effort to keep an eye on the activity in the park has resulted in over 25 years of dedicated service. Every year, a group of high school students from Ohio come on their spring vacation to help with some of the large garden projects.

A children's garden on the Forsyth Street side of the garden has a sand box, which is a rarity in the city these days (the garden has established a simple routine to keep the sand clean). Life-size stylized statues decorated with mosaic tiles stand in the children's garden, products of an art project just after 9/11 that allowed area children to express some of their concern and anxiety by creating art. The beds in the children's garden are edged with cobbles. Initially, the gardeners collected them from piles of discards they found on nearby streets; when the parks department realized that they were putting them to good use, they supplied them from renovation projects at other sites.

The city has built a senior center on the Delancey Street side of the garden. The seniors can use the garden any time, and Mr. Humber is building raised beds to make it easier for elderly or handicapped people to enjoy planting and caring for vegetables and flowers. Even though there are not very many open hours a week, the bright flowers and pleasing layout can be enjoyed from the sidewalks along Forsyth and Chrystie.

Lower East Side Community Gardens

Location: between Houston St. and E. 13th St. and First Ave. to Ave. D

Hours: generally, Sat.–Sun. 1:00pm–5:00pm; may also be open when
gardeners are on the grounds

Admission fee: no

Bus: M9, M14, M15, M21

Subway: L to First Ave.

Facilities: none

Best seasons: spring, summer

The community gardening movement in New York City was born on the Lower East Side in the early 1970s, and although the city now has hundreds of community gardens spread out over the five boroughs, this neighborhood still claims the highest concentration of them. The eclectic group of immigrants, artists, students, and activists who have lived in this neighborhood have inspired a series of spirited gardens that, though they span the spectrum of styles, share a common denominator: reliance on resourcefulness, not dollars. The imagination and originality of the creators seems to know no bounds, and a visit to the Lower East Side gardens can make you scratch your head, laugh out loud, or catch your breath.

In the 1970s, garbage-strewn vacant lots frequented by drug users and pushers were the norm on the Lower East Side. New York City was in fiscal trouble and unable to deal effectively with the situation. An artist named Liz Christy and a group of her friends used unorthodox methods to create guerilla gardens, often just climbing over fences and taking over vacant land. They would toss seed-filled water balloons into abandoned lots to encourage wildflower meadows and plant up window boxes and tree pits all over the neighborhood. Disgruntled residents joined in and started cleaning up themselves, building their own green spaces for recreation. It became apparent that the gardens filled a huge need in the neighborhoods for community gathering places.

Calling themselves the Green Guerillas, Liz Christy and her group of gardeners persuaded the city to rent them the plot on the corner of Bowery and Houston Streets, which was eventually named the Bowery Houston Farm and Garden (and then later the Liz Christy Bowery-Houston Community Garden, in honor of its founder). In 1978, the city administration, recognizing the value of the Lower East Side gardens, established the GreenThumb program, which still leases vacant lots to gardeners and provides assistance and expertise. Since those early days, many of the gardens on the Lower East Side have been given permanent status under the parks department, although others have been developed or continue to be in jeopardy. In 2002, there was a landmark settlement that affected community gardens citywide. Thanks to the intervention of a consortium of greening groups, among them the Trust for Public Land and the New York Restoration Project, more than 100 gardens were saved from destruction and permanently protected, and hundreds more were permanently transferred to the jurisdiction of the parks department—a huge step forward for the community gardening movement in the city. As a rule, members pay a small fee for the use of a garden, which entitles them to a key and, with luck, a plot of their own.

What follows is only a sampling of the community gardens

the Lower East Side has to offer. Part of what makes this area special is the sheer number of gardens; there seems to be one on almost every block. All are open to the public; hours are posted but vary according to the season. Most can be seen through their fences. The best time to visit is Saturday or Sunday afternoon, from spring to fall, when the gardens are usually

Other outstanding nearby community gardens to visit include Albert's Garden (16 E. 2nd St. between Bowery and Second Ave.); the Miracle Garden (E. 3rd St. between Avenues A and B); Ken-Keleba House Sculpture Garden (E. 3rd Street between Avenues B and C); Orchard Alley (E. 4th St. between Avenues C and D); El Jardin del Paraiso (706–718 E. 5th Street between Avenues C and D); Green Oasis (E. 8th St. between Avenues C and D); the Firemen's Memorial Garden (E. 8th St. between Avenues C and D); and El Sol Brillante (E. 12th St. between Avenues A and B).

open; however, at other times, if a member is present, he or she may be delighted to show visitors around.

Liz Christy Bowery-Houston Community Garden

Location: 110 East Houston St. between Second Ave. and Bowery

Hours: Sat. 12:00pm–4:00pm (all year); Sun. 12:00pm–4:00pm and
Tues. 6:00pm–dusk (May–September)

Web site: www.lizchristygarden.org

This is the community garden that started it all, the very first site that was officially approved as a community garden in 1974 by the city office of Housing Preservation and Development. Volunteers hauled away garbage and imported good soil, planted raised vegetable beds, and soon added trees, shrubs, and perennials. For many years it thrived, becoming a mature shade garden with handsome specimen trees. When plans for the AvalonBay complex next door were announced and it was clear that the building would seriously intrude into the garden, there was a huge outcry in support of this

Clockwise from left: Creative Little Garden; El Sol Brillante; Liz Christy Bowery-Houston Community Garden

local landmark. With the help of the parks department, an agreement was reached with the developer in 2005 that made sure the garden would be preserved. After being gated for two years, Liz Christy Bowery-Houston reopened in 2007, and you could almost hear the neighborhood breathe a collective sigh of relief. The huge dawn redwood still stands; the Blue Atlas cedar still stands; and the gardeners are learning to accommodate to the new, sunnier conditions.

A winding path leads from the entrance on Bowery, through the island beds, to a seating area with handsome benches near Second Avenue. This was once a separate garden called Rock 'n' Rose, but now restored to the Liz Christy garden it serves as a much-appreciated visiting spot. The individual plots, which are designed and maintained by the members, each tell a different story, but the garden is clearly home to some very sophisticated gardeners. The small sliver of a garden includes a birch grove, both ornamental and edible fruit trees, a berry patch, a cactus and moss collection, a native and wildflower garden, a pond (with a resident turtle), a beehive, and a wide variety of herbs and perennials. When they are at their peak in June, the climbing roses cascading over the pergola that forms the southern fence are easily the most beautiful sight on Houston Street.

Parque de Tranquilidad

Location: 314–318 E. 4th St. between Aves. C and D

Hours: Sat. and Sun. afternoon (summer)

Among the earliest gardens on the Lower East Side, Parque de Tranquilidad was founded on the former site of a synagogue, one of many that served the area's predominantly Jewish population. Architectural remnants from the previous structure are used throughout the space, which, like many gardens located in vacant lots, is deep and narrow. Often, community gardens focus on growing vegetables, but this one, as its name implies, is primarily a place of repose and pleasure. A path bordered by a rustic fence passes well-kept beds of hosta, euonymus, rhododendron, and azalea. A mature citrus tree occupies a sunny spot against a west wall and a birdbath fashioned from mosaics of broken glass provides a cheerful note. There are several seating areas along a path that eventually leads to a little plaza with a picnic table and a barbecue. Across the street from Tranquilidad is El Jardin del Paradiso, a larger but less intensively planted garden.

Creative Little Garden

Location: 530 E. 6th St. between Aves. A and B
Hours: Sat.–Sun. 12:00pm–5:00pm (summer)

For many years, the guiding light of this garden was an energetic Frenchwoman, Françoise Cachelin, who was a strong force not only for her own garden but also for other Lower East Side gardens as well. The hallmarks of this tiny space are shade, order, and tranquility. A gravel path winds through a grove of viburnum, azaleas, rhododendron, fern, and hosta to a small piazza shaded by a large willow. The large rocks placed at intervals were brought to the garden from Brooklyn. Over the years, many of the members have been artists who have endowed the space with a series of playful artworks. The garden is full of surprises: to the left of the entrance is a brick-wall sculpture in the shape of a niche; here someone has placed a small figure of a fox. Another artist has fashioned metal sculptures resembling stylized flowers. Some of these have been embedded in the gravel path; others peek out of the foliage. Tree stumps serve as plant stands throughout the garden. The piazza at the back is paved with samples of marble collected from building sites all over the world. The vividly painted benches were rescued from other locations as well.

6th and B Garden

Location: 78–92 Avenue B at 6th St.
Hours: Sat.–Sun. 1:00pm–6:00pm (summer)
Web site: www.6bgarden.org

Down the street from the Creative Little Garden is the larger and better-known 6th and B Garden, a major community center with active programming. Located on a large corner lot, it is relatively sunny and has individual plots as well as communal space. Some of the plots are dedicated to vegetables and others are filled with flowers and herbs. At the center of the garden is a large pergola and a stage, the scene of many community events and performances, including jazz, dance, and children's programs. A small playground was built in a corner of the garden in exchange for the city's donation of the land. A handsome fence with a motif of hands now encloses the garden, the result of garden members' successful solicitation of funding from various corporate and civic groups.

6BC Botanical Garden

Location: 624–628 E. 6th St. between Aves. B and C
Hours: Sat.–Sun. 1:00pm–4:00pm; Wed. 6:00pm to dusk (summer)
Web site: www.6bc.org

Just east of the 6th and B Garden is the complex, colorful, and elegantly designed 6BC Botanical Garden. A kaleidoscope of shapes and colors at first glance, this space eventually resolves into a series of smaller vignettes: a water feature, a rock garden, a woodland, perennial beds, and flowering trees. A number of architectural features, each finely executed, add structure to the intensively planted enclave. A long grape arbor on the diagonal makes a strong statement; solar panels on the roof of the arbor provide energy to run an adjacent waterfall and the garden's power tools. A mini-casita with a little front porch lies along the east wall of the garden (a second floor has been added to house a neighborhood environmental center), and at the far end of the garden is an elegant

In midsummer, the George Hecht Viewing Garden at the triangle formed by East 9th Street, Stuyvesant Place, and Third Avenue looks like a tightly packed bouquet offered to pedestrians and drivers whizzing along Third Avenue. Named for a public-spirited philanthropist who was an alumnus of nearby Cooper Union, the viewing garden includes sun-loving shrubs and ornamental grasses; a compass on the ground gives the true orientation of Stuyvesant Place, and a plaque explains that the garden pays homage to the city's Dutch heritage by "restoring a patch of greenery to what was in the 17th century part of Stuyvesant's bouwerie, or farm."

Chinese-inspired meditation pavilion, painted red. A picnic table is the site for a little trough garden; there is also a grotto with native plants and a woodland area. Although it may seem impossible to cram so many elements into a city lot and have the garden succeed, the number of elements all come together and actually makes it appear larger than it really is.

La Plaza Cultural de Armando Perez

Location: 632–650 E. 9th St. at Ave. C
Hours: Sat.–Sun. 12:00pm–5:00pm (summer)
Web site: www.laplazacultural.org

This open green space features two six-story willows planted in the late 1970s. Fed by underground springs, these trees have grown quickly to giant proportions. Two hundred years ago, this corner was a delta of the East River, at the confluence of two underground streams. Now it is a vibrant community resource, providing a full calendar of performing arts and educational programming. La Plaza Cultural is surrounded by a fence topped by brightly colored fantasy sculptures made up of flattened, cutout cans. This cheerful piece of folk art sets the tone for the plaza, which features a large lawn with seating under linden and willow trees and a terraced amphitheatre and stage made from rocks and rubble. More than 20 varieties of trees are scattered throughout.

9th Street Community Garden and Park
Location: 144 Ave. C at 9th St.
Hours: Sat.–Sun. 12:00pm–5:00pm (summer)
The half-acre 9th Street Community Garden and Park is one of the largest community gardens in the city, with more than 60 individual ten-by-ten-foot plots in which everything from papayas to flowers are grown. Here, as elsewhere, the plots express the individuality of the members, and a wealth of communal seating areas and nooks provide a balance between public and private spaces, a luxury made possible by the relatively large size of the garden. Many of the paths are paved with bricks and pavers rescued from nearby demolition work. Distinctive features of the garden include a towering willow, a wishing well covered with a spectacular display of the red rose Blaze (a memorial to a garden member); a goldfish pond edged in large rocks and surrounded by cattails and water lilies; a small shady nook paved with mosaics.

Merchant's House Museum

Location: 29 E. 4th St. between Lafayette St. and Bowery

Hours: Thurs.–Mon. 12:00pm–5:00pm

Garden info: (212) 777-1089

Web site: www.merchantshouse.org

Admission fee: yes

Bus: M1, M5, M6, M102

Subway: 6 to Astor Place; N, R to Eighth St.; F, B to Broadway/
    Lafayette St.

Facilities: rest rooms and telephones in museum

Best seasons: spring, summer

Gardens are notoriously ephemeral; most of those at historic sites are either interpretations of what the originals might have looked like or generic landscapes meant to create a pleasant setting for the house. The garden of the Merchant's House Museum, however, is a rarity—the real thing. The small backyard lot, with its bluestone flagging, narrow side borders, and two central parterres edged in stone, remains essentially as it was laid out in 1832 by its builder, Joseph Brewster.

In 1835, when a wealthy hardware merchant named Seabury Tredwell bought the attractive Greek Revival townhouse from Brewster, the neighborhood was an elegant enclave located just behind the fabled Lafayette Place, then one of the grandest addresses in the city. Although the center of fashionable life soon moved north, the Tredwells stayed and raised their children in the house. Gertrude, their eighth child, was born there in 1840, lived in the house all her life, and died in an upstairs bedroom in 1933. Three years later, the house, which had been preserved intact, became the Merchant's House Museum.

Gertrude Tredwell and her family kept everything "as Papa wanted it." The interior features what is thought to be the finest Greek Revival detailing left in the city and contains a fascinating collection of furniture, china, kitchen utensils, clothes, dance programs, diaries, and bills. Because the family kept voluminous records, quite a bit is known about what the Tredwells referred to as their "beautiful respite from the street."

This respite is a rectangular garden extending the full 25-foot width of the house and 60 feet in length. A small wooden room attached to the house was originally a loggia where the ladies could relax and admire their "vista." (Tredwell enclosed the loggia in 1848, turning it into a small dining parlor.) When the house was built it was one of a series of six identical residences whose back gardens were separated by white painted trelliswork. The trellises were pierced by as many as four arbors, or bowers, with small seats. In the 1860s the neighboring house was sold to a German association that erected a beer hall in the backyard; at that time brick walls were installed to insulate the garden from the noise and commotion next door. Originally the service entrance was at the northwest corner of the garden, a raised privy at the northeast corner. The present cinderblock and palisade rear wall, topped by a small rock garden, is a creation of the 1960s. The two central parterres were originally filled with grass (where the Tredwells would lay out their linens to be bleached by the sun); granite pavers replaced the grass in the 1980s, as it could not hold up to heavy foot traffic.

Although no other early plantings exist, historians have a fair idea of what grew here. The Tredwell girls were flower lovers and left four volumes of pressed flowers, many of them from the garden. The brick walls are now planted with vines, Boston ivy, grape, wisteria, and roses, and a mix of perennials, shrubs, and groundcovers fill the narrow beds. The intent is for the little garden to reflect what would have been fashionable in the 1890s, and thus many of the plants are tried and true plants that one's grandmother might have grown. The effect is of a cheerful cottage garden, and sitting in the sunny backyard and listening to the birds one could well imagine a different time and place. Curators know from contemporary accounts that the Tredwell garden was famous for its beautiful magnolias and that their flowering was a neighborhood event that attracted many visitors, including the Astors. The original pavers that still surround the parterres are mellow stones that pleasantly show their age and provide a gentle link connecting modern visitors to the Tredwells and the landscape they so enjoyed.

BRONX

1 The Rainforest Garden at
    Patterson Houses
2 Bronx County Courthouse
    Greenroof Garden
3 Taqwa Community Farm
4 Tremont Community Garden
5 Garden of Happiness
6 The New York Botanical Garden
7 The Enchanted Garden
8 Wave Hill
9 Bartow-Pell Mansion Museum

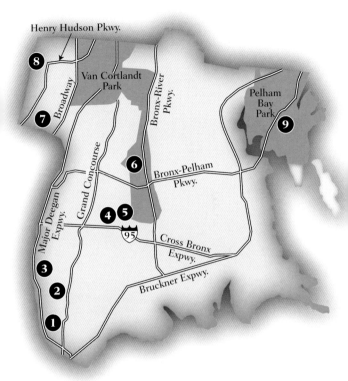

BRONX

From the New York Botanical Garden (NYBG) and Wave Hill, both stops on international horticultural tours, to community gardens like the Garden of Happiness and Taqwa Community Farm, to the green roof on the Bronx County Court House, the garden scene in the Bronx is as excellent as it is diverse. The community gardens are particularly vibrant, with innovative and successful programs, many of them focusing on urban farming and greenmarkets. Bronx Green-Up, an outreach program of NYBG, and GreenThumb, the city's garden assistance agency, have been instrumental in the success of many of them.

The Bronx is the smallest and the northernmost of the outer boroughs; it is also probably the greenest. Through the Bronx Initiative on Energy and the Environment, the Bronx county government has made possible the installation of 13 green roofs on buildings owned by nonprofits in the borough. One quarter of the landmass of the borough is parkland, thanks to the foresight of public officials in the 1880s who encouraged New York City to buy up open land in the Bronx while it was cheap. This, combined with the number of colleges and institutions that exist here (like Fordham University and the Bronx Zoo), gives the borough an unparalleled amount of green space, especially in the northern precincts.

Exciting greening initiatives are taking place in the South Bronx, which has much less access to green space and whose population has been victimized by proximity to heavy industry.

Here the nonprofit Sustainable South Bronx has launched a number of innovative initiatives to use green technology to improve the lives of local residents: building green roofs, training local youths in green technology, encouraging the creation of a Bronx Greenway and more local parks. The parks department has built several new waterfront parks in the South Bronx—Barretto Point Park, Hunts Point Riverside Park, and Concrete Plant Park—which show an exceptionally high level of design and greatly expand the neighborhood's access to the water. Another important organization is the Bronx River Alliance, which brings together stakeholders in the future of the Bronx River, the only freshwater river in the city. Eventually they hope to open up a river greenway from Westchester all the way down to the East River, creating a ribbon of green through the borough.

Wave Hill

The Rainforest Garden at Patterson Houses

Location: 140th St. and Third Ave., Mott Haven
Hours: always open as viewing garden; otherwise by appointment
Garden info: (212) 306-3268
Admission fee: no
Bus: Bx2, Bx21
Subway: 6 to 3rd Ave /138th St.
Facilities: none
Best season: summer

In midsummer, passersby can't help but notice the many small, bright gardens, each clearly identified by a vivid sign, on the grounds of the city's housing projects. Several good examples of these gardens can be found at the Patterson Houses in the Mott Haven section of the Bronx, where the McKay-Rodriguez Sunrise Garden features brick paths and colorful signs, and the luxuriant Rainforest Garden has colonized the entire western end of the property. These gardens are part of the citywide Tenant Gardening Program run by the New York City Housing Authority (NYCHA): 1,800 adults and 2,400 children participate in the gardening program every year, with about 600 tenant gardens spread though its vast system.

Begun in 1962, the Tenant Gardening Program was conceived as a way to beautify the projects' grounds and foster a sense of community. To encourage participation, the authority devised a yearly flower gardening competition that remains an important focus for tenants; a vegetable category was added in 1974 and, more recently, a category for children's gardens. Tenant gardeners now compete for regional and system-wide prizes, and the awards ceremony has become a major event. The gardeners are given seeds in the spring and bulbs in the fall, as well as gardening information. Throughout the year, the program organizes hands-on workshops and outings to other gardens, and at the end of the summer a panel of outside experts does the judging.

The Rainforest Garden, which has twice won the citywide flower competition, is larger than many other tenant gardens and is a memorial to Marta Diaz, who founded the garden in the mid 1990s. Along with a group of tenants that included her friend Grace Raynor, memorialized by a plaque in the garden, Diaz planted shrubs and trees, as well as the impressive roses that dot the grounds in bright yellow painted planters. Their first tree was a small yew that has now reached an impressive size. Diaz, who lived in Patterson Houses for 50 years, was originally from Puerto Rico, and the garden's name and the little casita she built recall her roots. Her children helped her, digging in the rocky soil and amending it, and moving plants around. When she fell ill, she continued to oversee the garden from her window, calling down instructions and directing the general design.

When Diaz died in 2007, her son and two sons-in-law continued her work. They built a large koi pond and waterfall by hand, using the rubble uncovered when they dug the gardens to shape the pond. The fat koi get larger every year. The pond and the waterfall are a memorial to Mrs. Diaz; there is another one in the middle of the large annual bed that occupies a prime space by Third Avenue.

Though the garden is shaded by London plane trees, Marta Diaz's son Ben has enlisted the children in the building to help him plant a vegetable garden. The children have put in tomatoes and peppers interspersed with marigolds in neat rectangular raised beds and, no doubt thinking of the children's garden competition, they decided to vary the design by adding two diamond-shaped beds.

The Diaz family has been gardening here for at least 15 years, and they have amassed an impressive collection of shrubs and trees, including a cut-leaf Japanese maple, hydrangeas, junipers, and lilacs, many by donation and as gifts. To thank their donors, the Diazes have put up the flags of the donors' countries of origin, so the flags of Puerto Rico, Israel, Italy, and Ireland fly proudly over their Rainforest Garden.

Bronx County Courthouse Greenroof Garden

Location: 851 Grand Concourse

Hours: Mon.–Fri. 9:00am–5:00pm (open only by appointment; call first to arrange visit)

Garden info: (718) 590-3498

Admission fee: no

Bus: Bx1, Bx6, Bx13

Subway: 4, C, D to 161st St. (Yankee Stadium)

Facilities: rest rooms

Best seasons: spring, summer, fall

Among many green initiatives, the Bronx boasts an exceptional 10,000-square-foot field of color on top of the Bronx County Courthouse, along with 13 other publicly funded green roofs, all on buildings housing nonprofits. At the time it was installed in 2006 the courthouse was only the second municipal building in the country with a green roof.

It all started in 2003 when a group in the Borough President's office formed the Bronx Initiative for Energy and the Environment. One of the ideas that intrigued them was planted roofs. The borough's president, Adolfo Carrion Jr., said, "Why not do one here?" So Kate Shackford, the executive vice president of the Bronx Overall Economic Development Corporation, started to do research. She was at a greening conference when she happened to hear a lecture on green roofs given by Peter Philippi of Green Roof Ser-

Around the corner from the Courthouse, on 161st Street between Morris and Sheridan, is the massive glass-curtained Bronx County Hall of Justice, which is a distinct departure from the other government buildings in the neighborhood. Designed by Rafael Viñoly, it opened in 2008. The complex wraps around a vast, sleekly modern civic plaza, which features light paving, a stylized bosque and a curiously large, squat, cylindrical building, which turns out to be the Jurors Hall. The Lego-like maze of the exterior staircases, visible through the glass walls, adds an important layer of interest to the site.

vice, and she knew that she had her man—and the right green roof technology to use on the site they had chosen, the roof of the imposing Bronx County Courthouse, a massive, square nine-story limestone structure built in 1933 and richly decorated with Art Moderne sculpture and reliefs.

It took a year and a half to get the permissions for the project. The city's Department of Citywide Administrative Services (DCAS) had no experience with green roofs and was skeptical. There were many, many approvals to be secured. Fortunately, structural engineers decided that the Bronx Courthouse was as solid as it looks, and the extra roof load was not going to be a problem. The DCAS signed on for the first green roof on a city-owned building. Even though this was conceived as a pilot project to show what might be possible, they knew that it had to work, it couldn't be an experiment.

The 10,000-square-foot planting occupies about a quarter of the courthouse roof. The first order of business, before putting on the green roof, was to test the existing roof for leaks. This proved prescient—they found 28. When the roof was watertight they installed the many layers that go into a planted roof: the root barrier, the protection fabric, the drainage layer made from recycled plastic, the filter layer, the soil medium, which here looks like tiny pebbles, and finally the plants. The soil medium is the key to a successful roof; it is a specific blend of very lightweight material that has excellent drainage and is also able to store a lot of water.

The plants, over 15,000 of them, were chosen for their toughness and tolerance for heat, cold, and drought. There are over ten different kinds of sedums, plus alliums, dianthus, and grasses. The design is simple: there is a small patio by the door, and a path of square pavers leading through the meadow planting. Two long, slightly bermed arcs, planted with grasses napped with allium and dianthus, provide a little visual structure and the rest of the flat roof is

Bronx County Courthouse Greenroof

a rich tapestry of sedums. In order to allow the grasses, dianthus, and allium to flourish, the berms have about 6 inches of growing medium, in comparison to the 3 inches of medium found elsewhere on the roof. The roof is a living system, and over time plants migrate and colonize different areas. It is an ever-changing kaleidoscope of greens, yellows, golds, reds, and pinks, and every inch of it is covered in plants; there are no bare spots. It's colorful, it's very attractive, and it works: since the installation of the roof, there have been no reported leaks.

Two research stations on the roof measure the temperature of the planted versus the conventional roof and the water retention properties of the new roof. On a hot summer day there is a 70-degree difference between the green roof and the conventional roof, and even in the most extreme rainstorm the planted roof captures 68 percent of storm water, in most cases it is 100 percent.

When a green roof is first installed it requires careful monitoring as the medium is by definition an ideal growing environment, for weeds as well as for sedums. Since the garden was installed in late June, it required irrigation to get through the first summer; now the system is working and there is no need for watering. After the installation, the contractor, under Peter Philippi's supervision, maintained the roof for two years. Green Roof Service did year three and then trained a team from SmartRoofs, a for-profit subsidiary of the Sustainable South Bronx, and now the local team is in charge.

Taqwa Community Farm

Location: 90 W. 164th St. at Ogden Ave., High Bridge
Hours: Mon., Wed., Fri. 9:00am–noon; Tues., Thurs. 4:00pm–7:00pm
Garden info: (718) 817-8026
Admission fee: no
Bus: BXM4A
Subway: 4 to 161 St./Yankee Stadium
Facilities: wheelchair accessible
Best season: summer

This is one garden that is guided to a remarkable degree by the strongly held philosophies of its gardeners. Abu Talib, one of the founders and its guiding spirit, sums up the feelings of the gardeners when he stresses that the garden truly has become sacred to the community. Particularly striking is Taqwa's Grow and Give program, through which the nearly 200 families who garden here donate to charity roughly 10,000 pounds of Taqwa's bounty—more than half its yearly production. Indeed, "farm" is an appropriate name for the tightly planted plots, which are among the most productive in the city.

Five white 40-foot-long tubes laid across brick piers are part of Taqwa's hydroponic farming system, which uses energy provided by solar panels. A system of growing plants in nutrient-rich water instead of soil, hydroponics requires maintaining a delicate balance of nutrients as well as constant supervision—a difficult task even with sophisticated equipment and under pristine conditions. But here at Taqwa, with help from the Cornell Cooperative Extension Service, gardeners are able to produce as many as three harvests per year of exceptionally tasty crops. Local youngsters, ages five to nineteen, are enlisted to run the hydroponics, feed the plants, and pick the produce; in exchange for their work, they are allowed to sell the produce at the farmers' market located at the garden on Saturdays and Sundays during the growing season. Nothing goes to waste in this all-organic garden. Bricks found on the site have been carefully stacked into a kind of hill, making use of material that might otherwise have become landfill. In another corner of the garden, there is brand-new playground equipment for the children. Although many people would consider mugwort a serious pest, at Taqwa it is treated with respect. The mugwort is clipped twice a year: the first batch is used for medicinal purposes, including mugwort tea, and the second for compost. Always expanding, the garden now boasts a chicken coop in a back corner, so that fresh eggs are available in the neighborhood.

Tremont Community Garden

Location: 1977 LaFontaine Ave. at E. 178th St., East Tremont

Hours: daily 8:00am–8:00pm (summer)

Admission fee: no

Bus: BxM4A

Subway: D to Tremont, then Bx40 bus

Facilities: none

Best season: summer

Running the entire length of a city block in the East Tremont section of the Bronx, Tremont is a neighborhood institution. On any fine afternoon during the growing season, a steady stream of people flows in and out. The gate is usually open, but if not, you just have to stand in front of it for a few moments looking curious and a member's head will pop out from one of the windows overlooking the garden and arrange to let you in. In midsummer, bins are bursting with vegetables, tomatoes, beans, peas, potatoes, and greens of all sorts, as well as herbs and flowers, and you are likely to see a group of gardeners sitting and visiting under the pavilion.

In the early 1980s this part of East Tremont, which once had been a solid, stable neighborhood, had deteriorated to the alarm of longtime residents who remembered better times. Although the area immediately surrounding the garden remained respectable, life was dangerous just a couple of blocks away. In 1983 a group of senior citizens from the Clinton Tremont Community Senior Citizen Center founded a community garden on what was then a trash- and crime-filled vacant lot at the corner of 178th Street and LaFontaine. They focused on aesthetics, planting flowers and cleaning up the site. Gradually, neighbors replaced the senior citizens, laying out boxes that they filled with vegetables. For 15 years the garden was the beloved preserve of a small group of volunteers, most of whom lived in the buildings immediately adjacent or across the street.

When the city planned to sell off a huge number of community gardens in 1998, Tremont was one of the gardens threatened with annihilation. This very real threat forced the garden leaders to focus on ways to protect what they had painstakingly built, and they looked to forge links with nearby gardens in similar circumstances. Under the auspices of Trust for Public Land's Neighborhood Open Space Program, nine gardens within walking distance of each other formed the advocacy group La Familia Verde, which not only provided a forum for exploring strategies to preserve the gardens, but also gave its members a broader and more sophisticated political presence in the heated citywide debate.

In 1999, TPL bought 62 of the endangered gardens, including Tremont, and this became a turning point for the garden: physical improvements were made and there was a shift from an informal leadership structure, where a few dedicated members did most of the work and made most of the decisions, to a more transparent and formalized structure. Even more dramatically, TPL helped them annex the adjacent empty lot, bounded by 178th and Monterey, which was filled with garbage—not just old coffee cups and cigarette butts but years of discarded cars, appliances, and furniture. The gardeners had been coveting this space, envisioning a place for children's activities, but the amount of work necessary to convert it had been daunting and beyond the resources of the most active of garden members. Countless truckloads of dirt and refuse were removed, and neighbors claimed the occasional working appliance or car part. Once the ground was leveled, six to twelve inches of new topsoil was added. Today all that remains is a white marker line about five feet up the side of the back wall of the garden, a reminder of the amount of junk that once was there.

The core of five or six members that remain from the early days of the garden all have their roots in the rural south, and planting a garden and growing food is an innate instinct to them. Most of them grow the same foods that they remember from their youth. They are acutely aware that there is a whole generation who have no relationship to the land, who didn't grow up on a farm or anywhere near a natural area, and who have no idea where food comes from. The Tremont gardeners work hard to educate and transfer their gardening skills and interest to newer members, and most especially to neighborhood children, and this mission gives them the knowledge that their work—and their garden—will continue to thrive in the future.

Garden of Happiness

Location: 2160 Prospect Ave. between 181st and 182nd Sts., East
   Tremont
Hours: Mon.–Fri. 9:00am–11:00am, 4:00pm–dusk; Sat.–Sun. 10:00am–
   dusk; weather permitting
Admission fee: no
Bus: Bx36
Subway: 2, 5 to E. Tremont. Ave.
Facilities: wheelchair accessible
Best season: summer

The Garden of Happiness brings to mind a rural village.
Children run up and down the beaten earth paths, calling
to each other and playing hide-and-seek between the square
raised beds bursting with vegetables, herbs, and flowers.
Their mothers check the crops or chat in the shade of the
little casita at the center of the garden. There are tomatillos,
popolo, and cilantro growing alongside cucumbers, cabbage,
squash, and okra. Roses, arborvitae, hydrangeas, and perennials line the perimeter bed, insulating the garden from the
street. Large blue plastic rain barrels are scattered around to
catch the rain. There are between 35 and 40 families gardening here, and about the same number at the garden's off-
shoot, the Garden of Youth, located just down the street.

   Like most of the community gardens in New York City, the
Garden of Happiness was once an abandoned lot. In 1988,
Karen Washington was at her kitchen sink when she noticed
a man with a hoe working across the street. She recalls that
this was a "light bulb" moment for her: she thought "garden"

right then and there, and she walked over to find out that the man was from Bronx Green-Up. The first members—all ten of them—were primarily African-Americans, with roots in the South, and Puerto Ricans. As the neighborhood has changed, so have the gardeners, and today they are mostly Mexican and African immigrants, although Washington (a born and bred New Yorker) has remained.

More than simply a place to grow tomatoes or an oasis in a desert of bricks and mortar, the Garden of Happiness plays an increasingly vital social role. It has become a de facto community center,

An increasing number of community gardens now operate summer farmers' markets. Two of the most successful are Bissell Gardens and Drew Gardens. Bissell Gardens extends for four city blocks in the shadow of a railway embankment in Wakefield, the northern reaches of the borough. In addition to vegetable farming, there is a children's garden and an extensive tree nursery. The market at Bissell Gardens is located on Baychester Avenue just south of 241st Street. At Drew Gardens, located in the West Farms section, gardeners have completely transformed the once-derelict shoreline of the Bronx River into a very attractive spot, with specimen trees dotting the grassy riverbank and an extensive and productive series of vegetable plots strung out along the top of the bank. Members from diverse backgrounds produce food and sell it at their West Farm Market, located just east of the intersection of East Tremont Street and Boston Road.

providing both a focus for neighborhood life and an important training ground for civic activists. As part of La Familia Verde, a coalition of Bronx community gardens, the garden has sponsored voter registration drives, health fairs, and neighborhood discussions as well as summer greenmarkets. And, because of La Familia Verde, the garden and its members are now linked to community-wide civic organizations. Karen Washington herself is now chair of the New York City Coalition of Community Gardens. The Garden of Happiness achieved permanent status in 1998.

The New York Botanical Garden

Location: 2694 Kazimiroff Blvd., 200th St. and Kazimiroff (Southern)
    Blvd., Bronx Park
Hours: Tues.–Sun. 10:00am–6:00pm; closed Mon.
Garden info: (718) 817-8700
Web site: www.nybg.org
Admission fee: yes
Train: Metro North (Harlem Line) from Grand Central Station to
    Botanical Garden
Bus: Bx26
Subway: 4, B, D to Bedford Park, transfer to Bx26 bus
Facilities: wheelchair accessible, café, picnic area, plant shop, rest rooms,
    telephones, tours, parking on-site
Best seasons: all seasons

Adjectives such as encyclopedic, first, oldest, and preeminent are applied liberally to the various programs, installations, and collections of the New York Botanical Garden, but for most of the 750,000 yearly visitors, the essence of NYBG is the simple beauty of the plants and their ability to stir the heart at every visit. Founded in 1891, this is the largest and oldest botanical garden in the country and a National Historic Landmark, occupying 250 acres in the Bronx. The collection of one million plants is displayed within 50 curated display gardens, plant collections, and a 50-acre remnant of old-growth forest. A leader in botanical research, home of the International Plant Science Center, NYBG boasts the largest herbarium in the Western Hemisphere (7.3 million plant and fungi specimens) and supports the oldest and largest publishing program of any botanical garden in the world, as well as the world's most important botanical and horticultural library. Although behind-the-scenes scientific endeavors are crucial to NYBG's mission, most of the Garden is open to the general public. A narrated tram tour is available to take visitors around the grounds, the signage is clear, and most of the exhibits are accompanied by ample didactic information.

At the end of the nineteenth century, a group of New Yorkers led by Columbia University botany professor Nathaniel Lord Britton and his wife, Elizabeth (herself an expert on mosses), lobbied for the creation of a botanical garden modeled after the Royal Botanical Gardens in Kew, England. In 1891 the state legislature incorporated the New York Botanical Garden and granted it 250 acres on the former Lorillard tobacco estate in the northern Bronx. A committee that included Calvert Vaux and Samuel Parsons Jr. made planning recommendations for the site, and the big names in New York philanthropy at the time—Carnegie, Vanderbilt, and Morgan—contributed funds to establish the garden. Britton was named director and immediately set up programs in plant exploration and collection as well as education and publishing, activities that continue to this day.

If ever there was a New York institution that deserved the term venerable, it is NYBG, but the garden has taken steps, even leaps, to engage the widest possible public and to ensure that its thinking, and its displays and exhibitions, are dynamic, and forward-thinking. There is an active program of special exhibits that range from the annual Orchid Show, which takes place each winter, to summer-long themed projects like the Edible Garden, to temporary art installations, featuring a range of artists from glass artist Dale Chihuly to sculptor Henry Moore.

Given the size and scope of the garden, one's first stop should be to one of the visitor information booths; although there is a pedestrian entrance at the Mosholu Gate, opposite the train station, the main visitor complex is at the Conservatory Gate on Kazimiroff Boulevard, where you will also find Shop in the Garden, a large garden store with a superb selection of books. Pick up maps (essential) and pamphlets (useful) describing individual gardens and collections, as well as updates about frequent special exhibitions.

At NYBG, as at many encyclopedic institutions, the journey can be as interesting as the destination, so if you have the energy, skip the tram and walk, or manage the visit in bite-size pieces. There are two main loci of activities: the western portion of the garden near the Enid A. Haupt Conservatory, where the Irwin Perennial Garden, the Home Gardening Center, the Ross Arboretum, and the Rock Garden are grouped, and a southeastern section where you will find the Peggy Rockefeller Rose Garden, the Benenson Ornamental Conifers collection, and the state-of-the-art Nolen Greenhouses for Living Collections, one unit of which is open to the public.

The Enid A. Haupt Conservatory

Sometimes described as New York's own Crystal Palace, the Enid A. Haupt Conservatory is the largest Victorian-style glasshouse in the country. Completed in 1902, it was designed by William Cobb for the preeminent greenhouse builder Lord and Burnham. This New York City landmark, designated in 1973, has been the symbol and glory of NYBG since its creation and remains the heart of the garden. Here, all the garden's varied initiatives come together: collecting (the garden's encyclopedic collection of tropical, subtropical, and desert plants is on display), research (the organization and substance of the display according to biomes and natural habitats highlights the work of its distinguished scientific staff), and education (the elaborate interpretive program is the most extensive of any glasshouse in the world). Throughout the year, the galleries host special installations, from a display of orchids to a highly informative ecotour of healing plants.

Although it looks like a Victorian architectural gem, the glasshouse is very much a twenty-first-century building

Enid A. Haupt Conservatory

with highly sophisticated ventilation, irrigation, and climate-control systems. Originally built of wood, glass, and cast iron, it has been renovated numerous times since its inception. Between 1994 and 1997, it was disassembled and repaired for what the administration hopes will be the last time. During the four-year, $25 million renovation under the guidance of restoration architect John Belle of Beyer Blinder Belle, the wooden and cast-iron members were rebuilt with aluminum and 17,000 panes of glass were replaced. In addition to the physical renovation, the conservatory was entirely reinstalled with A World of Plants exhibits.

The glittering U-shaped structure consists of a large domed palm house flanked by ten exhibition galleries. The main entrance is through the palm house, which is home to an impressive collection of American palms. Throughout the galleries, plants are grouped in ecosystems as they might occur in their natural habitat. As visitors circulate through the exhibits they proceed through different ecological zones and climates, moving from the lush humid jungle of the lowland and upland tropical forests to the aridity of the American and African deserts. Two galleries host special exhibitions and display exotic subtropicals from East Asia, Australia, California, and South Africa. Written materials and acoustiguides provide excellent background information on botany, ecology, ethnobiology, and conservation. Particularly useful is the plant quick-finder, which allows visitors to locate individual specimens that might be tucked away in the naturalistic displays.

The Jane Watson Irwin Perennial Garden and the Nancy Bryan Luce Herb Garden

In front of the conservatory is NYBG's perennial garden, designed by public garden designer Lynden B. Miller to demonstrate the wide range of possible plant combinations and compositions. Large pine trees shadow the beds, laid out on either side of a central axis that terminates in a large terracotta pot.

Using an extensive palette, Miller grouped plants according to different growing environments and color schemes. The repetition of gray- and red-leaved foliage plants, shrubs, grasses, and perennials—such as sedum Autumn Joy, hosta, miscanthus, oakleaf hydrangea, and red-leaf Japanese barberry—tie the disparate elements together. What sets this garden apart, however, is the attainment of true balance: size, texture, weight, and color all in perfect harmony.

Of particular interest is the area called the Fall Room, which peaks in late summer and fall. Autumn is generally not a focus of garden planning, but here the displays of asters, grasses, boltonia, and goldenrods, and the ruby fall color of the oakleaf hydrangea, supplemented by the intense blues of the half-hardy salvias, will convert even those who are convinced that a garden has nothing more to offer after the summer.

Nearby, Miller and the garden staff have collaborated and replanted the traditional Ladies' Border, first designed in 1933 by the great garden designer Ellen Biddle Shipman, with unusual half-hardy plants that can survive northern winters. The 260-foot-long garden has a protected southern exposure, and it is particularly worth a visit in the late winter when most other gardens are still fast asleep: camellias, witch hazel, and various viburnums are blooming along with the fragrant paper bush.

Attached to the perennial garden is the herb garden, designed by noted British writer and designer Penelope Hobhouse. The garden features a changing display of culinary herbs and other useful plants.

Ross Conifer Arboretum and the Benenson Ornamental Conifers

The garden has two important conifer collections; the oldest is the Arthur and Janet Ross Conifer Arboretum, previously known as the pinetum, which is the garden's oldest plant col-

New York Botanical Garden clockwise from left: Tanyosho pines; Rock Garden; Daffodil Hill; Jane Watson Irwin Perennial Garden

lection. Located to the southeast of the conservatory, it covers 37 acres and features 300 mature conifers with special emphasis on spruce, pine, and fir. Nathaniel Britton began the collection in 1901; it now includes trees from as far afield as the Himalayas and Mexico. Among the most outstanding trees is a grove of Tanyosho pines planted in 1908, which have a graceful multi-stem spreading form and beautiful red bark. They are particularly impressive in winter. Changing climatic conditions have proved challenging to the growing of conifers, however, and certain parts of the collection are at risk.

While the Ross collection is dedicated to species conifers, the 15-acre Benenson Ornamental Conifers collection, which includes 400 specimens, focuses on the wild, colorful, and sometimes weird world of ornamental conifers, and displays the wide range of colors, shapes, and sizes that conifer breeders have developed. This area was originally designed by Marian Cruger Coffin, a major figure in estate design in the first half of the twentieth century and one of the first women landscape architects, for a collection given to the garden in the thirties. It has been restored under the guidance of NYBG's experts, Towers/Golde Landscape Architects, and Patrick Chasse, a noted curator of historic gardens. Paths were widened, the original garden oval refurbished and pavilions created; dying trees were culled and many new features added, including a gardenesque dwarf conifer display that is intended to introduce the gardening public to the beauty of conifers.

Home Gardening Center

North of the conservatory is the Home Gardening Center,

which used to be known as the Demonstration Garden. Here, the staff at NYBG shares their gardening ideas with the public. There is plenty of inspiration for the home gardener, and the staff holds weekend demonstra-

Bronx Green-Up, NYBG's outreach program, has had a real impact on grass-roots gardening throughout the Bronx. It provides support, in the form of materials, technical advice, and environmental education, to almost 300 community gardens and urban farms in the borough. A particular focus is greening programs in Bronx schools.

tions at the Ken Roman Gazebo, which is smothered in sweet autumn clematis and is an excellent place to pause and rest and to collect informational pamphlets. One of the best features at the Home Gardening Center is the plant trials garden area where home gardeners now have a place to judge for themselves the relative merits of the latest in plant fashions. There is also a display of single-petalled Korean chrysanthemums. (The only other place in the city with Korean chrysanthemums this beautiful is the Conservatory Garden in Manhattan.)

The Rock Garden and Native Plant Garden

The Rock Garden is one of the must-sees at NYBG and spring is definitely its moment. At two and a half acres, not only is it large for a rock garden, but it succeeds in displaying a remarkably wide selection of delicate, often finicky plants to their best effect, in an environment that is anything but static. Rock outcroppings are woven together by finely textured plants, creating a colorful and delicate tapestry.

Conceived and built in the 1930s by Thomas H. Everett, then director of horticulture at NYBG, the Rock Garden is one of the glories of the garden. Ironically, although there are several natural rock outcroppings on the NYBG grounds, the Rock Garden was almost completely constructed. Large rocks were placed at the site to create the craggy mountain scenery of waterfalls, ledges, and outcrops. Because the rocks are placed on a deep soil base, a wider range of plants can be grown here than in the usually shallow soil around natural rock outcrops. The only natural rock in the garden appears at the top of the waterfall and behind the moraine.

Within the garden are a number of different habitats, including a pond and woodland garden where primroses flourish in the moist soil. A glade and waterfall form the backdrop for a striking display of moss phlox in the spring. An alpine meadow features small bulbs and ground cover, including thyme, pinks, and alpine scabiosa. A free-draining scree bed composed of gravel and sand that mimics alpine conditions is home to more than 150 types of alpines and a collection of encrusted saxifrages. There is also a heath bed filled with acid-loving plants such as rhododendron, azalea, and blueberry, as well as heaths and heather; a sand bed, which resembles the dry sandy slopes of the American West, featuring cactus, penstemons, yuccas, and other plants with deep root systems that thrive on limited amounts of water; and a bed that mimics a glacial moraine. The last is specially constructed with an underground watering system that keeps cool water circulating beneath the gravel, enabling the cultivation of many alpines that could not otherwise withstand the heat and humidity of a New York summer.

Adjacent to the Rock Garden is the Native Plant Garden. Here, the plants can seem coarse compared with the delicate alpines at the rock garden, but they display a welcome robustness, often with bold shapes grouped in vigorous stands. The garden is slated to be renovated and expanded by

2012. The renovated Native Plant Garden, designed by the firm of Oehme, van Sweden and Associates, will concentrate on using the right plant in the right place, demonstrating the wide possibilities of gardening with natives, so the public can better appreciate them and understand how we might use them in an environmentally responsible but also aesthetically pleasing manner.

The garden is adjacent to the Forest, one of NYBG's unsung treasures. One of the last vestiges of our true native landscape, the Forest is being restored by Garden staff. Invasive species are being removed and native trees, shrubs, and wildflowers planted in their place. Although most of the hemlocks have succumbed to disease, there remains a remarkable collection of old-growth trees, especially maples, tulip trees, and oaks, some as much as 300 years old.

The Peggy Rockefeller Rose Garden

This is the only example in New York City of the work of the pioneering landscape architect Beatrix Farrand, whose masterful Dumbarton Oaks garden in Washington, D.C., remains one of the great gardens in this country. The rose garden was originally designed in 1916, but only partially installed. In 1988, David and Peggy Rockefeller, stewards of another Beatrix Farrand garden in Maine, funded the completion of the rose garden from Farrand's plans, affording visitors a fascinating opportunity to see and evaluate an early-twentieth-century design that has been newly built.

Located on the eastern side of the NYBG grounds, it contains more than 600 varieties of roses and 3,500 individual bushes. The triangular garden is enclosed by an open-square ironwork wall interspersed with arches and painted a deep green. A round gazebo of more ornate ironwork is located at the apex of the triangle, surrounded by slim arc-shaped beds featuring climbing roses draped over pillars linked by chains, a Beatrix Farrand trademark. Eighty-three beds line three wide crushed-bluestone walkways radiating from the gazebo.

The movement toward sustainability and environmental stewardship is apparent here in the rose garden. Historically, the rose garden has been seen as a living catalog of roses available to the home gardener. Each rose has been evaluated for winter hardiness, disease resistance, quality of flowers and foliage, and consistency of bloom. The All-American Rose selection winners are here, the next year's winners appearing a full year before they are available for sale. All the roses are labeled and neatly laid out, so it is easy to distinguish one variety from another. Now there is an emphasis on experimenting with roses from all over the world that are as disease resistant as possible, and reducing or eliminating dependence on remedial sprays and pesticides.

Roses peak in early June, which is the best time to see any rose garden. This garden, however, has another peak period: the rosarians prune the plants back in the middle of the summer to produce another big flush of blooms in the fall, just in time for NYBG's annual Rose Garden Dinner Dance.

Collections

As befits a botanical garden with an encyclopedic range, NYBG has a number of discrete collections of plants, including crab apples, lilacs, and magnolias, as well as 100,000 narcissus, all of which create spectacular shows throughout the spring. Most of the large trees and shrubs of distinction are cataloged and can be located by checking the coordinates on

NYBG's Web site. Future plans include the transformation of Azalea Way, a collection of rhododendrons and azaleas, into an 11-acre garden with 2,500 new plants representing 300 varieties.

Everett Children's Adventure Garden

As part of its effort to attract families to its grounds, NYBG opened this indoor-outdoor museum of plant science in May 1998. Forty interactive exhibits for school-age children are interspersed with places such as the Boulder Maze and the traditional geometric Beth's Maze. The 12-acre site is often filled with active and excited children running through the many worthwhile displays. Adults wishing to view the gardens without distraction might be advised to go when school is in session.

A long, narrow trail between tightly planted beds leads to the various outdoor exhibits and to the labs and a herbarium of the Discovery Center. The exhibits each feature hands-on activities. Children can play with a large man-made flower with detachable parts, use a spotting scope to locate particular plants or birds in the wetlands, or scoop up water to examine microscopic aquatic life in the pond garden. The staff is informed and helpful and there are ample teaching materials. Five huge topiaries of garden creatures include two caterpillars and a fabulous frog with a tongue created entirely of the succulent rosettes of hen-and-chickens.

The Enchanted Garden

Location: 99 Terrace View Ave., south of 230th St., Kingsbridge
Hours: Mon.–Fri. 8:00am–4:00pm (school year); Mon.–Fri. 8:00am–
    noon (summer)
Garden info: (718) 562-5500
Web site: www.thomania.org/gardensite
Admission fee: no
Train: Metro North (Harlem line) from Grand Central Station to Marble
    Hill
Bus: Bx1, Bx7, Bx9, Bx20
Subway: 9 to W. 225th St., 1 to W. 231st St.
Facilities: wheelchair accessible
Best seasons: spring, summer

This is indeed an enchanted place, a many-faceted and deeply satisfying garden. It has moments of genuine beauty— a woodland path winding by a small pond, a butterfly garden, and a picturesque wetland. Remarkably, this is the work of high school students, who have brilliantly overcome the garden's unpromising location next to the school parking lot.

John F. Kennedy High School, with almost 4,000 pupils, is plunked down in a commercial wasteland at the confluence of the Hudson and Harlem Rivers on the edge of the Bronx. In 1995, a group of students tired of walking past an overgrown, garbage-strewn vacant lot near the school's entrance decided to clean it up. As work progressed, a small stream was discovered beneath the weeds and debris, a vestige of the ancient Spuyten Duyvil Creek that had been filled in when the city straightened out the shoreline. The creek became the backbone of the garden and the cattails that once grew there its symbol.

With the guidance of a dedicated teacher, the students, members of the school's environmental club, have done all the digging, planting, planning, design, fund-raising, and upkeep. The many different aspects of the garden are well integrated into its relatively small three-quarters of an acre. The wetland area, which now includes goldenrod, milkweed, marsh marigold, swamp willow, and elderberry, is where the garden began. Not only is it attractive in its own right, but the wetland also serves as a reminder of what this land looked like before the city existed. The first full-scale landscaping project was the woodland trail that runs beside the creek, leading through a forest that includes black locust, cottonwood, red maple, red oak, sassafras, and witch hazel. In the spring, the path is lined with bulbs. A line of lilacs has been put in along the tall iron fence next to the sidewalk, making the walk to school a special pleasure in May.

As the creek twists and turns, it passes a small rock-edged pond built in 1998 by five students who designed it with help from the environmental organization Open Road of New York. It is now one of the highlights of the garden, looking entirely natural in the landscape and creating a home for fish and frogs. A number of bridges cross the creek at various points. Along with the benches, seats, and decorated rocks, they attest to the high spirits and originality of the gardeners.

On the other side of the forest is a farm where students grow an impressive amount of food for themselves and a local soup kitchen. There are also herb beds and several fruit trees that produce apples, apricots, and peaches. A butterfly garden, filled with flowers such as butterfly weed, black-eyed Susan, and butterfly bushes, attracts monarchs and swallowtails and creates a colorful corner next to the farm. More color is provided by a modest rose garden.

A visit to this garden would not be complete without meeting the students who created it. Thirty to forty participate in the environmental club each year, working on various aspects of planning and maintenance. In the summer, they are employed to tend the garden and work on special projects. In its first five years, the garden gave the high school a new focus: it now boasts an Institute for Environmental Studies and the Urban Community and a series of courses relating to the environment.

Wave Hill

Location: W. 249th St. at Independence Ave., Riverdale
Hours: Tues.–Sun. 9:00am–5:30pm (April 15–October 14); Tues.–Sun.
    9:00am–4:30pm (October 15–April 14); greenhouses: 10:00am–
    noon, 2:00pm–4:00pm
Garden info: (718) 549-3200
Web site: www.wavehill.org
Admission fee: yes
Bus: BxM1, BxM2 from Manhattan
Subway: 1 to 242nd St. (shuttle bus available)
Facilities: mostly wheelchair accessible, café, rest rooms, telephones,
    free offsite parking
Best seasons: all seasons

Dramatic plantings, majestic trees, a velvet lawn, and a
drop-dead view—all combine to make Wave Hill an essential destination. Nowhere are the elements that make Wave
Hill unique more evident than in the opening tableau. Across
the sweeping lawn, a wide Italianate terrace holds a pergola
framing a long view of the Hudson River and the New Jersey
Palisades. Vines soften the outline of the structure, whose
sturdy shape and generous size mediate between the individual and the soaring vista. In summer, clusters of large pots
filled with a wild profusion of plants are grouped around the
base of the pillars. The plants may be unfamiliar to all but the
most erudite gardeners, but the compositions are inspired,
assertive in both shape and color, complementing rather than
competing with the view. This scene is always heart-catching

but perhaps most sublime in fall, when the flaming colors of the Palisades are echoed by the reds and bronzes, golds and purples of the plantings in the pots. It takes effort to remember that Wave Hill is within the city limits of New York.

Although it is now a public garden and cultural institution, Wave Hill retains the aura of a private estate, with its two mansions and rolling lawns. It is also a plant lover's paradise whose 28 acres of grounds feature 1,100 genera and more than 3,000 species, many of them unusual, combined in adventurous and sometimes provocative ways. The annual displays are often memorable, one year featuring orange cosmos and cannas, the next year different varieties of lettuce and chard and an entire hillside planted with pumpkins.

The site was farmed since before the Revolution, but Wave Hill House itself was built as a country home by William Lewis Morris, a New York lawyer, and his wife, Elizabeth, in 1843–44. Twenty years later it was sold to the publisher William Henry Appleton, who enlarged it and improved the grounds. Appleton was well-connected and entertained a series of distinguished visitors, including Charles Darwin and the naturalist Thomas Henry Huxley. In the summers of 1870–71 he rented the house to the parents of Theodore Roosevelt, and legend has it that young Roosevelt's time at Wave Hill fostered the deep love for nature that led him as president to support the acquisition and preservation of millions of acres of American parkland. Another famous inhabitant was Appleton's friend and client Samuel Clemens (Mark Twain), who leased the house from 1901 to 1903.

In 1903 the property was acquired by financier George W. Perkins, who had been amassing parcels of land along the river, including the adjacent property (what is now Glyndor

House). Perkins was the president of the Palisades Interstate Park Commission and instrumental in saving the Palisades from development, thereby preserving the magnificent view from his estate as well.

Over the years the property was constantly improved. Appleton built greenhouses and planted trees, but it was Perkins who transformed the property into a great estate, building a swimming pool and pergolas, adding to the greenhouses, contouring and terracing the hillside, and planting unusual varieties of trees and shrubs. One of his more dramatic changes was the creation of a recreation center below the lower terrace (now the ecology center) that included an indoor bowling alley and a squash court. Perkins, who lived at Glyndor House, rented Wave Hill house to Bashford Dean, a collector of European armor, who built the huge addition onto the north side of the house to display his extensive collection (much of which ended up in the Metropolitan Museum). The conductor Arturo Toscanini lived at Wave Hill from 1942 to 1945.

In 1960 the Perkins heirs deeded Wave Hill and its grounds to the city of New York. By 1965 it had been set up as a city-owned nonprofit cultural institution. Today it is a vibrant public garden with programs in horticulture, environmental education, and the visual and performing arts. In 1967 the horticulturist Marco Polo Stufano started work to renovate and reinvigorate the grounds, over time building a professional staff that included curator John Nally. If Wave Hill is now a mecca for plant lovers from all over the world, it is because Stufano, who trained at the New York Botanical Garden under the legendary T. H. Everett, is one of this country's premier plantsmen. For 34 years, from 1967 until

Wave Hill clockwise from left: pergola; Monocot Garden; Wild Garden; Flower Garden

his retirement in 2001, Stufano managed, in a traditional setting, to create bold and adventurous gardens full of risks. The tradition of innovation is still very much alive under the leadership of Director of Horticulture Scott Canning, and the gardens remain by turn playful, interesting, thought-provoking, and calm. Take a pad and paper and allow plenty of time to explore.

The Flower Garden

Formerly the estate's rose garden, the Flower Garden is enclosed with rustic cedar fencing inspired by the design of the original. In an updated version of the traditional cottage garden, the rigid symmetry of the 16 beds and the orderly path system are balanced by the colorful and informal planting. The foundation is a series of familiar garden favorites— foxglove, iris, peonies, and above all roses, many of which were growing in the garden when it was given to the city, including Mme. Gregoire Staechlin, New Dawn, Mary Wallace, and Silver Moon (this last found also on the arches in the Conservatory Garden in Central Park). There are at least two dozen varieties of clematis climbing over tripods, through bushes, and on top of fences. These old favorites form a comfortable framework for the rest of the plant material, which is often more obscure, a mix of perennials, tender perennials, and tender exotics that constantly change. Wave Hill has a permit to import seeds directly from abroad, and as a result the plant palette is unusually broad. Groupings of pots play a significant role in this garden, where changing arrangements anchor the centers of the beds. Sometimes the pots are full of vivid, dramatic flowers; at other times an installation of four tall yews lends an architectural element and focal point.

The Flower Garden forms the forecourt of the Marco Polo Stufano Conservatory. Once again the pots at the entrance merit attention. They are a hint of the plants to be seen inside. The small-scale Palm House contains unusual specimens, including *Anigozathus flavidus* and *Acacia baileyana*, a collection of South African bulbs that bloom profusely in the winter months, as well as ordinary garden plants, such as a five-foot-tall tower of sweet peas and standard rosemary and salvia. On one side of the Palm House is the conservatory for tropical plants, on the other are the cactus and succulents.

Up behind the greenhouse and in front of the T. H. Everett Alpine House are the Herb Garden and Dry Garden (in the ruins of a former greenhouse), which display a range of unusual herbs and plants. The vertical lines of junipers anchor the terraces. The Alpine House is designed so that the plants can be viewed from the outside. On its terrace a collection of troughs is massed in a sort of cubist arrangement. During most of the year, the alpines and tiny trough plants are probably most attractive to enthusiasts, but in the spring, which is their moment, the miniature landscapes are irresistible.

The Wild Garden

Now one of the most exciting areas at Wave Hill, the Wild Garden is the first one the new horticultural staff took on in the late 1960s. It is inspired in part by the theories of William Robinson, the irascible and influential nineteenth-century British garden writer who helped turn the focus of the gardening world from traditional bedding to the creation of more naturalistic settings. Wave Hill's Wild Garden tumbles down a hill from the estate's highest point, 250 feet above the river. A series of walks meander down from a rustic and picturesque gazebo, which is half buried by an ancient yew. The view from the gazebo is thrilling and, remarkably, the garden is so strong and vibrant that it more than holds its own against the Hudson and the Palisades. This was the site of Evelina Perkins's spring garden, and a gazebo has existed here since at least 1915. The hill is supported by a drystone retaining wall on its southern and western sides. When the transformation of the garden was begun, many of the beds were so choked with weeds that they had to be covered in black plastic for a season to be baked clean.

The horticultural staff inherited some weeds, but they also inherited a number of rare mature evergreens planted by the Perkins family. The differing colors, sizes, and densities of the evergreens give the garden a rich background and relate well to the mounds of densely textured and clipped little-leaf box, English yew, prostrate juniper, and creeping cotoneaster that dot the hillside, providing weight and contrasting with the plants with looser, freer habits. A large staghorn sumac makes a dramatic statement, its idiosyncratic branching pattern providing midstory interest. Plants appear to romp down the hillside, self-sowing at will. Woad, for instance, which a visitor might first have encountered in the herb garden, spreads all over the wild garden with its tall yellow spring flowers (belying its reputation as a source of blue dye). Foxgloves, mullein, and spiky Scotch thistle are other self-sowers that spring up where they want to. Big, strongly shaped plants seem to be encouraged; a series of yuccas, for instance, dominate a bed on the north side of the hill. Interspersed with the dramatic are the little treasures, such as a delicate white potentilla nestled in a corner or the scattered

love-in-a-mist. "Wild" here certainly does not mean untended; Robinson's point was that plants should be used in a way
that makes them look most natural. He himself was an avid
plant collector.

The gardens at Wave Hill continue to change and develop.
Beyond the Wild Garden, a series of pergolas are the site of
a collection that demonstrates the different methods vines
use to climb (by tendrils, suckers, twining, etc.). The upper
pergola surrounds the Aquatic Garden. In the same area is
the Monocot Garden, devoted to plants with parallel vena-
tion that produce one seed leaf upon germination. Here, a
surprising range of plants from lilies and grasses to asparagus
and corn are combined to dramatic effect. These gardens are
at their best in the late summer and fall, when the water lilies and then the grasses make their show. A woodland path
winds along the perimeter of the garden through groves of
witch hazel, yellowwood, and sweet gum.

A visit to Wave Hill should always include time to simply
relax and savor the atmosphere in one of the straight-back
chairs that dot the lawns. The scale here is very large and
the feeling of spaciousness is both soothing and invigorating.
Wave Hill has deliberately retained some of the attributes of
a great estate, so that everyone can enjoy the pleasures that
were once reserved for the privileged few.

Bartow-Pell Mansion Museum

Location: 895 Shore Rd., Pelham Bay Park

Hours: daily dawn to dusk (grounds); Wed., Sat., Sun. 12:00pm–4:00pm
(mansion)

Garden info: (718) 885-1461

Web site: www.bartowpellmansionmuseum.org

Admission fee: no (grounds); yes (mansion)

Bus: #45 Westchester Bee-Line bus

Subway: 6 to Pelham Station, transfer to #45 Westchester Bee-Line bus
to gates

Facilities: rest rooms (mansion); free parking

Best seasons: spring, summer

The garden at the Bartow-Pell Mansion is all about possibilities, the suggestion of what might have been, a sense of what has been lost. Truly romantic, it is the last of the many mansions that once graced the Pelham Bay area, and a stroll through the house and grounds is a journey back to a more elegant and genteel time. Not surprisingly, it is a highly sought-after site for garden weddings.

In 1654, Thomas Pell bought nearly 50,000 acres from the Siwanoy Indians (2,700 of those acres now comprise Pelham Bay Park), and ten years later received an official land grant from King Charles II. Four generations of Pells lived there until the American Revolution, when the original house was burned to the ground. After the war, the property, much reduced, passed into the hands of Robert Bartow, a Pell descendant, who built the present gray stone mansion with its Greek Revival interiors. The city acquired the house and land in 1888 and used it for a variety of purposes, including as Mayor Fiorello LaGuardia's summer office. It was opened as a museum in 1947.

Since 1914, the nine acres of house and grounds have been the domain of the International Garden Club (IGC), which was formed to promote an appreciation for horticulture, both here and abroad, and to create an American version of the Royal Botanical Gardens in Kew, England. The ladies of the club—many of them socially well-connected—originally planned to use the estate as their head-

Bartow-Pell Mansion Museum

quarters and hired the architectural firm of Delano and Aldrich to restore the mansion and design a garden that would be a showplace for a succession of seasonal exhibits of flowering plants and shrubs. Delano and Aldrich were aided by Arthur Herrington, who had been assistant to William Robinson, a dominant figure in British gardening at the time. Under Herrington's supervision, the stone walls surrounding the formal garden were built. At first only three feet high, the walls were raised another three feet several years later, supposedly to stop

In 1654, when Thomas Pell bought the first 900 acres of land from the Siwanoy Indians, he signed the treaty under a huge oak that became a local landmark known as the Treaty Tree. Later, the mansion was built not far from the tree, which stood in the front yard of the house until this century. The tree's historical importance was one of the reasons the garden club chose the mansion as its headquarters. The oak was protected by an iron fence, and when it was felled by lightning, another oak was planted in its place. During World War I, the fencing was removed by members of the club, who were worried that it would be stolen and sold for scrap, but it was carefully replaced after the war. Unfortunately, some years later, an observant visitor noticed that the fence had been put around an elm tree rather than an oak.

people on horseback from jumping them and thus wreaking havoc in the gardens. Herrington laid out the gardens as well and brought over a young Scotsman, James McGregor, as head gardener, a position he held for 47 years. In the late 1920s, the Garden Club hired the pioneering garden designer Ellen Biddle Shipman to draw up planting plans for the terrace. The result combined a formal style with a freer, more naturalistic grouping of plants. Shipman's plans now hang in the office of the director of the museum, but the gardens, unfortunately, never were built. Nor were the IGC's ambitious plans for horticultural exchange and display ever executed. Today the four-tiered formal garden, with its original terraces, high stone walls, and elaborate wrought-iron gates, can best be appreciated as the bones of a great garden. Even without flower beds, the garden is perfectly pleasing, primarily because of its beautiful proportions and materials. The wide, square-cut stone used for all the ground elements—the central terrace, the steps, paths, and edging around the pool—relate to the high flint-stone walls and visually unify the garden. The stonework of the steps has been restored thanks to a unique program of the Heritage Conservation Network, for volunteers who want to spend their holidays doing restoration work. Volunteers from France removed the mortar between the joints of the paving stones, which was not original to the construction, and replaced it with gallettes, small stones or gravel, which was the original specification.

Pelham Bay Park, the city's largest, contains several important historic sites as well a wealth of recreational facilities including two golf courses, bridle paths, and numerous hiking trails. The Appalachian Mountain Club and the parks department maintain the Siwanoy Hiking Trail, which passes through the woods close to Bartow-Pell.

From the steps, the visitor looks down over the terraces to a small, square pool; in the distance are the salt marshes bordering Long Island Sound. Six huge yews, planted in 1949 to replace the originals, stand in the quadrants of the garden and frame the ornate gates that lead to the extensive grounds. This juxtaposition of the cultivated walled garden and the surrounding wild landscape heightens the garden's special sense of privacy.

Delano and Aldrich's original design included a rose garden that never was built. Several small flower gardens, however, add to the period feeling of the grounds. Among these are a curved herb garden and a water garden, usually planted with brightly colored, sun-loving annuals such as zinnias, dahlias, and marigolds. An ancient mulberry sits close to the house and shades part of the upper terraces.

1 The Green Dome Garden

2 Brooklyn Heights Promenade

3 Columbia St. Waterfront District
    Community Gardens

4 Red Hook Gardens

5 The Brooklyn Bear's Community Gardens

6 Brooklyn Botanic Garden

7 Hattie Carthan Community Garden

8 Brooklyn Public Library, Saratoga Branch

9 The Floyd Bennett Gardens

10 The Narrows Botanical Gardens

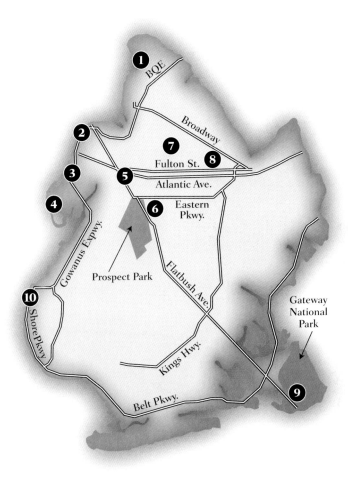

BQE

Broadway

② ⑦

③ Fulton St. ⑧

⑤

Atlantic Ave.

④

⑥ Eastern
Pkwy.

Gowanus Expwy.

Prospect Park

Flatbush Ave.

⑩

Gateway
National
Park

Shore Pkwy.

Kings Hwy.

⑨

Belt Pkwy.

BROOKLYN

Although it was annexed by the City of New York in 1898, Brooklyn's institutions, history, and personality require consideration on their own terms. For much of the nineteenth century, it was the third largest city in the country. Even now, its population is 2.5 million, down from a peak of 2.7 million in 1950, still larger than most major American cities.

As in all the boroughs, Brooklyn has seen a boom in park development, particularly along its waterfronts, which for so long were the industrial engine of the borough but have more recently fallen into disuse and disrepair. Phase one of the 85-acre Brooklyn Bridge Park opened in winter 2010, the biggest park project in the borough since Prospect Park. This being Brooklyn, the project has not been without controversy, but it will open up the waterfront to a wide range of recreational opportunities.

Brooklyn gardens reflect its topography and population patterns. In the northern neighborhoods, which are dense, urban, and partly industrial, the gardens are intimate and compact. The large and historic green spaces of Prospect Park and Green-Wood Cemetery provide acres of rolling land and splendid vistas in central Brooklyn. The southernmost part of the borough enjoys more than 60 miles of coastline; here gardens such as the Narrows Community

Garden in Bay Ridge and the Floyd Bennett Gardens can really spread out.

Brooklyn is justly famed for its domestic architecture, and many of the demure nineteenth-century facades of Greek Revival, Italianate, Anglo-Italianate, and Romanesque Revival row houses hide backyard gardens. Several blocks in Carroll Gardens also have beautiful gardens in their exceptionally deep front yards, thanks to an imaginative surveyor who laid out the neighborhood in 1846. Brooklyn's neighborhoods each have their own very distinctive character, and generations of immigrants continue to leave their stamps. The

Cherry trees at Brooklyn Botanic Garden

borough also has the largest concentration of community gardens in the city. From the smallest community plots to the expansive Brooklyn Botanic Garden, there is a pervasive sense of civic pride, as expressed by Marianne Moore when she wrote, "At all events there is in Brooklyn / something that makes me feel at home."

The Green Dome Garden

Location: N. 12th Ave. between Driggs and Union Aves.
Hours: daily 9:00am to dusk; closed in winter
Admission fee: no
Bus: B43, B48, B61
Subway: G to Nassau Ave.; L to Bedford Ave. or Lorimer St.
Facilities: none
Best seasons: spring, summer

For a plant person, Green Dome is a little bit of heaven, a series of totally satisfying garden moments. Each one of the lumpy hillocks that form the unusual topography of the garden provides its own little epiphany, which is exactly what the creators of this impressive garden in Greenpoint have been striving for since they started the garden in 1995. It has been a long and satisfying journey.

Back then, Greenpoint wasn't as gentrified as it is now. The garden site, a triangle of parkland adjacent to McCarren Park, was flat and featureless aside from some daffodils and the beautiful backdrop of the Russian Orthodox Cathedral of the Transfiguration with its five onion dome cupolas across the street. The garden founders, including Amir Yarkoni, a florist, Avigail Milder, a designer, and John Wright, an English professor who was also a talented stonemason, called their garden Green Dome—partially in homage to the then-green copper domes on the Cathedral, partially because it comes from the Latin word *domus*, or home. Right from the start, the gardeners wanted their garden to be a welcoming place.

The group spent the first three years ridding the ground of weeds and amending the soil. The parks department left them alone—they were definitely improving the area. When the site was properly prepared, they drew up a simple plan and got to work: Amir focused on plants, Avi on design with good circulation, and John on building the paths, using found materials, old cobbles, bricks, and some discarded granite slabs, and adapting the plan as he went.

The motto of the garden in its early days might have been "Be careful what you wish for." When a local contractor was excavating a basement nearby, the group asked if they could have a few of the boulders he was digging up. He said yes, but the boulders would come with some dirt on them. The gardeners arrived at the garden one day to discover that the contractor had dumped the entire contents of the basement excavation on their site, burying their garden under tons of clay. Faced with complete disaster, they persuaded the contractor to lend them a Bobcat and spent hours sculpting and shifting the clay with the help of about 30 volunteers from New York Cares. The parks department stepped in with soil, and all of a sudden the garden had elevation. An unexpected bonus of the added topography was that with the same perimeter there was a threefold increase in surface area for planting. Also, the new garden configuration made for a much healthier garden, since the original earth, now capped, turned out to have been heavily polluted.

The massive rocks that dot the garden were a different story. Keyspan was installing a gas line in the district, a very unpopular move among longtime residents. During the excavation they uncovered a number of huge boulders. The gardeners approached the contractors who were carrying out the work, and Keyspan agreed to use their construction crane to move two of the enormous rocks to the garden. A borrowed forklift shimmied them into the right spots. Wright, the stonemason, created a network of paths to wind through the garden; at times, the paths thread through narrow spaces between the huge boulders, at others they widen out to create seating areas.

The Green Dome gardeners are extraordinarily knowledgeable and creative, and have found ways to create various habitats within the small space, including an alpine garden and a bog garden. There is a large, preexisting pin oak that lends gravitas to the whole enterprise, and a wide variety of ornamental trees and shrubs both familiar and unusual, including a crape myrtle, several different viburnums, crab apples, an unusual sorrel tree, and a myriad of carefully chosen perennials. The garden was built by trial and error, and many of the specimens here have been moved three or four times until they are happy, both physically and aesthetically. The gardeners fall for the plant and then they look for the perfect spot, the ideal combination.

The results speak for themselves. The paths wind over the little hills, twisting and turning, widening and narrowing, encouraging visitors to stop and admire the many beautiful plant compositions that make up the garden. (The hills are particularly exciting for small children.) Although it was originally supposed to be a viewing garden, when the paths were built and the plants established well enough so that anyone could tell it was a garden, the founders opened it to the public, which responded by embracing it. The garden is still closed in the winter—the theory being that if people can really tell it's a garden that someone cares about they will respect it, but if there are no flowers and it looks bare, as gardens do in the winter, then vandalism is more likely to occur. Vandalism seems even more unlikely when you consider how important this garden has become to the neighborhood: children are welcome to scramble up

Stone path at the Green Dome Garden

and down the little hills, the paths are stroller-friendly, and the beauty of the plants themselves pulls people in. With its small but devoted core of gardeners, the Green Dome is an established destination now with legions of fans.

Brooklyn Heights Promenade

Location: west of Montague Terr., Pierrepont Place, and Columbia
   Heights, between Remsen and Orange Sts.

Hours: daily dawn to dusk

Admission fee: no

Bus: B51

Subway: 2, 3 to Clark St.

Facilities: wheelchair accessible from Montague Street

Best seasons: spring, summer, fall

Dedicated in 1950, the Promenade was a brilliant solution
to a problem caused by the creation of the Brooklyn-Queens
Expressway, which was slated by Robert Moses to turn the
western end of Brooklyn Heights into highway. Neighborhood opposition from the affluent Brooklyn Heights residents
killed the plan, which would have destroyed their gardens
and their peace. Compromise was reached: although the
original objectors to the plan lost their gardens anyway, they
gained a public esplanade, cantilevered over two levels of the
Brooklyn-Queens Expresssway, which almost appears as a
natural and elegant extension of its historic Brooklyn Heights
neighborhood.

The walkway's panoramic view of Manhattan and New
York Harbor encompasses the Statue of Liberty, the sky-
scrapers of lower Manhattan, Governor's Island, and the
Brooklyn Bridge. It is also the perfect place to see the
progress of Brooklyn Bridge Park spread out on the piers
below, not to mention the constant flow of river traffic.

Running the full length of the Promenade is a 30-foot-deep shrub and perennial border. Handsomely planted with a large display of shade-loving varieties, it forms an effective buffer between the public walk and the private houses to the east. Most of the shrub bed lies in the dappled shade of honey locusts and therefore its colors are somewhat muted, except in the spring, when midstory spring-blooming trees and shrubs put on a show, peaking before the honey locusts have established their canopy. Japanese dogwood, magnolia, weeping cherry, viburnum, forsythia, redbud, rhododendron, azalea, and laurel are underplanted with a generous bulb display.

Directly visible below the Promenade, Brooklyn Bridge Park will be 85 acres when it is finally completed. The park, which will run 1.3 miles along the shoreline, will include the existing Empire–Fulton Ferry State Park north of the Brooklyn Bridge as well as Piers 1–6 and their uplands to the south of the bridge. The piers portion of the park has been designed by Michael Van Valkenburgh Associates. The park incorporates salvaged materials from other city projects (i.e., granite from the Willis Avenue Bridge and also from the Roosevelt Island Bridge), making it the ultimate urban recycling effort. Salt marshes are being established to help jump-start the long-dormant waterside ecosystem. The outlines of the original piers will remain but as green parkland, their sharp industrial outline a permanent reminder of their past.

During the summer the garden is quieter. At intervals along the walk, pockets of variegated plants (dogwood, phalaris, ajuga, and hosta) lighten the picture. Over the years, residents and gardeners have left their mark on the garden, and new plantings pop up from time to time; an unknown enthusiast planted a huge stand of hollyhocks near the Remsen Street entrance, and midway along the Promenade, in the shrub bed, there is a kind of parterre, laid out in salvaged cobblestone, in the outline of a thunderbird. Built by three parks employees, it is a memorial to the Canarsie Indians who once lived in this area.

Although owned by the Department of Transportation, the Promenade is the responsibility of the parks department, and a public-private partnership with the Brooklyn Heights Association ensures a full-time gardener on the esplanade in the summer months. To mark the thirtieth anniversary of the establishment of the Landmarks Preservation Commission, the Brooklyn Heights Association commissioned a Texas rosarian to find an unnamed rose. A pink rose of exceptional size and vitality was sent to Brooklyn, named the Landmark Rose, and is now planted throughout the Promenade, where it flourishes.

There are a number of historical markers on the Promenade, the most interesting one by the flagpole notes the spot where the Four Chimneys house, George Washington's headquarters during the ill-fated Battle of Long Island, once stood.

Columbia Street Waterfront District Community Gardens

Location: see individual garden entries

Hours: see individual listings

Admission fee: no

Bus: B61

Subway: A, C, F to Jay St./Borough Hall, then the B61 bus

Facilities: none

Best season: summer

This quiet, offbeat corner of Brooklyn has weathered the ups and downs of city planning, and one of the surest signs of its present revival are these five thriving community gardens, all located within blocks of one another. Designated by city planners as the Columbia Waterfront District, its small red-brick nineteenth-century row houses are filled with a mix of recent arrivals and longtime residents, and Columbia Street, its backbone, now has both old businesses and trendy new restaurants and cafés.

Cut off from the rest of Carroll Gardens in the 1950s by the building of the Brooklyn Queens Expressway and the entrance to the Brooklyn Battery Tunnel, the Columbia district was further affronted when the city tore up Columbia Street to replace the sewers. The disruption lasted more than a year; the construction caused some houses to collapse and finished off many small businesses. To save what was left of the community, the city designated the area as a renewal district in the 1980s. Since then, there have been new housing starts and residents have united to preserve their human-scale neighborhood.

Human Compass

Location: 207–209 Columbia St. at the corner of Sackett St.
Hours: Sat.–Sun. 9:00am–noon

Founded in 1992 by a group of area residents, many of them artists, the Human Compass was the first community garden in the neighborhood. This deeply shaded spot—there are 22 varieties of trees in an area of less than an acre—nevertheless features a ravishing display of bright red roses in June. Several seating areas are furnished with elegant outdoor furniture, making the garden look more like a private backyard than a community garden. Each summer, it sponsors art classes for families, something of a neighborhood institution.

Summit Street

Location: 281–285 Columbia St. at the corner of Summit St.
Hours: Sat. 10:00am–2:00pm, Sun. 12:00pm–4:00pm Wed., Thurs.
    6:00pm–8:00pm

A grouping of pots and troughs at the entrance sets the tone for this sophisticated garden, which is filled with out-of-the-ordinary plants and combinations. Founded in 1993 on the site of a house that had been razed, the garden required many loads of fill to bring the land up to grade, and even after the cleanup rubble remained. Some of the bricks were used to make the wide patio, now shaded by clump birch, and some was piled up and covered with dirt to form a mound, an outstanding feature that can be found in the other Columbia gardens as well. The mound is planted with species that prefer lean soil and sharp drainage, including nepeta, artemisia, and pink evening primrose. Along with boxes for vegetables and flowers, there are a number of fruit-bearing trees, including cherry, elderberry, apple, and peach.

The Amazing Garden

Location: 261–265 Columbia St. at the corner of Carroll St.

Hours: Open April–October Sat.–Sun. 10:00am–6:00pm, Wed. 9:00am–6:00pm

Established in 1994 by several gardeners from the garden at Columbia and Summit Streets, the Amazing Garden consists of a number of lushly planted raised boxes filled with an orderly mix of flowers, herbs, and vegetables. Each year it holds a Christmas-tree shredding ceremony that supplies the community with invaluable mulch. In the summer, it hosts family barbecues and shows movies on an outdoor screen. Note the large fruit-bearing cherry tree on the Carroll Street side.

The Backyard Garden

Location: 61 73 Hamilton Ave. at the corner of Summit St.

Hours: Sat.–Sun. 10:00am–1:00pm (summer)

Set in a long triangular plot facing the marine terminal, this is the largest of the neighborhood gardens (it was once seven vacant lots). Founded by a group of gardeners from the Columbia and Summit garden, it is seriously eco-friendly, even by community garden standards. Its motto could be "Reduce, reuse, and recycle." The many compost bins are only the beginning. An attractive retaining wall built with salvaged bricks starts at the apex of the triangle and snakes through it, culminating in a rubble mound. Like the mounds in the neighboring gardens, this one is densely packed with poppies, pink evening primrose, artemisia, and nepeta. In the spring, there is a stand of McKana hybrid columbines, almost five feet tall, and a blush-colored rose that positively explodes against the gray of an adjacent wall. A tunnel, three feet in diameter, transverses the mound and looks like an inviting place for children to explore as the adults are digging and pruning. The tunnel is made from lengths of terra-cotta pipe that were rescued when the city switched to cement water lines. The wooden seats inserted in the outside walls of the tunnel are made from reused lumber from the Brooklyn Bridge. In the center of the garden members grow vegetables and flowers in a number of raised hexagonal planters. Beyond the planters is a haphazard collection of trees of all sizes, from seedlings to saplings, part of the Backyard Garden's Tree Outgrow program. Members receive seedlings from the National Tree Trust, grow them to saplings, and distribute them to a range of public spaces, from community gardens to Gateway National Park.

Cabrini Green Urban Meadow

Location: corner of Van Brunt and President Sts.

Hours: no fixed hours

This 8,000-square-foot green space began life in 2005 as a temporary landscape several blocks away at Columbia and Sackett. Created by Julie Farris of XS Space and called "Temporary Landscape: A Pasture for an Urban Space," it consisted of a small grassy mound bounded by a split-rail fence set in front of a large wall onto which was projected a film depicting pastoral scenes. It was a big hit in the neighborhood and beyond.

The earth was then recycled to a second site at Van Brunt and President Streets, where initially it was going to be a second temporary landscape, but it was so popular that it was adopted by GreenThumb, which runs the city's community gardening programs, and given permanent status.

Designed by Julie Farris and Balmori Associates, the meadow was installed in the spring of 2007. A wildflower meadow arcs around a rolling grassy lawn dotted with pink flowering dogwoods. There are two large panels at the entrance that explain with admirable scientific gravity the benefits of greening public space. The community has embraced the project, fund-raising is ongoing, and there are community workdays to keep the meadow flowery and the grass green. It is also the venue for a local summer jazz festival.

Red Hook Gardens

Location: Van Brunt to Beard Sts., waterfront to Columbia St.
Hours: daily dawn to dusk
Admission fee: no
Bus: B77, B61
Subway: A, C, F, 2, 3, 4, 5 to Borough Hall or M, N, R to Court Street
    then B61; F, G or Smith Street and 9th then B77
Water taxi: from Pier 11 in Manhattan (Wall St. Ferry Pier) to Ikea
Best seasons: spring, summer, fall

Red Hook, Brooklyn's blue-collar maritime community that seems perpetually on the brink of gentrification but never quite succumbs, is a fascinating destination for students of contemporary urban landscape design. Within a few blocks of one another, and in the presence of some of New York's most beautiful nineteenth-century buildings, are a superb mixed flower and shrub border in a small waterfront park, a clever and expansive contemporary park, and a large urban farm.

One hundred years ago Red Hook was one of the busiest ports in the country. Ships from all over the world loaded and unloaded cargo at its docks; the goods were stored in the large red-brick warehouses that crowded its shores. The teeming streets were lined with row houses built to lodge the Italian dockworkers who had settled here. A rough and vibrant community, Red Hook was Al Capone's home before he moved to Chicago. The construction of the Brooklyn-Queens Expressway and the Brooklyn Battery Tunnel in the 1950s and 60s sliced the area off from the rest of Brooklyn, bisecting communities and isolating residents. The advent of container shipping brought further changes to the port as the industry moved across the water to the new container terminals of New Jersey. As the great warehouses and docks emptied, the discrete neighborhoods that once made up Red Hook withered. In some ways, the isolation was probably a good thing: the waterfront, with its distinctive redbrick warehouses adorned with large arched and shuttered black-iron windows and doors, was left alone, and while the vitality of the neighborhood was entirely sapped, the fabric remained, untouched and unwanted.

Untouched and unwanted, that is, until the 1990s when an entrepreneur and former police officer Gregory O'Connell began buying up many of the properties along the waterfront, including the old Beard and Robinson Stores (actually, warehouses) built in 1869 to meet the increased demand in port activity after the Civil War. O'Connell rented space to small manufacturers, artists, and businesses, and the neighborhood came alive, albeit on a quieter scale than in earlier days. Then came Fairway in 2006, the discount food emporium inhabiting another of the dramatic warehouse buildings, and finally IKEA, the giant Swedish box store with its vast yellow and blue warehouse, opening at the former Todd Shipyard site in 2008, amid howls of protest and tears of regret by lovers of the "old waterfront." But along with all this upheaval have come more green spaces than this neighborhood has seen for generations.

Pier 41 Waterfront Garden

Location: 290 Conover St. at Pier 44

O'Connell had promised the community a park and he delivered, commissioning public garden designer Lynden B. Miller to design the Pier 41 Waterfront Garden. It is the first part of a half-mile public walkway between the Beard Street Warehouse Promenade (beside Fairway, at the foot of Van Brunt Street) and Pier 41 at Van Dyke.

The garden is right at the water's edge, and the view—of the Pier 41 warehouses, the harbor, the Verrazano-Narrows Bridge, and the Statue of Liberty seen face on—is nothing less than stunning. Miller has created a serpentine walk backed by fairly narrow beds, culminating in a naturalized clover meadow and a windswept seating area on the point with benches and rocks. O'Connell and his crew, with his son running the backhoe, did the 2004 installation of the garden, with Miller directing the troops. When she found an old bollard in the bushes, they hauled it out and made it a centerpiece for the sitting area. The beds are beautifully planted with species that do well in difficult seaside conditions, including a vibrant blue catmint, repeated continuously throughout the garden, which bears no resemblance to the washed-out stalwart grown in most gardens. The plant palette is blue-collar, although there are moments of gentrification (just like the neighborhood). Sturdy plants like goldenrod, willow, sedums, grasses, and chokecherries form an attractive matrix punctuated in spring by the vivid blue catmint and a delicate bearded iris. Miller also designed the plantings at the nearby Fairway store.

Erie Basin State Park

Location: 1 Beard St.

A few short blocks away from Pier 41, the Swedish furniture maker IKEA, as part of a deal with the city that allowed them to put in a giant store and parking lot on the former Todd Shipyard property, commissioned Lee Weintraub Landscape Architecture to design the 6.5 acre Erie Basin Park. Even the preservationists who mourn the passing of the shipyard, once one of the most important on the East Coast, are thrilled with the esplanade park that opens up almost a mile of waterfront and celebrates the industrial culture of old Red Hook.

The Erie Basin is a large protected harbor that was created by the canny and successful Edward Beard (of the Beard and Robinson Stores) in the mid-nineteenth century. He charged incoming vessels to discharge their ballast when they arrived at his docks to load up on freight bound for Europe. The ballast, old rocks and cobbles, was piled up in a scythe shape and eventually formed the large breakwater that creates the basin. The protection afforded by the breakwater made it ideal for ship repair operations, which need space for storage and dry docks. The once prosperous Todd Shipyard, which occupied 20 acres on the basin, closed in 1986.

Before the site was completely razed to make way for IKEA, a design team walked the site and collected two containers full of tools and artifacts they found in the yard. The loss of the giant graving, or dry dock, was particularly painful to preservationists, but its shape can be seen outlined in the IKEA parking lot. Weintraub's design goal was to tie in as much history as possible to the new park, and it is hard to walk through the bright and breezy site without feeling a bit of nostalgia for a lost industry: the materials and tools so

Pier 41 Waterfront Garden

lovingly displayed were not so long ago the means of men's livelihoods and are potent symbols of a more muscular economic era.

Erie Basin, technically a privately owned public space, will eventually be part of the Brooklyn Greenway. Hugging the shoreline, the park is dominated by four huge cranes, their operator cabins and movement arms intact, standing like sentinels on three piers that have been preserved. At the entrance to the piers the architects have designed raised disks that present, as in a museum display, the items collected from the shipyard—bollards and cleats, once used to tie up ships, large coils of rope, an arrangement of shackles, old winches. An array of chocs, concrete cubes that were lowered into the water to steady ships going into dry dock, are displayed as well. Some are used as a retaining wall, with the names of many of the ships repaired here bolted onto their cracked concrete surfaces. Archival photographs and accounts from Pino Deserio, the former foreman of the shipyard, are displayed on placards attached to the railing throughout the park, personalizing the historical perspective in the park's design. Abstract patterns of white lines criss-cross the paths and plazas, a reference to shadows cast by the masts and rigging of the thousands of ships that had been here. This same criss-cross pattern is echoed in the large abstract sculpture that serves as the park's logo. Near the entrance to the park a large compass is embedded in the walkway.

The park is fairly narrow where it starts as a band around the IKEA parking lot, but it widens to a grassy knoll at its southern end. Erie Basin is not all about nostalgia and history. There are 558 trees and over 900 shrubs and perennials here. The designers, veterans of other forward-thinking parks (Weintraub was one of the team that created Gantry Plaza State Park in Queens), have created little nooks outlined in boulders, each with specifically created, and very hip, furniture. Each nook offers visitors a protected retreat where they can enjoy the harbor, which is still alive with tugboats and barges chugging back and forth across the inlet.

Red Hook Community Farm

Location: entrance at corner of Otsego and Van Dyke Sts.
Web site: www.added-value.org

If Erie Basin Park is an ode to the industrial past, the Red Hook Community Farm is a modern-day example of a movement that has appeared in the city in various incarnations since the turn of the twentieth century—city farming as a tool for social change, a way to encourage healthier living for families, specifically children, in at-risk neighborhoods. In

The Red Hook farmers share an interest with their neighbors on the other side of Brooklyn, in East New York. Founded in 1995, the nonprofit East New York Farms! runs farms and a farmers' market that brings fresh food to an underserved population, recruiting community gardeners to grow and sell crops. Their youth internship program provides leadership training and sets up young people to work in their own youth farm and sell their produce, in addition to helping seniors with their farming. East New York Farms! also provides agricultural training with an emphasis on sustainable practices.

1908, there were over 80 farm garden programs in schools throughout the city, and Red Hook Community Farm is their very modern successor.

Right across the street from the bright-blue IKEA store, the nonprofit Added Value has transformed a big, old city playground into a real urban farm with rectangular fields raked with long furrows of crops. Founded in 2001 by youth workers Ian Marvy and Michael Hurwitz, Added Value's stated goal is "youth empowerment and urban agriculture for a sustainable Brooklyn." Each year up to 30 teenagers participate in the farm as part of a leadership training program; there is an active program for elementary school kids; and almost 14,000 students visit the farm yearly. It's not that Added Value thinks that the teenagers working here will become farmers, but they will have a clearer understanding of a wide range of issues, from sustainable agricultural practices to economic models (they sell the food at a weekly farmers' market) to community building. It's a grassroots effort to make better citizens and, along the way, it provides fresh food to a community that had little access to reasonably priced fresh produce before.

The Red Hook Farm's growing beds have been built on top of the original asphalt; the 2.75-acre site, an entire city block, had been a rail changing yard before it was a playground. At the time the farm started, organizers had $5,000 for the whole operation and there was no question of paying to rip up the asphalt, but they figured out a way to get compost for free, to enhance the 18 inches of topsoil placed on top of the asphalt. Each year there is approximately one acre under production; leaf mold, woodchips, and compost from the Bronx Zoo are used to top-dress the growing beds. The compost pile in the old batting cage is truly impressive. The farm produces about 6,500 pounds of food a year—from seed to market, working with a little greenhouse to get a jump on the season. Along with the farmers' market, the gardeners also sell to area restaurants, and they have set up a Community-Supported Agriculture program, where supporters receive a box of fresh produce each week during the growing season. The founders called their nonprofit Added Value because they hoped to be able to add value to both the food cycle and the wider community, and it is clear that they have succeeded in that and more.

The Brooklyn Bear's Community Gardens

Location: see individual garden entries
Hours: Sat.–Sun. 10:00am–2:00pm (hours subject to change)
Web site: www.brooklynbears.wordpress.com
Admission fee: no
Bus & Subway: see individual garden entries
Best season: summer

These three gardens near the Brooklyn Academy of Music are the work of a band of garden activists called the Brooklyn Bears. Two of the gardens are in locations where commercial and residential neighborhoods intersect, and one is a little farther away in the Fort Greene section. The dramatic clock tower of the Williamsburgh Savings Bank looms over all three.

The first Brooklyn Bear site was a former parking lot that had become a notorious center of prostitution and drug sales. In 1982, neighborhood groups, including the Brooklyn Academy of Music and the Pacific Street Block Association, were searching for a way to improve the neighborhood when a group of activists began clearing the site for a garden. When someone found a teddy bear in the weeds, a garden member made up a sign saying, "'Please Don't Litter in the Garden,' signed *The Brooklyn Bear*," thereby giving a name to the group. All three of the gardens are now permanent; Pacific is part of the Brooklyn Queens Land Trust, and Carlton and Rockwell have permanent parks department status.

Pacific Street Garden

Location: corner of Flatbush Ave. and Pacific St.

Bus: B41, B45, B67

Subway: B, Q, 2, 3, 4, 5, LIRR to Atlantic Ave.; D, M, N, R to Pacific St.

The original garden was 7,500 square feet, but as often happens, once the neighborhood was improved, the land became attractive to developers. In 1990, when plans were made to develop the site, members started a campaign to preserve the garden. A compromise plan was worked out whereby the developer would build on part of the land and some space would be saved for a garden. The development never materialized, however, and the garden continued to thrive until 1998, when, without warning, a tractor drove through the fence and workers commenced taking core samples for construction. Scrambling to save the garden, the Bears again enlisted the help of the community and the borough president; eventually a compromise similar to the first was worked out. This time the site was redeveloped, and the Bears had to pot up and move all their plants to another location, where they stayed for the duration of the construction. The Bears returned to a smaller space of about 5,000 square feet, but before long the garden looked just as lush as ever, with a variegated beech tree, winding paths, free-form beds, and a little wisteria-covered pergola.

Rockwell Place Garden

Location: 104 Rockwell Place

Bus: B103, B37, B45, B67

Subway: 2, 3, 4, 5 to Nevins Street; B, M, Q, R to DeKalb

This garden was founded in 1980 but taken over by the Bears in 1992 when the original gardeners moved away. The original Rockwell garden was a quiet woodland triangle in the middle of a lot of traffic, with a weeping beech and several linden trees, benches, and winding woodchip paths. History repeated itself, and like the Pacific site this garden was razed for a construction project. Here, the Metropolitan Transportation Authority needed to install an underground fan room for the nearby subway. After three years of construction, the MTA restored the garden, actually improving the physical site with a serpentine brick path, a large wooden trellis, lighting, a shed, and most exciting of all, a water source. The woodland is gone but the garden lives on.

Carlton Avenue Garden
Location: 397–401 Carlton Avenue
Bus: B38, B52
Subway: C to Lafayette, G to Classon Ave.

The Carlton Street Garden was colonized by Pacific Street gardeners the first time their garden was threatened in 1991. The city offered them this spot for the duration of the construction. The construction never materialized, but the gardeners stayed put. There are sidewalk beds of bright native plantings, but a lot of the emphasis here is on vegetables, as Fort Greene is a residential neighborhood. Members share giant boxes, which are divided up into smaller sections, and there is a large oval for community vegetables. A mural depicting a winged mantis completes the picture. Watering is a perennial problem in community gardens, so members harvest water from surrounding roofs and store it in a cistern. The gardeners have built the Rolls-Royce of compost systems—impressive "rat-proof" compost bins that look much sturdier than the average pergola; they accept neighborhood home compost collected at the farmers' market in Fort Greene Park and turn it into rich garden soil.

Brooklyn Botanic Garden

Location: 900 Washington Ave. between Eastern Pkwy. and Empire
    Blvd.; visitor entrances on Flatbush Ave. and Eastern Pkwy.
Hours: Tues.–Fri. 8:00am–6:00pm, weekends and holidays 10:00am–
    6:00pm; closed Monday
Garden info: (718) 623-7200
Web site: www.bbg.org
Admission fee: yes
Bus: B41, B45, B48
Subway: B, Q to Prospect Park; 2, 3 to Eastern Pkwy.; 4 to Franklin Ave.
Facilities: wheelchair accessible, café, rest rooms, telephones, parking,
    guided tours on weekends
Best seasons: all seasons

From the billowing profusion of April's delicate cherry blossoms to June's extravagant roses and the brilliant fall colors of the maples in the Japanese Hill-and-Pond Garden, Brooklyn Botanic Garden (BBG) offers a series of memorable moments despite its relatively modest size. These delights, coupled with its educational activities, and friendly, approachable staff, make BBG a beloved community resource as well as one of the city's premier cultural institutions and an internationally known center of horticulture.

    Although there are several entrances to the garden, including a convenient one by the parking lot it shares with the Brooklyn Museum, the most dramatic approach is from the Eastern Parkway Gate redesigned by Polshek Partnership Architects in 2005. Passing between the two massive curved walls that form the entrance of the garden into the Osborne

Brooklyn Botanic Garden clockwise from left: Japanese Hill-and-Pond Garden; Bluebell Wood; Cranford Rose Garden

Garden, the visitor moves between two worlds. The traffic recedes and the stately aura of the Italian-inspired Osborne Garden sets a calm tone. Designed by landscape architect Harold A. Caparn, it was built by workers from the WPA and opened in 1939 (renovated in 2004). The long narrow *tapis vert* is banded by a series of ten wisteria-covered pergolas, which make a magnificent display in the spring. At the southern end of the garden are a fountain and a terrace overlook that afford a good view of the garden and an especially pleasing perspective of the Cherry Esplanade.

BBG was conceived in the 1890s when Brooklyn was the third largest city in the country, a vast, bustling hub of immigrants and industry in competition with its flashy neighbor across the East River. In 1910, philanthropist Alfred T. White raised $25,000 to establish the garden on 39 rubble-strewn acres next to Prospect Park. The site, filled with boulders deposited by glaciers during the last ice age, had long been a dumping ground; a seepage pit would later become the Japanese Pond.

The proud civic leaders driving the project engaged the best designers for their new garden. The Olmsted brothers laid out and graded the site, and in 1912 Harold A. Caparn took over. An Englishman trained at the École des Beaux-Arts in Paris, Caparn is responsible for most of BBG's features, including the rose garden and the systematic display of plant families. McKim, Mead and White designed the administration building and the Palm House.

The garden, which has grown to 52 acres, attracts more than 750,000 visitors a year. It has 12,000 kinds of plants in its collection and an impressive record of firsts in horticultural display. The children's garden, created in 1914 by the schoolteacher Ellen Eddy Shaw, is the oldest of its kind in continuous operation in the country. Here, hundreds of plots are available for children to grow vegetables, flowers, and herbs. It has now hosted many generations of children—in fact, one of the early young gardeners was Alice R. Ireys, who went on to become a distinguished landscape architect and to design the BBG fragrance garden in 1955. Another first, the fragrance garden was specifically created for the blind. Plants, in raised beds 28 inches high, were chosen for texture as well as fragrance, so that visitors can feel silky lamb's ears or smell the pungent odor of marigolds. Information about various species is embossed in braille on a continuous metal railing that runs atop the stone planters. This innovative garden has been much copied and was one of Ireys's proudest achievements; it was renamed in her honor in 2000.

Set within a woodland border and incorporating the glacial boulders that littered the site, the rock garden was established in 1916 and was the first in an American botanical garden. One of the rocks has been linked to a formation 250 miles away in the Adirondacks. Unlike conventional rock gardens, which are dominated by alpines, this one includes a wide range of small or miniature plants—dwarf conifers, azaleas, rhododendrons—as well as the more typical scree plants, all nestled among the ancient boulders.

The Steinhardt Conservatory houses BBG's collection of indoor plants (2,700 taxa) in realistic environments simulating their native habitats. Opened in 1988, the three triangular pavilions each replicate a different region—desert, tropical, and warm temperate. The largest, at 6,000 square feet, is the tropical pavilion that houses a luxuriant rainforest, including towering trees that almost reach the top of the 65-foot-high ceiling. The country's largest collection of bonsai can be found at the C. V. Starr Bonsai Museum, started in 1925 with a gift of 25 plants. It was redesigned in 2007, and the fascinating miniatures are displayed in a clean Japanese-inspired setting that encourages visitors to admire the form of the individual specimens.

The most expansive display at BBG is the Plant Family Collection, which occupies nearly half the garden. Plants grouped to display their evolutionary progression wind throughout the grounds, starting in the northern section near the Japanese Hill-and-Pond Garden with a huge stand of lady ferns and scented ferns. The exhibit continues nearby with conifers (note the dramatic weeping hemlock) and moves to the gingko triangle. Also included in this collection are magnolias, elms, and oaks, heaths, roses, legumes, honeysuckles, daisies, and monocots. A visitor who reads the labels while touring the exhibit will receive a thorough education in plant evolution.

The Japanese Hill-and-Pond Garden

The pride of BBG, the Japanese Hill-and-Pond Garden was built in 1914 on three and one-half acres, the first Japanese garden within an American public garden. This was the masterpiece of landscape designer Takeo Shiota, who planned it loosely as a stroll garden. The garden represents an unusual intersection of immigrant forces. Although Shiota was Japanese, most of the workmen were local Italian laborers and stoneworkers, and scholars have noted that the waterfalls bear an uncanny resemblance to the grottoes and stonework found in classic Italian gardens. Be that as it may, the garden contains many of the traditional elements of Japanese gardens, including a pond, two waterfalls, an island, carefully placed rocks, a viewing pavilion, stone lanterns, and a torrii, a large red gate-like structure that indicates a nearby Shinto shrine. A path leads around the large pond, past a series of scenes and views that change with the differing elevations and orientations. The key to enjoying this garden is to go slowly and savor individual moments—the image of the weeping cherry mirrored in the pond, the severely pruned evergreens, the way the russets of the maples in autumn echo the red of the torrii gate.

Considered by many to be Olmsted and Vaux's masterpiece, Prospect Park occupies 526 rolling acres in Central Brooklyn, across Flatbush Avenue from BBG (which was built on land originally set aside for Prospect Park in a design proposal of 1860). Frederick Law Olmsted and Calvert Vaux designed what they described as a "pastoral landscape." It took eight years and 2,000 workers to transform the site into what is still one of the most sublime of urban parks. Perhaps the crowning glory is the 90-acre long meadow, a gently undulating sea of green called by the designers a "greensward." Protected from the sights and sounds of the street by berms and edged with stately trees, the meadow was Olmsted and Vaux's ultimate antidote to the congestion of the city. Although a number of changes have been made to the original design, and some new buildings erected, the park remains a gem, albeit one that needs a tremendous amount of care.

In fact, the trees are the true pride of this garden. Many have been "cloud pruned" to suggest shapes of nature, giving them a controlled cohesion that contrasts with the giant pine trees that form much of the backdrop. In the spring, the different tones of the Japanese maples, ranging from light green to deepest red, are the perfect foil for the soft pinks of the cherry trees.

The garden underwent a $3.2 million restoration in 1999 and 2000, when the one-and-a-half-acre pond was rebuilt, the path system redone and made wheelchair accessible, the slopes stabilized to prevent erosion, the perimeter fence redesigned and extended, and the viewing pavilion's pergola restored. Many new trees were added as well, including Japanese maples and Japanese cherries, especially weeping varieties.

The Cranford Rose Garden

This classic, romantic garden was established in 1927. Donated by a New York City contractor named Walter V. Cranford, who built many of Brooklyn's subway tunnels, it contains more than 5,000 bushes representing nearly 1,200 varieties. Harold A. Caparn designed the garden, whose satisfying structure makes this an attractive place at any time and a magnificent site in June when the roses are at peak. A one-acre rectangle, it is enclosed by a white lattice fence; a raised latticework pavilion near the southern end affords a view of the entire garden, with its 15 rectangular beds divided by panels of grass. Caparn disliked modern roses, finding their foliage scraggly and unappealing; he therefore surrounded these central beds, full of leggy modern roses, with a framework of bushier old garden roses—gallicas, damasks, centifolias, and mosses.

Originally, the central beds were meant to illustrate the gradual development of the modern rose in chronological order. During the first winter, however, nearly all the tea roses died because they were not hardy enough for Brooklyn. As the years passed, many others died as well, and the scheme was modified. Today, the central beds, each 10 by 50 feet, feature hardy modern roses; the side beds, old garden roses and species roses; the posts, climbers; and the trellised walls of the garden, ramblers and climbers. The pavilion, too, is covered with climbers, many of them developed by W. Van

Fleet, a famous American rosarian. The rose garden is closed in the winter.

Cherry Walk and Esplanade

The most popular annual event at the garden is the Sakura Matsuri, or Cherry Blossom Festival, which celebrates Japanese culture. The two-day festival takes place each spring at the peak of the cherry blossom season (usually late April or early May), attracting up to 40,000 visitors. There are a host of activities and demonstrations, but visitors come mainly to admire the more than 200 cherry trees in the garden's extensive collection, including more than 40 varieties of Oriental flowering cherry trees. Many overhang the gently winding Cherry Walk, which leads to the Cherry Esplanade, where 76 Kwanzan cherries are laid out on either side of a wide lawn. The exact bloom time of the cherry trees is a subject of much speculation among cherry blossom lovers, and the garden's Web site tracks each individual tree as it approaches perfection. Originally the cherries were backed by rows of towering red Norway maples, the burgundy of the leaves providing a stunning backdrop to the cherries. They were known as the Armistice grove, since they were planted on the last day of World War I. Time and ecological correctness, however, converged. The 80-year-old maples needed to be replaced, and because the Norway maples have come to be seen as an invasive species, 88 Scarlett oaks, a native species, were chosen to replace them.

Collections

Nearby, the Louisa Clark Spencer Lilac Collection features approximately 150 species and cultivars in a spectrum of colors from white through lilac to pink and burgundy. The lilacs begin blooming as the cherry blossoms fade, but there is a brief overlap in May, when a visitor can experience both the delicacy of some of the weeping cherries as well as the heady fragrance of the lilacs in bloom.

Although the cherry display is justly praised, some think that the greatest moment at BBG occurs in late May in the wood just south of the Cherry Esplanade, when 45,000 bluebells carpet the forest floor and the tree trunks rise like sculpture out of a sea of deepest sapphire. It is a thrilling sight in a woodland that is quiet the rest of the year.

Starting in early spring, the BBG's magnolia collection, first planted in 1932 (restored 2004), is full of blossoms and fragrance. The Judith Zuk Magnolia Plaza, named for a beloved former director of the garden was like the rose garden, originally designed by Harold A. Caparn in a formal style that complemented the administration building that overlooks it. Seventeen varieties of magnolias are represented, including the star magnolia, which begins blooming in March, followed by the saucer magnolia in April and the sweet-bay in June. The well-known yellow-flowered magnolia, Elizabeth, which was developed at BBG and patented in 1977, is also prominently displayed.

Hattie Carthan Community Garden

Location: Marcy Ave. between Lafayette Ave. and Clifton Place,
    Bedford-Stuyvesant
Hours: no fixed hours (very active)
Garden info: (212) 788-8070
Admission fee: no
Bus: B38
Subway: G to Bedford/Nostrand Aves.
Facilities: none
Best season: summer

Friends and colleagues remember Hattie Carthan simultaneously charming and challenging city officials with her two
favorite expressions: "You wouldn't want to disappoint an
old lady, would you?" and "Look, we've got to get this done
because I have one foot in the grave and one on a banana
peel." At stake in the beginning was one very special tree,
a rare Southern magnolia threatened by development. The
magnificent tree had grown from a slip brought to Brooklyn in
1855 from North Carolina. In the 1960s, fed up with watching her neighborhood deteriorate around her, Hattie Carthan
led a fight to preserve not only the tree but the three nineteenth-century buildings behind it at 677 Lafayette Street.
Carthan, who took on the fight to save the magnolia when she
was 68 years old, was remarkably successful with city officials, and in 1972 she succeeded in having the tree declared
the first Living Landmark in the city. Credited with helping
revitalize this Bedford-Stuyvesant neighborhood, she went on

to found the Magnolia Tree Earth Center, which administers the garden that bears her name and promotes environmental programs throughout the community. One of its most innovative programs, Tree Corps, developed into the Urban Tree Corps, which trains young people to look after street trees. She died in 1989, the same year the Hattie Carthan Community Garden was established.

This was the third attempt to start a community garden on this sizeable lot, originally the site of the Church of St. Augustine, which burned down. The garden's members enjoy the great luxury of its spaciousness: this site is one of the largest GreenThumb community gardens in the city. The atmosphere is friendly and relaxed. There is a gazebo, and groves of trees, including a striking group of purple-leaved plums, provide shade for the benches, which are placed strategically around the garden. There are well-used barbecue and picnic areas and a large compost operation.

Scattered throughout are fruit-bearing trees, including peach, apple, cherry, and fig. The striking aspects of this garden are the individual plots, most of which are given over to vegetables. Here, in the middle of Bedford-Stuyvesant, a visitor can see corn as high as that in Iowa; there are also several other crops not usually found in the city, including peanuts, indicating gardening techniques well beyond the basic.

The 60-member garden just keeps expanding: in 2009, after a year of hard work, an adjacent empty lot was transformed to an urban farm and the site of a farmers' market. Local youths work in partnership with garden members to run the market. The garden has also added a hoop house so that members can grow seeds right through the winter. There is a children's garden on land that was once a dumping pit; the gardeners turned it into a place where elementary school children come to learn about growing plants and food and also get to pump water from an old-fashioned hand pump. Like most successful community gardens, this one flourishes because of the symbiosis between the agricultural and horticultural programs and the spirit of community-building that prevails.

After visiting the Hattie Carthan garden, walk down the block to the Magnolia Tree Earth center at 677 Lafayette Street to learn more about Hattie Carthan's mission. Make sure to look for the large southern magnolia that started it all.

Hattie Carthan mural

Clockwise from left: Green Dome Garden; Pier 41 Waterfront Garden in Red Hook; the Green Dome Garden

Brooklyn Public Library, Saratoga Branch

Location: 8 Thomas S. Boyland St., near Broadway, Bedford-Stuyvesant
Hours: Mon., Wed., Fri. 9:00am–6:00pm; Tues. 1:00pm–8:00pm;
      Thurs. 1:00pm–6:00pm; Sat. 10:00am–5:00pm; closed Sun.
Garden info: (718) 573-5224
Web site: www.brooklynpubliclibrary.org
Admission fee: no
Bus: B7, B20, B26, B60, Q24
Subway: J to Halsey St.
Facilities: wheelchair accessible, telephone, rest rooms
Best season: summer

Behind this pocket-sized branch of the Brooklyn Public Library lies a serene reading garden, a simple oval of grass enclosed by shrubs and perennials, with a pergola at one end offering shade to the sun-weary. Both the library and the garden are aesthetic standouts in this section of Brooklyn.

A happy result of the confluence of enlightened philanthropy and civic pride, the Saratoga branch was built in 1908, one of 61 public libraries funded by the steel magnate Andrew Carnegie, who insisted that the best architects, contractors, and materials be used in their construction. As a result, these libraries brought to the working-class neighborhoods they served a level of architecture rarely seen there. The Saratoga branch, designed by the firm of Davis and Otto, is a one-story red-brick Classical Revival building with exceptionally fine grillwork and iron railings inside. It was renovated in 1994. Between 1997 and 1998 the Horticultural Society of New York installed a viewing garden at the front and a reading garden in the unused space at the rear of the building. These installations were the first projects in the GreenBranches program, which creates gardens in libraries around the city, especially in neighborhoods with few green spaces or amenities.

The Horticultural Society also sponsors a very successful gardening program at Rikers Island. The GreenHouse project enrolls up to two dozen inmates and, using a one-and-a-half-acre plot as a laboratory, prepares them for horticultural jobs on the outside. The inmates have built a series of gardens, complete with paths, planters, and 100 different kinds of plants, many of which are unusual varieties from Rockefeller Center displays.

One enters the reading garden through the library, presumably collecting one's book along the way. Although the materials used in the garden are not unusual, they are handled with care. The corrugated iron fence is painted a maritime blue and further adorned with panels of Boston ivy, turning what could have been an eyesore into an asset. The path that circles the lawn is brick laid in a running bond pattern. At the far end of the garden a redwood gazebo, covered in roses and trumpet vine, provides shade and adds an important architectural focal point to the space. A broad variety of shrubs chosen for continuous bloom and attractive foliage fills the beds surrounding the lawn, including hydrangea, yew, lilac, juniper, dogwood, holly, arborvitae, spirea, and rose of Sharon. Handsome wooden benches are placed strategically along the path, far enough apart so that readers can have space and privacy. The two small viewing gardens at the front of the library, contemporary versions of a parterre, feature formal beds of periwinkle partially enclosing an annual bed flanked by peonies, astilbe, and lady's mantle.

The Floyd Bennett Gardens

Location: 1 Ryan Visitor's Center, Floyd Bennett Field, Gateway
   National Recreation Area, south of Shore Pkwy. at the end of
   Rockaway Pkwy.
Hours: daily dawn to dusk
Garden info: (718) 338-3799
Web site: www.fbga.net
Admission fee: no
Bus: Q35
Subway: 2, 5 to Flatbush Ave., then Q35 bus to the marina
Facilities: none; rest rooms and telephones at Gateway offices
Best season: summer

On first viewing, this is a curiously forlorn spot. Grass pushes
through cracks in the runway of this former municipal air-
port, where celebrity pilots Amelia Earhart and Howard
Hughes once flew; the land stretches out flat and empty to
the horizon. On a clear day, the faint outline of the Manhattan skyline can be glimpsed a long way to the north. It is only
when one moves close to the site that a hodgepodge patch-
work quilt of fences, pergolas, and bizarre structures appears
and then resolves itself into orderly rows, and the tremendous
vitality of an enormous garden becomes apparent.

Floyd Bennett bills itself as one of the largest community
gardens in the country, and with nearly 600 ten-by-twenty-
foot plots on more than five acres of land, this could well be
true. Founded by the Cornell Agricultural Extension Service
in 1970, it includes members from every borough. Since a

Floyd Bennett Gardens

sports center opened in the old air terminal, the garden has been inundated with requests for plots and there is a two-year waiting list to garden here.

For the student of human nature, this is the place to go. Each garden has its own personality and reflects the sensibility, tastes, and even the eating habits of its owners. Double plots are available, and groups can band together to form a small empire of as many as four plots. On one pergola an artist has hung a string of cobalt blue bottles that tinkle and sparkle in the sun; down the path, a couple has built an elaborate potting bench and planting boxes painted a stylish dark green. Other gardens are salad bowls, entirely dedicated to an assortment of delicate greens that look as if they could land directly on a luncheon plate at the Four Seasons. Although many of the gardeners grow flowers, the emphasis is on vegetables. Many of the members manage three harvests a year, thanks to good technique and an emphasis on soil improvement. The native sand has been amended liberally with manure from the local stables and rich, black compost. The association sponsors a series of workshops on subjects ranging from companion planting to canning. Making the most of a small space is a popular subject, ergo a course called The Lasagna Garden: How to Grow Things Right in Your Compost Pile and Have the Best of Both.

The Narrows Botanical Gardens

Location: Shore Rd. between Bayridge Ave. and 72nd St.

Hours: daily dawn to dusk

Web site: www.narrowsbg.org

Admission fee: no

Bus: B1, B9, B27, B37

Subway: R to Bay Ridge

Facilities: none

Best seasons: spring, summer

Although dog owners and garden lovers are often at odds in New York City parks, here dog owners have taken the initiative and turned an ordinary city park into an ambitious horticultural showpiece. The redesign and replanting, begun in 1995 by a small group of Bay Ridge residents—among them two dog lovers, a garden designer, a horticulturist and a teacher—has expanded to fill more than four acres. The park has been transformed into a varied landscape, with an ever-increasing number of garden areas as well as space for neighborhood cultural events and an active educational program.

The site, a long piece of land that serves as a buffer between the residential Shore Drive and the busy Belt Parkway at the water's edge, is several feet below the grade of the street and has a fine view of the Narrows and Staten Island. There are two entrances, both from Shore Drive—a simple path at the north end near the native plant habitat and a more formal one through an allée of little-leaf linden at the south end of the garden (note the various kinds of ivy that form a tapestry under the lindens).

The public part of the garden consists of a large oval lawn and paths circled by themed plantings and smaller gardens; each one is a destination in itself. South of the native plant garden along the western side of the site is a tightly planted alpine garden; across the path, there is an unusual fastigiate tree grove that includes hornbeam beech and pine; and in the southern section of the garden, there is a corresponding collection of weeping trees.

Among the outstanding features of the garden is the 380-foot Fragrant Path. A deep bed planted with shrubs and perennials provides four seasons of interest and three seasons of delicious smells. The planting recalls the billowing waves of color that are the outstanding features of the English perennial garden. Plants include lilac, mock orange, lavender, honeysuckle, viburnum, jasmine, vitex, mahonia, and thorny eleagnus, the last producing a wonderful scent in October and November, when nothing else is blooming.

The Fragrant Path blends into a colorful butterfly garden, which includes butterfly bushes (self-sown to great effect), mallow, a giant stand of *Verbena bonariensis* (also self-sown), and black-eyed Susans. Eighty percent of the flowers in the butterfly garden were started from seeds. This garden then morphs into a meadow. Other small but ambitious gardens include a Zen garden, which has become the garden's memorial to the events of 9/11, a moon garden that features silver and white plants, and a dry garden installed in a 50-foot-long drystone wall, built by the gardeners themselves. Two rose gardens occupy small ovals, facing one another. One features fragrant tea roses, many of them donated by the supplier

Jackson and Perkins; the other is filled with old-fashioned shrub roses. Above the garden, on the sidewalk along Shore Drive, is a lily pond, actually a simple, square tank filled with water lilies, which can be enjoyed by all who pass by. Because of the fragile nature of its ecosystem, the native plant habitat at the extreme northern end of the park is fenced off and used only for educational programs.

This is one of the few gardens in New York that is truly dog-friendly. There are cleverly constructed plastic-bag dispensers located throughout the grounds, so that visitors can easily clean up after their dogs. The dispensers are kept filled by senior citizens who recycle plastic bags as part of their contribution to the upkeep of the garden.

1 Isamu Noguchi Garden Museum

2 Gantry Plaza State Park

3 Queens Botanical Garden

4 Queens County Farm Museum

5 Veterans Memorial Garden

6 Mother Carter Garden

7 Curtis "50 Cent" Jackson Community Garden

8 Merrick Marsden Community Garden

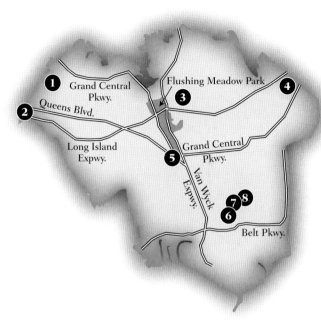

Grand Central
Pkwy.

Queens Blvd.

Long Island
Expwy.

Flushing Meadow Park

Grand Central
Pkwy.

Van Wyck
Expwy.

Belt Pkwy.

QUEENS

Queens is blessed with a rich, loamy soil courtesy of the last ice age. (It sits at the foot of the terminal moraine and is the head point of the outwash plain.) The effect of the soil can be seen throughout the borough, from the lush plantings of the Queens Botanical Garden to the neighborhood yards where giant dahlias jostle with impossibly abundant roses.

Sometimes described as the birthplace of American horticulture, Queens was the site of the first commercial nursery for trees and plants in America, opened in Flushing in 1737 by William Prince. Through the eighteenth and nineteenth centuries, countless nurseries and farms took advantage of the excellent soil and proximity to New York and established themselves in those small communities of Long Island that eventually united to form Queens. There is even a neighborhood known as Floral Park, named for a large commercial nursery grower once located there. The garden theme has remained prevalent in Queens; in the 1920s a whole neighborhood of garden apartments was developed, with magnificently planted central courtyards. Today, the yearly Jackson Heights Garden Tour, where nonresidents can get a look at these private edens, is a much-anticipated event.

The farms and nurseries have all moved on, squeezed out by a burgeoning population, formed in great part by waves of immigrants that have made Queens the most ethnically diverse county in the nation. The western edge of the borough along the East River is heavily industrialized, yet it remains a predominantly residential borough. But Queens is not immune to the cycle of industrialization and decay that plagues the urban landscape. This is especially true in Long Island City and in the parts of the borough nearest the East River. Yet these areas are also the scene of creative uses of discarded or unused industrial sites. Artists have established a showcase for contemporary sculpture, the Socrates Sculpture Park, on a piece of wasteland at the river's edge, in a neighborhood of old factories and warehouses. At the huge Queens West development in Hunter's Point, an abandoned, dilapidated shoreline is being turned into an extensive park. It seems fitting that the birthplace of American horticulture should also be the site of these new beginnings.

Queens Botanical Garden

Isamu Noguchi Garden Museum

Location: 32–37 Vernon Blvd. at 33rd Rd., Long Island City
Hours: Wed., Thurs., Fri. 10:00am–5:00pm; Sat.–Sun. 11:00am–6:00pm
Garden info: (718) 204-7088; shuttle bus information {718} 721-1932
Web site: www.noguchi.org
Admission fee: yes
Bus: Q69, Q103 (courtesy shuttle bus is available on Sundays from Asia
    Society in Manhattan)
Subway: N, W to Broadway
Facilities: wheelchair accessible, café, rest rooms, telephones, parking
Best seasons: spring, summer, fall

To Western visitors, the Isamu Noguchi Garden Museum
suggests the influence of Japanese tradition; to Japanese
visitors, the garden seems to reflect a Western aesthetic. Its
creator, the famed sculptor Isamu Noguchi, was a product of
both cultures, and the museum, he explained, was an attempt
to define his role "as a crossing where inward and outward
meet, East and West."

The son of a Japanese poet and an American writer, Noguchi designed some of the twentieth century's most influential
garden spaces. His interest in gardens stemmed from his
work in stage design (he designed many sets for Martha Graham). Unlike the gardens he created for Chase Manhattan
Plaza in downtown New York or for UNESCO headquarters
in Paris, this space is specifically intended as an environment
for viewing his sculpture in changing perspectives. It is Noguchi's stage set for his own work.

The artist moved his studio from Manhattan to this industrial area in Long Island City in the 1960s. In 1975, he bought an old brick photoengraving plant here, which he used as an office, studio, and storage facility. When he began to build the museum, this two-story brick structure become its core, and a cinderblock wing was added. It opened to the public in 1985 and now houses more than 200 of Noguchi's sculptures as well as plans and models for his gardens, playgrounds, and stage and dance sets.

The galleries lead directly out from the entrance hall. Although they have walls and a roof, a clerestory window the length of one wall is permanently open, and a graceful birch grows in a corner, bringing the outside inside. The galleries, featuring large stone sculptures that the artist created late in his life, flow into the walled garden itself.

Meditative is perhaps the word that best describes the garden. It encourages reflection and contemplation. Noguchi created a simple triangular space and clothed the walls with ivy. The carefully chosen trees—katsura, magnolia, birch, maple, weeping cherry, black pine, and bamboo—share the garden with the sculpture, their differing shapes and textures playing off the eloquent shapes and textures of the stone.

Through his work with gardens, Noguchi became more and more intrigued by stone, especially the hard granites and basalts found in Japan. He was fond of the traditional saying "Stone is the affection of old men," and in his later years clearly relished the challenge of finding the sculpture within the stone, or, as he put it, "leaving nature's mark." Several of the works here are tsukubai—naturally hollowed-out stones into which water trickles—that are traditional features of Japanese gardens. Noguchi inverted the concept by

Two blocks from the Noguchi museum another famous artist has established a rugged, thought-provoking exhibition space for sculpture. The sculptor Mark Di Suvero created the Socrates Sculpture Park in 1986 on five acres of abandoned industrial land next to his studio on the shores of the East River (31–42 Vernon Blvd. between Broadway and 31st Street Drive; 718-956-1819; open daily, 10:00am–sunset). The sculptures—often large-scale works of cutting-edge artists—change twice a year: most of the exhibitors are chosen by other artists. With little signage and no written material, the park forces the viewer to respond to the work itself rather than to a label.

omitting the elements of age and naturalness so prized by the Japanese when he used machinery to fashion two tsukubai. With another, made specifically for this garden, Noguchi again reimagined the principle: instead of trickling in, the water flows out, creating an exceptionally beautiful fountain.

Noguchi's appreciation of texture and the relationship between the man-made and the natural is evident in the elements that make up the ground plane. The path through the garden is concrete; other large areas are paved with coarse gravel edged in granite. The large pieces of gravel—a dark, cold gray set in amorphic-shaped beds—contrast with the straighter lines of the concrete walkway and the green beds of ground cover that includes vinca, moss, and ivy. Throughout, the rounded shapes of some of the sculptures are echoed in the soft, cloudlike forms of mounded juniper and pine.

Noguchi remains here in spirit and in fact: after he died in 1988, half his ashes were buried in his garden in Japan and half were buried at the far end of this garden beneath the magnolia tree.

Gantry Plaza State Park

Location: between 50th Ave. and Center Blvd., Hunters Point
Hours: daily dawn until 10:00pm
Garden info: (718) 786-6385
Admission fee: no
Bus: Q103
Subway: 7 to Vernon Blvd./Jackson Ave.
Facilities: wheelchair accessible, rest rooms, telephones
Best season: summer

Queens West, an Empire State Development Corporation project, is transforming a portion of the Queens waterfront in Hunters Point from a derelict post-industrial mess to a desirable if sometimes predictable modern neighborhood of mixed residential and commercial towers with a huge bonus—dramatic, even extraordinary, views across the East River to the Manhattan skyline. Gantry Plaza State Park, which has been developed in phases, serves as the waterside "front yard" for this new neighborhood and has become a popular destination in its own right.

Phase one of the park, a two-and-a-half acre section designed with a sure yet playful touch by Thomas Balsley Associates, Lee Weintraub Landscape Architecture, and architect Richard Sullivan, features many of the design elements—the jetties, the site-specific furniture, the touches of humor—that have become familiar in New York's park design vocabulary, but when Gantry opened in 1998, they were new and very exciting. The emblems and most striking

Down the street from Gantry is the Long Island City Community Garden (49th Avenue between Vernon Boulevard and Fifth Street) which features handsome trees—redbud, weeping cherry, shadblow—as well as plenty of flowers. A curved mulch path leads to vegetable boxes in the back. Note the random tile pieces in the walkway.

elements of the park are the two hulking black steel gantries that loom over the site. Elevators once used to load railroad freight onto barges, they are remnants of the site's earlier incarnation and stand like triumphal arches at the edge of the river facing Manhattan. The words "Long Island" are painted in red outlined with white on the river face of the gantries, proclaiming in no uncertain terms their physical location, but also, in the boldness of the graphics, the rebirth of the waterfront.

Four piers jut out into the river, linked by a wide ribbon of paths and plantings. The design of the piers is lighthearted, as is evidenced by the fanciful furniture used throughout. Each has a different shape and function, but all are built of the same materials, stylistically linked by metal balustrades topped by large, rounded wood railings. The Café Pier features a stylized stainless-steel arc of a lunch counter with attached seating, under a complicated metal structure that suggests an awning. The Sunning Pier zigzags out into the river, ending in a square platform containing four hugely oversized wooden chaises. The Fishing Pier, the pièce de résistance, offers a large fish-shaped table for cleaning fish. People use these piers: they fish, sunbathe on the chaises, and eat lunch at the café tables. First-time visitors can be heard chuckling as they examine the furnishings; regulars go directly to a favorite spot.

At the edge of the plaza, beside the Café Pier, the granite blocks tumble down the shore to a little rocky beach, and from there a bridge curves out over a river inlet to the base of the second gantry. Split granite blocks, each with one polished face and the other sides left rough, are scattered throughout for seating. Visitors can actually put their feet in the water. This intimacy—the sound of the irregular lapping of the water against the shore, the sight of the wind rippling on the water—provides a unique connection between the individual and the river that is as powerful as it is rare in New York City.

Around the corner on 48th Avenue, on a long, narrow strip of land between Fifth Street and Vernon Boulevard, lies the former Hunters Point Community Park, now part of the larger Gantry Plaza State Park. Opened in 1996 and also designed by Thomas Balsley Associates, it anticipated many of the elements of Gantry Park: the stainless-steel street furniture punched out with geometric patterns, the sail-shaped canopies, the bright colors. This is an active-use recreation area, and it manages to bow to the basic industrial nature of the area while offering the public a clean, modern, and amusing neighborhood amenity.

Several gravel paths lead from the plaza through asymmetrical beds. The plantings, designed by horticulturist Billie Cohen, are deliberately wild, as if the natural vegetation that grew up when the site was abandoned had simply taken over. The wide plant palette includes ornamental grasses; perennials such as iris, veronica, gaura, and nepeta; and shrubs such as abelia, rugosa roses, viburnum, bay, shadblow, willows, and azaleas. Height is provided by several red maples and oaks. On a hot summer day, the mist rising from the round stone table on the northern side of a grove of red maples provides cooling moisture.

Two sets of railroad tracks slice through the planting beds, pointing toward the gantries. Elements such as these call to mind the site's history and roots. But there is a freshness about the place, a combination of elegance and playfulness,

Clockwise from left: Gantry Plaza State Park; Curtis "50 Cent" Jackson Community Garden; Merrick Marsden Community Garden

natural wildness and man-made structure, all set against the magnificence of the New York skyline, that has nothing to do with the past and everything to do with the future.

At the northern end of Gantry, Peninsula Park features a large grassy mound with a perimeter path, with sets of specially designed deck chairs, and offers sunbathing, ball playing, and terrific views of the United Nations buildings across the river.

After many years of planning and then site remediation, the first part of phase two of Gantry opened in July 2009. Part of a five-acre parcel to the north of the gantries, it was designed by Able Bainnson Butz. A continuous wooden esplanade of 21,000 linear feet offers visitors intimate views of a constructed wetland as well as a sweeping vista of the East River and the Manhattan skyline. This phase also has site-specific furniture and features a big children's playground and an earth form that dominates the main green.

There is no question that the best part of the Queens West development is the greening of the shoreline: even if the developers had simply put in a huge lawn, the spectacular views would have made this shoreline a destination. But Gantry Plaza State Park is more than that. With a myriad of experiences to offer—from viewing the wetlands to the lawns to the rocky shoreline in the shadow of the gantries—it goes a long way to making this a first-class project and sets a high bar for this changing neighborhood.

Queens Botanical Garden

Location: 43–50 Main St. between Dahlia and Elder Aves., Flushing

Hours: Tues.–Fri. 8:00am–6:00pm; Sat.–Sun. 8:00am–6:00pm (April–
    October): Tues.–Sun. 8:00am–4:30pm (November–March);
    closed Mon. (except holidays)

Garden info: (718) 886-3800

Web site: www.queensbotanical.org

Admission fee: no

Train: LIRR to Flushing

Bus: Q20, Q44

Subway: 7 to Main St./Flushing

Facilities: wheelchair accessible, garden shop, rest rooms, telephones,
    parking

Best seasons: spring, summer, fall

Queens is the most ethnically diverse county in the United
States and throughout the 39 acre grounds of Queens Botan
ical Garden this diversity is everywhere apparent—in the signage; in the brochures printed in English, Spanish, Korean,
and Chinese; in the gardens themselves; and especially in
the visitors, whose nationalities cover a considerable spectrum. Serving this diverse population is an important part of
the garden's core vision, which is to present plants as unique
expressions of cultural traditions.

Equally important is the garden's commitment to responsible stewardship, and here QBG is most definitely walking
the walk as well as talking the talk. The administration building is the first new public building to be LEED Platinum

Queens Botanical Garden

certified in New York City. With features like a planted roof and fully recycled stormwater runoff and gray-water collection systems, this building puts Queens Botanical Garden in the vanguard of institutions committed to responsible stewardship, and this commitment continues in the sustainable horticulture practiced in the surrounding gardens.

QBG began as a five-acre horticultural extravaganza, the Gardens on Parade exhibit at the 1939–40 New York World's Fair. After the fair closed, local residents continued to garden on the grounds, and in 1946 a group of them became incorporated as the Queens Botanical Garden Society and expanded Gardens on Parade to 20 acres. In the early 1960s the garden was moved to its present location, which had originally been used as a dumping area, to make room for the 1964–65 World's Fair.

The theme for the 1939 World's Fair was innovation, and it is this concept that inspired the present generation at

Queens Botanical Garden to embark on their journey toward environmental sustainability. As long ago as 1998 some board members and managers decided that Queens could be in the forefront of the green movement, and this, in conjunction with its continuing mission to serve its diverse public, might give Queens its own niche among the many botanical gardens of its size. The result of this farsighted policy is an all-encompassing initiative, whose centerpiece is the 16,000-square-foot Visitor & Administration Building designed by BKSK Architects, with its green roof and enclosed water systems, solar panels, geothermal heat, and native plantings. When it opened in 2007 it was the most advanced green building in the city and has served as a model for groups from all over the world. There are a number of ways that horticulture is integral to these new green systems.

Water is a unifying element. The administration building has two separate water systems, but each uses plants to naturally clean the water. The gray water from sinks, dishwashers, and washing machines is carried to a settling tank, where impurities sink to the bottom; it is then piped to a constructed wetland, located for all to see at the entrance plaza. The wetland slopes gently back towards the building. The gray water is released at the high end of the wetland and is purified as it moves through layers of gravel and plant roots, slowly making its way downhill back to the building where it is collected and used to flush the toilets.

Stormwater-runoff management is an increasing problem, especially in cities, where most of the surfaces are paved and there is no place for water to go except into sewers. A heavy storm can easily overcome the sewer system, and water loaded with impurities and toxins then flows into local waterways. QBG is committed to keeping all of its storm water on site. All the rainwater from the roofs and terrace canopy of the administration building is collected in a rainwater harvest system and runs through the cleansing Biotope Garden located just to the west of the Visitor & Administration building. The biotope is closely planted with native wetland species that filter the rainwater, which then flows to the fountain at the entry plaza. The fountain provides a good "teaching moment": because it depends on rainwater to function, it bubbles furiously if there has been lots of rain, but a portion of the system is dry during droughts. From the fountain, the water flows through the decorative water channels back to the pools at the base of the administration building. There are also several bioswales, depressions planted with species that absorb water and can survive being flooded—one just to the west of the administration building. These swales are made from soil that is specially composed to retain water, and they are an integral part of the new parking lot gardens that also feature permeable paving.

The landscape plan for the administration building subtly supports the ideas that informed the entire project: around the contemporary structure are gardens of native plant communities organized by families. These gardens, which include 800 native species, are often aesthetically quieter than traditional gardens, and here too there is an educational component, as the public is asked to appreciate, close up, the more restrained beauties of our native species. QBG has plans to install a "green trail" that will include markers giving information about different aspects of the sustainability initiative.

The 3,000-square-foot green roof acts as a ramp that starts at ground level and rises to the second floor of the build-

Queens Botanical Garden Greenroof

ing (the ramp forms the roof of the auditorium). A pathway leads visitors through the planting so they can see close-up the mostly native plants growing on the six inches of growing medium, and watch it evolve over the year. Moving beyond the now-familiar all-sedum roof planting plan, the QBG roof, which requires minimum watering, includes plants like little bluestem, prairie dropseed, and butterfly weed. At the foot of the ramp is a small garden of woodland plants, with ferns, wildflowers, and native shrubs.

For those gardeners who, while appreciating subtlety, still love show and color, QBG has not abandoned its traditional gardens. The collection comprises 18 acres of gardens, including a wedding garden, teaching collections, backyard demonstration gardens, rose gardens, and a 21-acre arboretum and meadow linking the garden to Flushing Meadows Corona Park. The theme gardens, and their configuration in a spiral form around the Cherry Circle, were inspired by the layout and themes of the original Gardens on Parade.

Throughout the garden, the visitor will notice how satisfyingly healthy the plants look—not just well cared for but unusually large and sturdy. Remember that Queens was once a center for the nursery business and still boasts exceptional soil and growing conditions. Three large Blue Atlas cedars from the 1939–40 World's Fair greet visitors as they enter the front gates. There is an impressive allée of oak trees. To the south lies the Cherry Circle surrounding the Great Lawn; adjacent is the pinetum.

The residents of Queens really use their garden, which is the only source of horticultural and botanical information in the borough. The demonstration gardens are all practical and useful, as befits a borough where many residents have backyards. One is the All-America Garden, which exhibits annuals and perennials selected each year as best and easiest to grow by All-America Selections, an organization of nurserymen. The woodland garden features a number of backyard environments familiar to homeowners, including dry shade and boggy soil. The Backyard Gardens exhibit features several small-scale ideas for backyards that were originally planted by member nurseries. QBG also runs a borough-wide program to encourage backyard composting and has created a compost garden that suggests alternatives to traditional yard turf, using groundcovers, perennials, and wildflowers.

One of the most unusual of the teaching collections is the Bee Garden, which features working hives. The garden is filled with plants that attract bees, including hollyhocks, fruit trees, peonies, coreopsis, and daisies. Its gate is usually locked to keep onlookers at a safe distance.

The QBG rose collection is comprised of more than 1,400 plants, many of them originally donated by the Oregon rose nursery Jackson & Perkins, honoring the company's beginnings in Queens. As part of QBG's sustainability initiative, the rose garden was moved to a location with better growing conditions and replanted with specimens that are more sustainable.

The most elaborate display is undoubtedly the Wedding Garden. The one-acre enclave, richly planted, is a veritable potpourri of garden features. Surrounded by a white picket fence, its myriad attractions include a bridge, a garden swing, a gazebo, a Japanese lantern, statuary, a small waterfall, and a little pond with a smaller Japanese lantern. Wide beds of brightly colored annuals and smaller borders of traditional perennials such as iris and peonies join a range of white-flowered shrubs, including double-file viburnum, rose of Sharon, and white hydrangea. Weeping willows sit in one corner, weeping cherries in another. This garden is extremely popular, especially in June, when it is usually booked solid for ceremonies and photo sessions (there are often as many as 500 weddings in a year). Although it is closed to the general public, most of it can be seen over the low picket fence.

When QBG made its commitment to responsible stewardship, it hoped that beyond doing the right thing, the initiative would give Queens its own important place among midsize botanical gardens and raise its profile in the community. That hope has become a reality—not only has QBG been recognized nationally for its green building, but attendance at its programs has risen by a dramatic 46 percent, proving that virtue does have its rewards.

Queens County Farm Museum

Location: 73–50 Little Neck Parkway, Glen Oaks

Hours: grounds only: Mon.–Fri. 9am–5pm; Sat.–Sun. 10:00am–5:00pm

Garden info: (718) 347-FARM

Web site: www.queensfarm.org

Admission fee: no (grounds); yes (museum)

Bus: Q46

Subway: E or F to Kew Gardens/Union Turnpike, then Q46 to Little
    Neck Parkway

Facilities: rest rooms and telephones; wheelchair accessible; gift shop;
    seasonal farm-fresh produce and eggs for sale (when available)

Best seasons: summer, fall

This is the last vestige of Queens County's agricultural past.
Its flat, well drained, and extremely fertile soil, along with
its location next to the huge population centers of Brooklyn
and Manhattan, made Queens an ideal spot for farming as
far back as the early eighteenth century. Sadly, the pressure of an expanding population gradually squeezed out the
orchards, truck farms, greenhouses, and flower nurseries that
used to supply vegetables, fruit, and flowers to Manhattan,
and by 1920 they were mostly gone.

   The museum, on 47 acres in Floral Park, is a remnant of
a much larger farm established in 1772 by Jacob and Cath-
erine Adriance. They built the Flemish-style farmhouse that
still stands, although subsequent owners have added on to it.
By 1900 the farm was the second largest in Queens, and was
valued at $32,000. In 1926 the owner sold the property to

the State of New York, which made it part of the Creedmoor Psychiatric Center. The farm provided fresh produce for the institution, and working in the fields and with the livestock was considered therapy for the patients. Creedmoor stopped farming in 1960, and in 1973 the state put the property up for sale. Area residents banded together to save the farm and the open land, and they succeeded in having it turned into a city park. The farmhouse, its outbuildings, and the seven acres around it make up the farm museum, which is a national and city landmark.

The museum's mission is to teach visitors—many of them children—about the rich agricultural history of the borough. To that end, there is a working orchard (three acres of apple, pear, peach, and plum trees) and plenty of livestock, including several Suffolk sheep, Old Spot pigs, an Ayrshire cow, and a hundred or so laying hens. Two acres of planting fields are filled with crops—pumpkins, beans, squash, corn, eggplant, and tomatoes—much as they would be on a typical truck farm. The staff and volunteers hand-weed the fields, employ natural pest-control techniques, and spread compost from their own barnyards. Beehives produce honey; the duck pond is home to a number of ducks and geese. There is also a greenhouse on site dating to the Creedmoor period, which has been rebuilt so that the farmers can raise seedlings and year-round crops.

Behind the farmhouse is a small herb garden, surrounded by a traditional picket fence and filled with plants used in the eighteenth and nineteenth centuries for medicinal purposes, dying yarns, brewing teas, and flavoring food. Although there are no records of an herb garden in precisely this spot, farms typically had this kind of garden near the house, so

Queens Botanical Garden clockwise from left: Cherry Circle; Wedding Garden; Visitor and Administration Building

that the herbs that were used in everyday household activities were readily available. Besides the herbs, the beds are filled with strawberries, rhubarb, asparagus, lavender, asters, and hollyhocks.

The Queens County Farm Museum has a dedicated staff that seems to take care of the visitors and the farm with equal enthusiasm. In 2008, the museum hired a full-time director of agriculture, who has significantly expanded the capacity of the farm, using sustainable practices. Along with selling produce at the farm, the museum also now sells at the Union Square Greenmarket and donates its extra bounty to local community food banks. To many of the visitors, especially children from New York City schools, this is a unique experience, and it is a tribute to the staff that despite half a million visitors a year, it still does feel and smell like a working farm.

Veterans Memorial Garden

Location: Queens Borough Hall, 120–155 Queens Blvd., Kew Gardens

Hours: Mon.–Fri. 9:00am–5:00pm (call first to make sure garden is
    open)

Garden info: (718) 286-3000

Admission fee: no

Bus: QM1A, Q46

Subway: E to Union Turnpike

Facilities: partially wheelchair accessible, rest rooms, telephones

Best seasons: spring, summer

The lawns and forecourts of public buildings are generally
dead spaces that serve only the formal purpose of setting off
the architecture—the more impressive the lawn, the more
important the building. Here, however, a different, somewhat innovative approach has resulted in a lush sunken
garden sited right in front of the south wing of the Queens
Borough Hall. Worth noting is that this well-executed design
is the work of the in-house landscape architects of the city's
Department of General Services.

    Sunk four feet below the sidewalk and the building's entry
plaza, the garden is a long rectangle lying parallel to Queens
Boulevard on one side and the busy office building on the
other. Hidden from the street by a screen of cherry trees,
honey locusts, and shrubs, which also serve to muffle noise,
it is laid out along a central axis on two levels. Two circular
seating areas and a narrow corridor make up the open area of
the garden, which is surrounded by deep beds of shrubs and

perennials. The red brick and the pink and gray granite in the paths and seating areas echo the materials used in Queens Borough Hall. Inspirational quotations are sandblasted into the granite features, on benches, walls, and curbs, to reinforce the memorial theme of the garden.

Despite the institutional setting, the designers' choice of perennials lends the space an informal and intimate appeal. The beds are thickly planted with hydrangea, azaleas, astilbe, euonymous, lilies, coneflowers, rhododendron, and ornamental grasses. Although there are some bright flowers and an extensive bulb display in the spring, the overall tone of the garden is calm, with cooler pale colors and green predominating.

Mother Carter Garden

Location: 122nd Ave. at 155th St., South Jamaica
Hours: daily dawn to dusk
Admission fee: no
Subway: E to Sutphin Blvd. (transfer to Q6 bus)
Facilities: none
Best seasons: spring, summer, fall

The only thing that disturbs the long views and restful atmosphere at Baisley Pond Park is the sound of ducks, geese, and seagulls landing in the water and, on summer weekends, the cheers of spectators who have gathered to watch white-clad cricketers play in the pitches set aside for them at the edge of the park. A small, handsome flower garden is set on the western bank of the 30-acre pond, which was created by local farmers in the eighteenth century by damming three streams to get power for a grain mill. The garden replaced an aging playground, addressing the neighborhood's need for a quiet seating area with a view of the water. It was named for civic activist Laura Carter, who died in 1999. By all accounts a dynamo, she championed not only green spaces but also women's rights and programs for the neighborhood's young people. The well-kept park, which features rolling lawns and stately shade trees surrounding the long, narrow pond, is her legacy.

Dedicated in August 2001, Mother Carter Garden covers a third of an acre and consists of a series of curvilinear beds grouped around a central gazebo and surrounded by a high

Initially laid out in the 1920s and 1930s, the quiet, residential community of Laurelton, with its wide, tree-lined streets, is located on the Queens-Nassau line not far from Mother Carter Garden. More than 50 of the community's 76 malls are brightened up by gaily planted flower gardens, which are the work of the Garden Club of Laurelton, formed in 1986 to counter neglect and area crime in the wake of a city fiscal crisis. The largest of the Club's projects is the garden at the traffic circle at 225th Street and 141st Avenue, where a colorful mix of perennials and annuals, along with cannas and yew, are planted on the bermed traffic island, creating a dramatic introduction to the community.

black iron fence. The beds are planted with sweeps of perennials, notably sedums, daylilies, purple cone-flower, and Siberian iris. Roses climb over the perimeter fence, and spring-flowering redbud, shadblow, and crab apple provide vertical elements. The designers have made good use of preexisting trees; the muscled gray bark of an ironwood thrusts up from a bed of shade-loving shrubs and perennials, lending weight to the young plantings, and the mitten-shaped leaves of a large sassafras shade another area of the garden.

Wide paths and benches encourage both strolling and contemplation. The large gazebo, painted brown with green trim and floored with bluestone, is topped by a weather vane in the shape of an angel blowing a trumpet, an allusion to Mother Carter's guardianship of this green space. In another fanciful touch, the gates are decorated with ironwork ivy and the outline of a small bird. Unfortunately, the flower beds are confined by knee-high barriers, which are quite obtrusive, but they are a parks department requirement designed to stop people from trampling the beds.

Curtis "50 Cent" Jackson Community Garden

Location: 117–119 165th St. at Foch Ave., Jamaica

Hours: irregular (when gardeners are present), but can be seen as viewing garden

Admission fee: no

Web site: www.nyrp.org

Subway: E to Jamaica Center, then Q113 bus

Facilities: none

Best season: summer

The star power that went into this little garden, which opened in the fall of 2008, has been put to good use: the 15,000-square-foot community garden is a standout both in its neighborhood and among community gardens in general. Bright and lively, yet practical, the "50 Cent" garden takes a familiar collection of community garden features and turns them into something that looks like a cheerful contemporary art installation, taking inspiration from classic French parterres as well as modern silhouettes and design.

The garden was funded by the hip-hop star Curtis "50 Cent" Jackson, through his G-Unity Foundation, and designed by Walter Hood, a renowned name in contemporary landscape architecture. Hood was looking for something special that would capture the imagination; after consultation with the gardeners, whose biggest wish was convenient watering, he devised what turned out to be the signature feature of the garden, a rainwater collection system. It gathers water in six bright-blue, ten-foot-high martini-glass-shaped towers that are really funnels; the water pours down them into an underground cistern. A bright red hand pump, a tip of the hat to the "olden days," brings the water up for watering.

Approaching the garden through the neighborhood of small, tidy houses, the large blue towers make quite an impact. Closer inspection reveals other touches that take this garden out of the ordinary. At one side of the long, trapezoidal garden there are planting beds of various odd shapes edged in clipped boxwood. Think of this as updating the famous French potager in Villandry. Fruit trees, many of them saved from the original garden on this site, are dotted around the box-edged beds. The garden lies just beside the LIRR rail embankment, and there are references to the railroad everywhere. The linear aspects of the tracks are echoed by the pergola that edges the garden along the 165th Street sidewalk; an old box car is used as a tool shed. "50 Cent" has a number of raised beds, as is traditional in community gardens, but here they are raised waist-high, since many of the gardeners are retirees and it's much easier to garden if you don't have to bend to the ground.

Although it looks as though design considerations must have been first and foremost in the renovation of this space, in fact Hood worked hard to respond faithfully to the needs of its users, some of whom had been with the garden for many years. Before 1992, this site was a neighborhood eyesore, and neighbors would walk their children past it and fume. Eventually, one of the neighbors, Gertrude Duncan, persuaded the GreenThumb program to help make it a community garden. When, in 1999, it was acquired by Bette Midler's New York Restoration Project, they collaborated with Ms. Duncan and the other gardeners to develop the design. Now that it is up and running, it is clear that "50 Cent" is an outstanding example of a design that springs from the needs of the community, and then rises to a level of entertaining sophistication that surprises and delights its visitors and users.

Merrick Marsden Community Garden

Location: Roy Wilkins State Park at 175th St. between 115th and 116th
　　　Aves., St. Alban's
Hours: daily dawn to dusk, in good weather
Garden info: (718) 276-4630
Admission fee: no
Bus: Q4, Q5, Q84, Q85
Subway: E, Z to Parsons Blvd./Archer Ave., transfer to Q5 or Q85 bus
Facilities: none
Best season: summer

This unusual garden, located on eight flat and featureless
acres surrounded by a high chain-link fence and scrubby
trees, is one of the largest community gardens in the city,
with 400 plots. It is home to a group of determined seniors,
who spend their days here, slowly and methodically working
the soil, mounding it up in long, neat rows of butter beans,
collards, sweet potatoes, and peanuts. "We grow everything
you can eat here," one said, "and, if I wasn't doing this, what
else would I be doing?" They take time out to visit with one
another, leaning their hoes on the side of the cars dusty from
the dirt kicked up on the unpaved roads that surround the
field. Drawing on memories of youth spent in the country,
the gardeners here concentrate on food production, using
tried and true methods. Unlike the usual community garden
jumble of beds, here the rows of crops march evenly down
the entire length of the field, divided into 30-by-15-foot plots.
Two gardening associations share the space, a seniors club

and a regular community garden, both under the auspices of the Southern Queens Park Association. There is a clear demarcation line between the two groups. The gates are opened with the first gardener, often by 6am in the summer, and closed when the last one leaves in the evening. The garden produces more food than can be eaten by the gardeners and their families, so the surplus is given to friends and local churches. Most of the problems they encounter are familiar to all gardeners, but there are some that are particular to city life; instead of coping with woodchucks or raccoons, the gardeners here are plagued with rats, which seem to love the cucumbers and melons.

A community garden of sorts has been on this site for 30 years. Originally, the site was part of the St. Alban's Golf Club, which was sold to the U.S. Navy in the 1920s and became the St. Alban's Naval Hospital. When the barracks on the hospital grounds were abandoned, neighbors started cultivating vegetables on the flat land. The city took over the hospital grounds in 1977 and created the 54-acre Roy Wilkins Park, setting aside land for the community garden. The park, which in addition to the community garden has a host of sports facilities, has also recently added 400 new trees from the MillionTreesNYC program.

World Trade Center Educational Tribute Center at Snug Harbor Cultural Center and Botanical Garden

STATEN ISLAND

1 Snug Harbor Cultural Center
      and Botanical Garden
2 Jacques Marchais Museum
      of Tibetan Art
3 Stephens-Prier House at Historic
      Richmond Town
4 Bayview Habitat
5 The Conference House Park

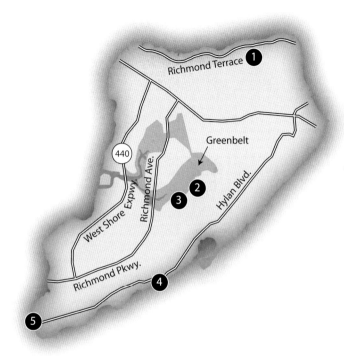

Richmond Terrace

Greenbelt

440

West Shore Expwy.

Richmond Ave.

Hylan Blvd.

Richmond Pkwy.

STATEN ISLAND

Although it is five miles across the water from Manhattan, Staten Island has been a part of New York since colonial times and played a large role in the Revolutionary and Civil War history of the region. Throughout the nineteenth century, the southern shore of Staten Island attracted wealthy New Yorkers, among them Nathaniel Lord Britton, the founder of the New York Botanical Garden, and the young Frederick Law Olmsted, who established an experimental farm called Tosomock where he planted fruit trees imported from France and studied landscaping improvements. Still the least populated of the five boroughs, Staten Island retained a rural character well into the 1960s, when the Verrazano Bridge was completed, providing a commuter link through Brooklyn and spurring on acres of new housing.

Here, amid closely knit suburban communities, much remains of the natural world. Its remarkable Greenbelt consists of 2,800 acres of preserved land in the heart of the island, including salt and freshwater wetlands, ponds, brooks, forest, and grasslands, all linked by a 35-mile foot trail network. The borough's gardens are varied, including a historic village, an up-and-coming botanical garden, and two centers of Asian art and culture.

For 53 years, Staten Island also had the unfortunate dis-

Black swan at Snug Harbor

tinction of being the site of the Fresh Kills Landfill, for a time the largest landfill in the world. But construction has begun on the 2,200-acre Fresh Kills Park, which over a 30-year period will transform what was once mounds of garbage up to 220 feet high into a vast and varied rolling landscape. The acclaimed design, by James Corner Field Operations, was chosen by international competition.

The best way to visit Staten Island is really by car, although a combination of the ferry and local buses can get you where you want to go, albeit slowly. Another possibility for the more energetic would be to take bicycles, although beware: the island is fourteen miles long by seven miles wide and quite hilly in places.

Snug Harbor Cultural Center and Botanical Garden

Location: 1000 Richmond Terrace at Snug Harbor Road, Livingston

Hours: grounds, daily dawn to dusk; the New York Chinese Scholar's Garden and Richmond County Savings Foundation Tuscan Garden, Tues.–Sun. 10:00am–5:00pm (April 1–October 31); Tues.–Sun. 10:00am–5:00pm (November 1–March 31)

Garden info: (718) 448-2500

Web site: www.snug-harbor.org

Admission fee: no (grounds); fees charged for Scholar's Garden and Tuscan Garden

Bus: S40

Ferry: Staten Island ferry, transfer to S40 bus for a ten-minute trip

Facilities: Wheelchair accessible, café, restrooms, telephones, botanical library

Best season: all seasons

The Snug Harbor Cultural Center and Botanical Garden is a treasure trove of Greek Revival, Victorian, and early-twentieth-century architecture, interspersed with an expanding number of display gardens, all set on a 83-acre campus. Although it can be a challenge to get there, it is well worth the effort. Located in a mixed residential and light-industrial section of Richmond Terrace, this was originally a self-sufficient retirement home for "aged, decrepit and worn-out" sailors. The architecture is an eclectic mix of tiny, picturesque brick cottages and elaborate and imposing stone buildings, the earliest dating from the 1830s. The Staten Island Botanical Garden was established in 1977 on the grounds of Snug Harbor, by then a cultural center. The cultural center and botanical garden merged in 2008. The gardens, because they are laid out amid this fascinating collection of historic buildings, have a patina of age that befits a long-established institution.

Established by a bequest in 1801 from Robert Richard Randall, whose fortune was made in the sea trade, Snug Harbor remained one of the city's richest charitable institutions throughout the nineteenth century. At its height, it was home to 1,000 sailors. Theodore Dreiser described a visit in 1923: "Though the surroundings are pastoral, the appearance of the inmates of this retreat, as well as their conversation, is of the sea, salty. . . . To the passer-by without the walls they are visible lounging under the trees, their loose-fitting blue suits fluttering light with every breeze and their slouch hats pulled rakishly over their eyes, an abandon characteristic of men whose lives have been spent more or less in direct contact with wind and rain."* By the 1940s, however, the enrollment was less than 400 men (in part due to new systems of pension plans and Social Security), and endowment funds couldn't keep up with the enormous maintenance requirements of the campus. For 20 years, the institution struggled to continue its mission; it was forced to raze some buildings when repairs were too costly. In 1966 the entire campus was perilously close to being dismantled, when the newly formed New York City Landmarks Commission stepped in and designated it a city landmark, mak-

*Theodore Dreiser, *The Color of a Great City* (New York: Boni and Liveright, 1923).

Snug Harbor Cultural Center and Botanical Garden clockwise from left: impatiens; hornbeam tunnel; decorative detail at Chinese Scholar's Garden

ing it very difficult for the Snug Harbor trustees to continue with their plan to raze the complex. Ultimately, the sailors' retirement home was moved to North Carolina, and the city took over the property and created the Snug Harbor Cultural Center and Botanical Garden.

With the opening of the much-acclaimed Chinese Scholar's Garden in 1999, the Botanical Garden put itself on the city's horticultural map and leaders at the garden adopted the concept of "Gardens of the World" as a guiding principle for long-term expansion. The next flagship garden to open was an Italian Renaissance garden in 2010. The Italian Renaissance was chosen because, like the classical Chinese garden, it has had a seminal influence in the history of garden design.

The mix of eclectic Victorian architecture and the wide variety of gardens make the grounds a unique destination. In front of some of the buildings, the horticultural staff lays out bedding plants, recalling techniques that were used in Victorian times. Since the gardens are quite spread out, a map of the grounds, available at the Visitors' Center, is useful.

The Pond Garden

Closest to the entrance and garden parking, this is the first garden a visitor encounters, marked by an enormous stand of epimedium under the trees by the parking lot. The retired sailors dug the pond and used it to sail their model boats. A brick path circles the formal pond, which is edged with brick coping and richly planted; one side features the dogwood collection, the other side European beech, ironwood, and sassafras underplanted with perennials. In the summer, water lilies provide a burst of color. The pond is home to a pair of handsome black swans; it also attracts a wide array of migratory birds. Look for the topiary Sailor and Child and a restored miniature lighthouse.

The Heritage Rose Garden

The traditional hedging and white trelliswork of this garden complement the Victorian architecture of the former Governor's House next door. More than 140 different varieties of heirloom roses, all developed before 1910, can be admired from the elaborate Lutyens-style benches. Many of these old roses are fragrant; most of them bloom only once a year, in late May and June. Visitors interested in rose history should note that one of the beds includes each variety of rose used in creating the famous hybrid Queen Elizabeth. Snug Harbor's small horticultural staff is augmented with dedicated volunteers. The garden relies on them for many tasks, including propagation and seed starting. A small group focuses on the Heritage Rose Garden and keeps it in top shape.

Perennial Garden and Carl Grillo Glass House

Deep and well-planted perennial beds edge the lawn in front of the Glass House. Backed by a low, green fence, they contain more than 60 different cultivars—mostly yellow, orange, and blue—chosen to provide the longest possible season of bloom. This was the first installation at the botanical garden. Note the unusual yellow butterfly bushes and the fall-blooming camellias.

The Carl Grillo Glass House, named after a local political figure, is a replica of a Victorian glasshouse. One of the wings features tropical plants, the other subtropicals; the central dome area offers changing displays. In addition, the propagating greenhouse for the garden occupies the rear wing of the building. Beside the greenhouse is an orderly potager, and behind it is an extensive tree peony collection, barely noticeable most of the year, but spectacular when the eighty cultivars are in bloom.

The White Garden

For those who can't get to Vita Sackville-West's famous white garden at Sissinghurst, England, this version provides plenty of ideas and inspiration. The garden wraps around a trellised folly, meant to evoke European follies of the past. Even though the color palette is restricted to shades of white and light gray, the planting includes more than 40 varieties. Shape becomes a vital element in the composition, as can be seen in the spiky yucca and the mushroom-shaped artemisia, the sword-shaped iris foliage and fountain-like grasses, as well as assertive flowers such as coneflowers and lilies. The gray trellis is covered with several different vines, including clematis, silver fleece, climbing roses, and an unusual white akebia. White-flowered shrubs—lilac, rose, viburnum, rose of Sharon, and two tree wisteria—encircle the garden.

The Lions' Sensory Garden

A hornbeam tunnel leads to a garden created to enhance the experience of people with disabilities by emphasizing smell, touch, and sound. The sensory garden is located next to one of the prettiest buildings on the Snug Harbor campus, a small cottage painted light blue and white with a little cross over the entrance, originally the morgue of the sailors' community. As is traditional, it is set slightly askew in order to stop any evil spirits from moving through the building. (The entrance to the complex is askew for the same reason.) The cottage is now the World Trade Center Educational Tribute Center, and contains a moving exhibit of portraits, artifacts and materials relating to the disaster. The cottage is a perfect foil for the planting, which includes a big annual moment in the summer with lush tropical plants and gigantic deep-red dahlias. The dahlias were a gift from the Sea-Tac Dahlia Gardens, a nursery in Seattle, Washington, in memory of the World Trade Center attacks. The cultivar is called FDNY, and the original six tubers were placed, as requested, near a bronze statue of a firefighter. The six have multiplied, and the intensely colored dahlias, many of them over six feet tall, are now planted throughout the garden. There is a spectacular bulb display in the spring, when tulips, daffodils, and hundreds of scented hyacinths bloom with the intensely fragrant viburnum, a combination that is both visually and olfactorily stunning. Rocks and waist-high boulders line the paths of the sensory garden, contrasting in texture with the plants. The sound of water tumbling from the waterfall fills the air. Among the highly scented plantings are lilac, heliotrope, fringe tree, and Japanese snowbell. Also nearby is a butterfly garden, planted with abundant butterfly bush and salvia, and a shade garden.

The New York Chinese Scholar's Garden

This is the first authentic classical Chinese garden in the United States. Opened in 1999, it was conceived in 1984 by Frances X. Huber, then director of the Staten Island Botanical Garden, now president of the Snug Harbor Cultural Center and Botanic Garden. The garden began to take shape in 1998, when 40 artists and artisans were brought over from the southern Chinese city of Suzhou. Living in cottages near the site at Snug Harbor and fed by a chef who came with them from China, they settled down to their painstaking task. The work, accomplished in only six months, was done in the traditional manner, almost entirely by hand; the wooden elements all were joined with mortise and tenon, and no glue or nails were used in the fabrication. All the architectural components came from China, including roof tiles, floor tiles, columns, and beams. Many of the all-important rocks were taken from Lake Tai, considered the finest source of eroded rocks in China (and also the source of the rocks at Astor Court, the Metropolitan Museum of Art's replica of a scholar's garden).

The classic Chinese scholar's garden, brought to perfection in Suzhou during the Ming dynasty (1368–1644), is a rarefied environment to which the scholar can withdraw from the hurly-burly of everyday life; the beauty and quiet of the setting embody the finer, more spiritual aspects of Chinese culture. Traditionally, the serene atmosphere has been achieved using certain strict principles, among them yin/yang, the principle of opposing concepts that finds expression in the juxtaposition of water and rock, shadow and light, high and low. Here, the entrance path winds along a wavy wall, past a series of vignettes: a still pool edged with chunky, dark red rocks hugs the whitewashed wall; a small balcony with a dramatic Chinese roof projects over the pond; a single pine, bent as if by the wind, is silhouetted against a wall. The path continues through a small glade of flowering fruit trees, then to an austere entry where a wooden screen blocks the passage of evil spirits. Once around the screen, the visitor finds a large, formal courtyard surrounding a lake, the edge of which is piled with the whitish, fantastically eroded rocks from Lake

Tai, some jutting up out of the water, others nearby on the shore. Across the lake, another small lake is visible through a moon gate, and a single flowering shrub adds a note of color. A series of walls, pavilions, and corridors radiates from the courtyard, each gate or window offering a glimpse of other rooms in the complex or the landscape of the outside world. Circulating, the visitor comes upon a remarkable series of episodes, including "borrowed views," where a distant perspective is incorporated into the immediate composition, and "hidden views" framed by a moon gate or floral window. These different garden scenes, which change with the viewer's perspective, promote a sense of infinite space within a confined area, one of the hallmarks of this genre of garden. Indeed, this entire complex—comprising three courtyards, a teahouse, three bridges, and five pavilions, not to mention three ponds, waterfalls, and a stream—fills only an acre.

Although at first glance the scholar's garden seems to be about rocks and buildings, it is clear that the plants are an equally important element in the design, and in fact there is a remarkably wide selection of unusual plants, each treated as a precious specimen. The garden provides an excellent planting guide, identifying more than 80 species growing here. Form, color, and fragrance, as well as bloom time, have all been taken into account. (Thus, along with the expected rhododendron, peonies, magnolias, Japanese maples, and pines, there are the flowering apricots at the entrance, which bloom in late February, and wintersweet, whose waxy delicate flowers hanging from bare branches have a particularly clean, sweet, piercing fragrance.) Most of the species have their origins in Asia, although there are some North American natives such as flowering dogwood. Each specimen is placed to best advantage, creating some memorable pictures, such as the huge, intensely green leaves of the banana plant positioned against a bare white wall in a side courtyard.

Connie Gretz's Secret Garden

The make-believe castle gatehouse at the entrance to the Secret Garden is 30 feet high and can be seen from far away on the grounds. Inspired by Frances Hodgson Burnett's children's classic, *The Secret Garden*, this is a twenty-first-century take on a seventeenth-century French or English garden folly. The magical feature here is a child-size maze, created from evergreens about three feet high. The reward for making it to the end of the maze is a small, walled, cheerfully planted "secret garden."

The Healing Garden

This tranquil, one-acre hillside garden commemorates the 267 Staten Islanders killed in the World Trade Center attacks. It is an effort by many groups, the garden staff, borough leaders, residents, and the members of Rescue 5, to create a place of healing for the community. The garden overlooks the serene landscape of a twenty-acre wetland. At the top of the hill a simple stone trough initiates the water feature: a gentle stream flows in a stone rill shadowing a wide path that zigzags down the slope. At the turns of the zigzags, landings furnished with rustic benches provide an opportunity for contemplation. Woodland plants and shrubs line the paths and dot the hillside.

Richmond County Savings Foundation's Tuscan Garden

The Tuscan Garden comes, literally, straight from Italy. Modeled on the Villa Gamberaia in Florence and its famous water parterre, the design was overseen by Mariella Zopi, Tuscany's minister of culture, and Florence's leading preservation architect, Enrica Buccioni. Great care has been taken to make this an authentic Renaissance garden; the plants are authentic, and those that can't survive a New York winter, like the thirteen lemon trees, are potted so they can be brought inside a small orangerie during the colder months. The simple plant palette includes boxwood, yew, Leyland cypress, iris, lavender, and standard white roses. Even the statuary comes from Italy, replicas of famous Florentine statues. The design is classically geometric, but in the forecourt between the villa and the garden the designers have chosen to preserve four large London plane trees, which, while not strictly aligned, go a long way in making this new garden look at home in its setting.

Fortunately, Snug Harbor already had a Renaissance-style building, a former nurses' dormitory, and this has been transformed into the garden's villa, now being used as an administration center and exhibition space for all things Italian. A small amphitheatre hosts concerts, plays, and other events that celebrate Italy.

The concept behind the garden is that, like its historical model, it is a celebration of the best parts of an entire culture and will draw visitors eager to learn about all aspects of Italian heritage.

Jacques Marchais Museum of Tibetan Art

Location: 338 Lighthouse Ave., Lighthouse Hill
Hours: Wed.–Sun. 1:00pm–5:00pm
Garden info: (718) 987-3500
Web site: www.tibetanmuseum.org
Admission fee: yes
Bus: S74
Ferry: Staten Island Ferry, transfer to S74 bus
Facilities: restrooms, telephones

To come across this building, which resembles a Tibetan Buddhist temple, on a suburban street in Staten Island is unexpected, to say the least. Indeed, both the building and its garden have a certain otherworldly aura. As one enters, the world inside seems to move more slowly and gently, and the plantings outside, though not at all exotic, have a quality often missing in more conventional, horticulturally superior gardens: there is a palpable sense of place that encourages a visitor to pause at the wide stone table on the terrace and contemplate the woodland view across Staten Island toward the water.

The museum was established between 1945 and 1947 by Jacques Marchais, an accomplished woman who had amassed one of the largest privately owned collections of Tibetan art outside Tibet and a library of over 1,000 volumes. Marchais, who was born in the Midwest, was a child actor, and came to New York City in 1915. Captivated by the spirituality of the Tibetan culture and religion she became a major dealer in Tibetan art, and in the 1920s and 30s had a gallery on East 51st Street. To house her collection, Marchais built a museum beside her house in this suburban neighborhood on the side of a steep hill in Staten Island. The inspiration for the museum was a small mountain temple. Marchais, who never got to Tibet herself, had pictures of temples in her extensive library, and she designed the museum to be as faithful as possible to the original. The result is a sturdy stone building with squat square windows and bell-shaped brown window casements that does indeed look to the untutored eye like the austere monasteries of the Himalayas.

Designed by Marchais herself, the garden is located to the side of the house. When the museum first opened, the approach was from down below, and visitors had to make the steep ascent to the monastery/museum up through a series of terraces. Now her house is no longer part of the complex, and the lower terraces and approach have grown over. Only the top terraces around the museum remain in use. When it was built in the 1940s the site was quite open, with a distant view of lower New York Bay, but it is now surrounded by woods. The flagstone terraces, shaded by oak, black locust, and spruce trees, are surrounded by shade plantings: rhododendrons and azalea, as well as iris, peony, and ferns. There is a small fish pond featuring lotus and water lilies, and the pleasant sound of running water. In the center of the terrace is a massive stone table with stone benches. A white marble buddha at the end of the terraces glows in the green shade of the trees and serenely presides over the gardens, usually holding a small offering of money or flowers. The spirituality that Marchais craved seems quite near.

Clockwise from left: Jacques Marchais Museum of Tibetan Art; New York Chinese Scholar's Garden; Bayview Habitat

Stephens-Prier House at Historic Richmond Town

Location: Historic Richmond Town, 441 Clarke Ave. near Arthur Kill
   Rd., Richmondtown

Hours: Wed.–Sun. 1:00pm–5:00pm; July and August: Thurs.–Fri.
   11:00am–3:00pm, Sat.–Sun. 1:00pm–5:00pm

Garden info: (718) 351-1611

Web site: www.historicrichmondtown.org

Admission fee: yes

Bus: S74

Ferry: Staten Island Ferry, transfer to S74 bus

Facilities: wheelchair accessible, restaurant, rest rooms, telephones

Best seasons: summer for the gardens

Richmond Town is New York City's own historic village. Refreshingly low-key, it offers quiet streets and grassy grounds dotted with 28 houses, many of which have been relocated from other parts of the island. The 25-acre restoration is seldom busy and visitors can saunter through the site, looking at buildings ranging from a fieldstone cottage (circa 1670) to Public School 28 (1907). Some of the houses are furnished with period pieces and are open for visits or occasional craft demonstrations. The excellent museum displays maps, paintings, furniture, and artifacts from 300 years of life in Staten Island, including a fine display of agricultural tools. Stephens-Prier House, down the street from the museum, makes an enjoyable side trip. It serves as the office of the

Staten Island Historical Association and features a pleasant, old-fashioned garden that is in keeping with the turn-of-the-century grounds.

Although the Stephens-Prier House is open by appointment only, the garden can be visited at any time. Located in front and to the side of the house (a brown and tan Italianate wood-frame gentleman's residence built in 1857 by Daniel Lake Stephens), the garden was installed in the early 1990s to fit into the overall restoration. Inspiration for the planting list came from the pages of a gardening manual published in Staten Island in 1871—*Gardening Made Easy for the Million: Every Man His Own Gardener* by J. C. Thompson (price, ten cents). There are several copies of this little book, which was written to encourage market gardening on the island, displayed at the museum.

The grounds are divided in two by the front walk. To the left as one faces the house is the ornamental flower garden, cared for by volunteers. The simple oval-in-a-square layout is reminiscent of Victorian landscape design. Two small ornamental cherries frame the entrance. Beds surrounding the lawn are filled with traditional shrubs such as lilac and azalea, as well as perennials, including peonies, foxglove, lamb's ears, roses, daylilies, and hollyhocks. Annuals such as cannas, impatiens, and ageratum round out the picture. To the right of the walk is the working garden, set in the shade of a large ash.

Bayview Habitat

Location: corner of Bayview and Holdridge Aves., Arden
Hours: Wed.–Thurs. 8:00am–4:00pm in season
Admission fee: no
Bus: S78
Ferry: Staten Island Ferry, transfer to S78 bus
Facilities: none
Best season: summer

A sweeping view of the ocean, the scent of salt, and a sea breeze provide the stunning backdrop to this well-kept garden, which has a cohesion and polish rarely found in the rough-and-tumble world of community gardening.

Located in a wealthy pocket of shiny new homes, many of them quite elaborate, this strip of land had been abandoned by the city and used as a dumping ground for construction debris. In 1991 a small group of neighbors pitched in to clean up the strip, installing a couple of planting boxes on the newly cleared land. After three years, the city asked the gardeners to leave, but by then the group had put down roots, both literally and figuratively. With the help of community leaders they succeeded in having responsibility for the land transferred to the parks department. "A couple of planting boxes" has become an extensive showplace that stretches about a block along the ocean.

The dozen or so members of the garden resist the temptation to fill up every inch of the 250-by-100-foot site with plantings; an inviting lawn at the southern end of the site is oriented toward the water and fringed by an unobtrusive mix of shrubs and perennials. Just inside the gate is a small pond with an elaborate fountain that was originally a large puddle with an abandoned refrigerator in the middle. The fridge was removed, the puddle was extended a bit, and the water is topped up from time to time. A highly textured planting of ornamental grasses, barberry, iris, and roses now surrounds what was previously an eyesore.

A large part of what gives Staten Island a rural feeling is the Greenbelt, a 2,800-acre network of wilderness, parks, open fields, marshes, and forests that winds through the heart of the island. The open space provides opportunities for outdoor activities as well as protected habitats for native wildlife and resting places for migratory birds. Hiking maps can be obtained at many local sites on Staten Island or on the Greenbelt Web site, www.sigreenbelt.org.

The pond and its plantings, with a line of espaliered Blue Atlas cedars and fruit trees, provide an excellent transition from the lawn to the area dedicated to crops. A stone and gravel path leads through the shrubs and perennials to the numerous vegetable boxes, which are neatly arranged and stained pale gray to match the garden shed.

Each year, the members decide what crops to plant and establish a planting schedule. One year they might plant sweet potatoes or tomatillos, another a bumper crop of plum tomatoes, basil, and tromboncino squash. A variety of planting theories are accommodated; some gardeners like to plant by the phases of the moon, others have more conventional preferences. Members here are not just garden lovers but also bird lovers. Birdhouses dot the grounds, including hanging gourds for swallows and multistory purple martin apartment hotels.

The Conference House Park

Location: 298 Satterlee St., Tottenville
Hours: daily dawn to dusk (grounds); house: Fri.–Sun. 1:00pm–4:00pm
    (April–December)
Garden info: (718) 984-6046
Web site: www.conferencehouse.org
Admission fee: no (grounds); yes (house)
Bus: S59, S78
Ferry: Staten Island Ferry, transfer to S59, S78
Facilities: restrooms in house, telephones
Best season: summer

The Conference House looks much as it must have to Captain Christopher Billopp, who built this two-story stone manor in the 1680s. Surrounded on three sides by forest, with a wide lawn stretching down to the water, it is now a museum owned by the city and restored and maintained by volunteers. It sits in the middle of the 226-acre Conference House Park, at the southern tip of Staten Island, nearly the southernmost point of New York State. The park includes three other historic houses besides Conference House, all in the process of renovation. There is also a reconstructed viewing pavilion on the shoreline, originally built in the thirties, but in Victorian gingerbread style. This is an idyllic spot to picnic on the lawn or read in the shade of magnificent trees (note the very old white mulberry and mottled sycamores), imagining life in Staten Island hundreds of years ago. On a clear day, the power plants and chimneys of Perth Amboy are visible in the distance, but in the ocean haze they look more evanescent than real. The gardens themselves, in combination with the grounds and the house, make a pleasing destination.

The Conference House earned its name during the Revolutionary War, when it was the site of the Staten Island Peace Conference held on September 11, 1776. Captain Christopher Billopp, an English naval officer, built the house on 998 acres of land that had been granted to him by the Crown. At the time of the Revolution, the house belonged to his grandson, Colonel Christopher Billopp, a staunch Tory. When Lord Admiral Richard Howe was looking for a venue for a peace conference with the American colonists, he chose Billopp House. Benjamin Franklin and John Adams were included in the diplomatic mission that arrived by barge from New Jersey. We have Adams's diary entry: "We walked up to the house between lines of guards of grenadiers, looking fierce as ten Furies, and making all the grimaces, and gestures and motions of their muskets, with bayonets fixed, which, I suppose, military etiquette requires, but which we neither understood nor regarded." Although Adams remarked that the house was as "dirty as a stable," Howe had "prepared a large handsome room by spreading a carpet of moss and green sprigs," which made it "romantically elegant." The two sides ate a delicious meal, "good Claret, good Bread, cold Jam, Tongues and Mutton," and then began the conference.* Although the meal was a success the conference was a failure, and after three hours the Americans left and the war

*Fred Horn, *The Conference House Revisited: A History of the Billopp Manor House* (New York: The Conference House Association, 1990).

continued: so much for the house's moment of fame. The house and grounds passed out of the Billopp family in 1781 but remained in private hands until it was given to the City of New York in 1925.

There are two garden projects on the grounds of Conference House; much of the park itself has been designated Forever Wild. Since 1929, the nonprofit Conference House Association has been responsible for the site's upkeep and programming. In addition to addressing constant maintenance and restoration issues, the all-volunteer group staffs the house with guides in period costumes and sponsors demonstrations of colonial spinning, embroidery, and cooking techniques. The major event in the Conference House year is the September lawn party commemorating the peace conference. The Staten Island Herb Society maintains a Colonial herb garden to the west of the rear entrance, which seems a natural extension of the interpretive spirit of the house, with its fencing, neat bricked pathways, and rectangular parterre beds. The plants are grouped by use: culinary, medicinal, herbs used for dyeing, and ornamentals. There is also a section for Native American herbs, featuring plants such as black cohosh, wild ginger, and herb Robert. Near the visitors' center, the Herb Society has planted an exuberant native plant garden, featuring plants native to Staten Island or that Native Americans might have used. The garden includes the three "sisters": corn, beans, and squash. Native plants also decorate the parking lot in front of the visitors' center. The Herb Society conducts guided tours of the Colonial and Native American gardens.

Listings by Category

Not-to-Be-Missed Gardens
Battery Park City
Brooklyn Botanic Garden
The Cloisters
The Conservatory Garden
The Gardens at the Battery
The High Line
Lower East Side Community Gardens
The New York Botanical Garden
Wave Hill

Asian Gardens
Astor Court at the Metropolitan Museum of Art
The Japanese Hill-and-Pond Garden at Brooklyn Botanic
    Garden
Isamu Noguchi Garden Museum
The Japan Society
The New York Chinese Scholar's Garden

Best Vegetable Gardens
Bayview Habitat
The Floyd Bennett Gardens
Garden of Happiness
Hattie Carthan Community Garden
Lenape Edible Estate
Queens County Farm Museum
Red Hook Community Farm
Taqwa Community Farm

Birding Gardens

Bartow-Pell Mansion Museum
Battery Park City
Bayview Habitat
Brooklyn Botanic Garden
Central Park Wildlife Center
Clinton Community Garden
The Conference House Park
The Conservatory Garden
The Floyd Bennett Gardens
The Garden at the Church of St. Luke in the Fields
The Gardens at the Battery
The Heather Garden
Mother Carter Garden
The New York Botanical Garden
Shakespeare Garden
Wave Hill
West Side Community Garden

Child-Friendly Gardens

Battery Park City
Brooklyn Botanic Garden
Cathedral Church of St. John the Divine
Central Park Wildlife Center
The Gardens at the Battery
The Green Dome Garden
M'Finda Kalunga Garden
The Howard A. Rusk Institute of Rehabilitative Medicine
The New York Botanical Garden
Queens Botanical Garden
Snug Harbor Cultural Center and Botanical Garden

Swindler Cove Park
Washington Market Park

Church Gardens
Cathedral Church of St. John the Divine
Eighth Church of Christ, Scientist
First Presbyterian Church
The Garden at the Church of St. Luke in the Fields
General Theological Seminary
Mary's Garden

Community Gardens
The W. 87th Street Park & Garden
Bayview Habitat
Bissel Gardens
The Brooklyn Bear's Community Gardens
Clinton Community Garden
Columbia Street Waterfront District Community Gardens
Convent Garden
Curtis "50 Cent" Jackson Community Garden
Drew Gardens
The Enchanted Garden
Five-Star Community Garden
The Floyd Bennett Gardens
Garden of Happiness
The Green Dome Garden
Hattie Carthan Community Garden
Jefferson Market Garden
Liz Christy Bowery-Houston Community Garden
Lower East Side Community Gardens
The Lotus Garden

Merrick-Marsden Community Garden
M'finda Kalunga Garden
The Narrows Botanical Gardens
The 91st Street Garden
Pleasant Village Community Garden
RING Community Garden
Riverside Valley Community Garden
Rodale Pleasant Park Community Garden
Taqwa Community Farm
Tremont Community Garden
West Side Community Garden

Fall Gardens
Battery Park City
Brooklyn Botanic Garden
Bryant Park
Central Park Wildlife Center
The Conservatory Garden
The Elevated Acre
The Gardens at the Battery
The Heather Garden
The High Line
Hudson River Park
Isamu Noguchi Garden Museum
Mother Carter Garden
The New York Botanical Garden
The 91st Street Garden
Queens Botanical Garden
Snug Harbor Cultural Center and Botanical Garden
Wave Hill

Gardens for Plant Lovers

6BC Botanical Garden
Battery Park City
Brooklyn Botanic Garden
Clinton Community Garden
The Cloisters
The Conservatory Garden
The Gardens at the Battery
The Green Dome Garden
The Heather Garden
The High Line
Liz Christy Bowery-Houston Community Garden
The Narrows Botanical Gardens
The New York Botanical Garden
The 91st Street Garden
Queens Botanical Garden
Snug Harbor Cultural Center and Botanical Garden
Wave Hill

Gardens with a View

Battery Park City
Bayview Habitat
Brooklyn Heights Promenade
The Cloisters
The Conference House Park
The Elevated Acre
Erie Basin State Park
Gantry Plaza State Park
The Gardens at the Battery
The Heather Garden
The High Line

The Iris and B. Gerald Cantor Roof Garden at the
    Metropolitan Museum of Art
The Narrows Botanical Gardens
The 91st Street Garden
Red Hook Pier 41 Waterfront Garden
Swindler Cove Park
Wave Hill

Gardens with Restaurants
Battery Park City
Brooklyn Botanic Garden
Bryant Park
Central Park Wildlife Center
The Cloisters
The Gardens at the Battery
The Heather Garden
The High Line
The Metropolitan Museum of Art
The New York Botanical Garden
Wave Hill

Herb Gardens
Brooklyn Botanic Garden
Clinton Community Garden
The Cloisters
The Conference House Park
Hattie Carthan Community Garden
Queens Botanical Garden
The New York Botanical Garden
Snug Harbor Cultural Center and Botanical Garden
Wave Hill

Historic House Gardens

Bartow-Pell Mansion Museum
The Conference House Park
Dyckman Farmhouse Museum
Merchant's House Museum
Morris-Jumel Mansion
Mount Vernon Hotel Museum & Garden
Queens County Farm Museum
Stephens-Prier House at Historic Richmond Town

Indoor Gardens

Enid A. Haupt Conservatory at the New York Botanical
    Garden
The Ford Foundation
The Japan Society
The Howard A. Rusk Institute of Rehabilitation Medicine
Steinhardt Conservatory at Brooklyn Botanic Garden

Modern Gardens

Arthur Ross Terrace at the American Museum of Natural
    History
Balsley Park
Battery Park City
Bronx County Courthouse Greenroof Garden
The Elevated Acre
Erie Basin State Park
Federal Plaza
Gantry Plaza State Park
The Gardens at the Battery
Greenacre Park
The High Line

Isamu Noguchi Garden Museum
The Museum of Modern Art
Samuel Paley Plaza

Museum Gardens

Bartow-Pell Mansion Museum
The Cloisters
Cooper-Hewitt, National Design Museum, Smithsonian
    Institution
The Frick Collection
Isamu Noguchi Garden Museum
Jacques Marchais Museum of Tibetan Art
Merchant's House Museum
The Metropolitan Museum of Art
The Museum of Modern Art
Queens County Farm Museum

Native Plant Gardens

6BC Botanical Garden
Brooklyn Botanic Garden
Clinton Community Garden
The Conference House Park
Lenape Edible Estate
The Narrows Botanical Gardens
The New York Botanical Garden
Snug Harbor Cultural Center and Botanical Garden

Rock Gardens

Alpine Garden at Fort Tryon Park
Brooklyn Botanic Garden
Clinton Community Garden

The Green Dome Garden
The New York Botanical Garden
The 91st Street Garden
Sheridan Square Viewing Garden
Wave Hill
West Side Community Garden

Rooftop Gardens
Bronx County Courthouse Greenroof Garden
The Iris and B. Gerald Cantor Roof Garden at the
    Metropolitan Museum of Art
The Lotus Garden
Queens Botanical Garden

Rose Gardens
Brooklyn Botanic Garden
Queens Botanical Garden
The New York Botanical Garden
Snug Harbor Cultural Center and Botanical Garden

Sculpture Gardens
Battery Park City
Isamu Noguchi Garden Museum
The Iris and B. Gerald Cantor Roof Garden at the
    Metropolitan Museum of Art
The Museum of Modern Art
Socrates Sculpture Park

Wedding Gardens
Bartow-Pell Mansion Museum
Bronx County Courthouse Greenroof Garden

Brooklyn Botanic Garden
Queens Botanical Garden
The Conservatory Garden
The New York Botanical Garden
Shakespeare Garden
Snug Harbor Cultural Center and Botanical Garden
Wave Hill

Greening Organizations

Added Value
(718) 855-5531
www.added-value.org

Alley Pond Environmental Center
(718) 229-4000
www.alleypond.com

Brooklyn GreenBridge
(718) 623-7250
www.bbg.org/edu/greenbridge

Bronx Green-Up
(718) 817-8026
www.nybg.org/green_up

Brooklyn Greenway Initiative
(718) 522-0193
www.brooklyngreenway.org

Bronx River Alliance
(718) 430-4665
www.bronxriver.org

Central Park Conservancy
(212) 310-6600
www.centralparknyc.org

Citizens Committee for NYC
(212) 989-0909
www.citizensnyc.org

City of New York Parks and Recreation
Central Horticulture
(212) 639-9675 or 311 within NYC
www.nycgovparks.org

City Parks Foundation
(212) 360-1399
www.cityparksfoundation.org

Cornell Cooperative Extension
(212) 340-2910
www.nyc.cce.cornell.edu

The Council on the Environment of NYC
(212) 788-7900
www.cenyc.org

Earth Celebrations
The NYC Garden Preservation Coalition
(212) 777-7969
www.earthcelebrations.com

Earthpledge
(212) 725-6611
www.earthpledge.org

East New York Farms!
(718) 649-7979
www.eastnewyorkfarms.org

Greenbelt Conservancy
(718) 667-2165
www.sigreenbelt.org

Greenacre Foundation
(212) 649-5691

GreenGuerrillas
(212) 594-2155
www.greenguerillas.org

GreenThumb
(212) 788-8070
www.greenthumbnyc.org

The Horticultural Society of NY
(212) 757-0915
www.hsny.org

Just Food
(212) 645-9880
www.justfood.org

La Familia Verde
www.lafamiliaverde.org

Magnolia Tree Earth Center
(718) 387-2116
www.magnoliatreeearthcenter.org

Metro Hort Group
(212) 877-4433
www.metrohort.org

MillionTreesNYC
www.milliontreesnyc.org

More Gardens!
(718) 665-3999
www.moregardens.org

The Municipal Art Society
(212) 935-3960
www.mas.org

Neighborhood Open Space Coalition
(212) 228-3126
www.treebranch.com

NYC Audubon Society
(212) 691-7483
www.nycaudubon.org

NYC Community Garden Coalition
(212) 926-8648
www.nyccgc.org

NYC Compost Project
www.nyccompost.org

NYC Environmental Justice Alliance
(212) 239-8882
www.nyceja.org

NYC Housing Authority Gardening Program
(212) 306-3268
www.nyc.gov/html/nycha/html/community/garden.shtml

NYC Park Advocates
www.nycparkadvocates.org
(212) 987-0565

New York Restoration Project
(212) 333-2552
www.nyrp.org

New Yorkers for Parks
(212) 838-9410
www.ny4p.org/

Open Road of New York
www.playgrounddesign.blogspot.com

Park Avenue Malls Project
(212) 705-4237
www.fundforparkavenue.org

Partnership for Parks
(212) 360-1310
www.itsmypark.org

PlaNYC
www.nyc.gov/2030

Project for Public Spaces
(212) 620-5660
www.pps.org

Prospect Park Alliance
(718) 965-8951
www.prospectpark.org

Riverside Park Fund
(212) 870-3070
www.riversideparkfund.org

Staten Island Greenbelt
(718) 667-2165
www.sigreenbelt.org

Student Environmental Action Coalition
www.seac.org

Sustainable South Bronx
(646) 400-5430
www.ssbx.org

Trees New York
(212) 227-1887
www.treesny.com

The Trust for Public Land
(212) 677-7171
www.tpl.org

Waterfront Alliance
(212) 935-9831
www.waterfrontalliance.org

Wild Metro
(212) 308-9453
www.wildmetro.org

Photo Credits

Page 207 (top): Photograph of the Elevated Acre © Peter Mauss/ESTO. Courtesy of Ken Smith Landscape Architect.

Page 347: Photograph of Curtis "50 Cent" Jackson Community Garden © Jimmy Asnes. Courtesy of New York Restoration Project.

Pages 206 and 207 (bottom): Photographs of the Gardens at The Battery © Ilana Marks

All other photographs by Joseph De Sciose.

Decorative gate at 6th and B Garden (see page 226)

Index of gardens, designers, and artists

Photographs are indicated by page numbers in *italic type*.

Abramson, Mallory, 155
Amazing Garden, 297
Amster Yard, 124
Anderson & Ray, 71
Armajani, Siah, 198
Arthur Ross Terrace, American
        Museum of Natural History,
        70–72

Backyard Garden, 297–298
Balmori Associates, 299
Balsley, Thomas, 128. *See also*
        Thomas Balsley Associates
Balsley Park, 157–158
Bannerman, Isabel and Julian, 212
Bartow-Pell Mansion Museum,
        278–281, *279*
Battery Park City, 192–201
    Hudson River Esplanade, 199
    Irish Hunger Memorial, *185*,
        196–197
    North Cove Harbor, 197–198
    Rector Park, 199–200
    Rockefeller Park, 194
    South Cove, *185*, 200–201
    Teardrop Park, *185*, 194–196
    Wagner Park, *184*, 201

Baucher, David, 94
Bayview Habitat, *391*, 394–395
Berdan, Pamela, 174–176
Bertoia, Harry, 122
Bissell Gardens, 251
BKSK Architects, 351
Bogardus Triangle, 181
British Memorial Garden, Hanover
        Square, 211–213
Bronx County Courthouse
        Greenroof Garden, *233*,
        241–244, *243*
Brooklyn Bear's Community
        Gardens, 308–310
    Carlton Avenue Garden, 310
    Pacific Street Garden, 309
    Rockwell Place Garden, 309–310
Brooklyn Botanic Garden, 287,
        311–320
    Bluebell Wood, *313*
    Cherry Walk and Esplanade, 319
    Collections, 319–320
    Cranford Rose Garden, *313*,
        318–319
    Japanese Hill-and-Pond Garden,
        312, 316–318
    Osborne Garden, 283
Brooklyn Bridge Park, 293
Brooklyn Heights Promenade, 83,
        292–294
Brooklyn Public Library, Saratoga
        Branch, 326–327

Bryant Park, *4*, 83, 147–151, *148, 152, 153*
Buccioni, Enrica, 387
Bullard, Helen Elise, 46
Burton, Scott, 198
Butz, Able Bainnson, 348

Cabrini Green Urban Meadow, 298–299
Canal Park, 180–183
Caparn, Harold A., 314, 318, 320
Carles, Antonin Jean, 145
Carlton Avenue Garden, 310
Cathedral Church of St. John the Divine, 52–55
  Biblical Garden, *38*
  Pulpit Lawn, 53
Cavala Park, 182
Central Park Wildlife Center, *99*, 104–105
Chambellan, Rene Paul, 114
Child, Susan, 200
Church of St. Luke in the Fields, 178–179
Clarke, Gilmore D., 81, 83, 149
Clinton Community Garden, 154–156, *156*
Cloisters, 33–37, 137
  Bonnefont Cloister Herb Garden, 35–37, *39*
  Cuxa Cloister Garth Garden, 34–35, *39*
  Trie Cloister Garden, 37
Cobb, William, 254
Coffin, Marian Cruger, 260
Cohen, Billie, 51, 345

Columbia Street Waterfront District Community Gardens, 295–299
  Amazing Garden, 297
  Backyard Garden, 297–298
  Cabrini Green Urban Meadow, 298–299
  Human Compass, 296
  Summit Street, 296–297
Columbia University, 54
Conference House Park, 396–398
Conservatory Garden, 80–86, *82, 90, 91*
  Central Garden, 82–83
  North Garden, 83–84, *91*
  South Garden, 84–86, *85, 90*
Convent Garden, 45
Cooper, Eckstut Associates, 199. *See also* Eckstut, Stanton
Cooper-Hewitt, National Design Museum, Smithsonian Institution, 87–89, *89*
Corlett, Keith, 53–54
Corner, James. *See* James Corner Field Operations
Crawford, Stuart, 198
Creative Little Garden, *222*, 225–226
Curtis "50 Cent" Jackson Community Garden, *347*, 365–367

Dag Hammarskjold Plaza & Katherine Hepburn Garden, 126–127
Delano and Aldrich, 279, 281

Diller Scofidio + Renfro, 165
Di Suvero, Mark, 342
Dome Community Garden, 67, *291*
Doyle, Alexander, 146
Drew Gardens, 251
Duane Park, 180–183
Dyckman Farmhouse Museum,
    31–32

Eckstut, Stanton, 200. *See also*
    Cooper, Eckstut Associates
Eighth Church of Christ, Scientist
    Garden, 97
Elevated Acre, *19*, *207*, 209–210
1100 Architects, 197
Embury, Aymar, 104
Enchanted Garden, 266–268
Erie Basin State Park, 303–305
Everett, Thomas H., 261

Family Garden, 49–51
Fanning, James, 116
Farrand, Beatrix, 263–264
Farris, Julie, 298–299
Federal Plaza and City Hall Park,
    214–216
First Presbyterian Church, 171
Fischer, R. M., 199
Floyd Bennett Gardens, 328–330,
    329
Ford Foundation, 130–131
Fort Tryon Park, 28
Fort Washington Park, 28
Frick Collection, *99*, 101–103
    Courtyard Garden, 77

Friedberg, M. Paul, 128

Gantry Plaza State Park, 343–345,
    346, 348
Garden of Happiness, 250–251
Gardens at the Battery, 202–205,
    206, *207*, 208
General Theological Seminary,
    141–143
George Hecht Viewing Garden, 227
George Washington Carver
    Community Garden, 100
Golden Swan, 177
Goldsworthy, Andy, 200
Gramercy Park, 138–140
Greeley Square, 144–146
Greenacre Park, *109*, 123–124
Green Dome Garden, 288–291,
    324, 325
Gustafson, Kathryn, 71

Haeg, Fritz, 163
Hamilton, Anne, 195
Hancock, Ralph, 114
Hanna/Olin, 199. *See also* Olin,
    Laurie
Hattie Carthan Community
    Garden, 321–323
Heather Garden, 23, 40–43, *43*
Heinz, Judith, 70
Herald Square, 144–146, *153*
Herrington, Arthur, 279–280
Highbridge Park, 28
High Line, *159*, 162–165, *164*, *166*,
    167, 168–169

Hobhouse, Penelope, 257
Hood, Walter, 365
Howard A. Rusk Institute of
    Rehabilitation Medicine,
    135–137
Howells and Stokes, 53
Hudson River Esplanade, 199
Hudson River Park, 188–191
Human Compass, 296
Hunters Point Community Park,
    345

Innocenti-Webel, 199
Ireys, Alice, 107, 315
Irish Hunger Memorial, *185*,
    196–197
Isamu Noguchi Garden Museum,
    335, 340–342

Jacques Marchais Museum of
    Tibetan Art, 388–389, *390*
James Corner Field Operations,
    165, 375
Japan Society, 127–128
Jefferson Market Garden, 173–174
Johansson, Sonja, 137
Johnson, Philip, 116–117

Kapoor, Anish, 113, 212
Kelly, Bruce, 74, 75
Ken Smith Landscape Architect,
    209
Kevin Roche John Dinkeloo and
    Associates, 105

Kiley, Dan, 130
Koons, Jeff, 113

LaGuardia Corner Gardens, 230
Lee Weintraub Landscape
    Architecture, 303, 343. *See
    also* Weintraub, Lee
Lenape Edible Estate, 163
Linville, Anne Warner, 61
Liz Christy Bowery-Houston
    Community Garden, 221,
    223, 224
Lolup, Wopo, 204
Long Island City Community
    Garden, 344
Loring, John, 51
Lotus Garden, 60–62
Lower East Side Community
    Gardens, 219–228
  Creative Little Garden, *222*,
    225–226
  Liz Christy Bowery-Houston
    Community Garden, 221,
    223, 224
  9th Street Community Garden
    and Park, 228
  Parque de Tranquilidad, 224–225
  Plaza Cultural de Armando
    Perez, 227–228
  6th and B Garden, 226
  Sol Brillante, 223

Machado, Rodolfo, 201
Madison Square Park, 150
Marchais, Jacques, 388–389

Mary's Garden, 128–129
Mathews Nielsen Landscape
        Architects, 190. *See also*
        Nielsen, Signe
Maynard, Penelope, 86
McCarren Park, 290
McKim, Mead and White, 203, 314
Merchant's House Museum,
        229–231
Mercil, Michael, 195
Merrick Marsden Community
        Garden, 347, 368–369
Metropolitan Museum of Art,
        92–95
    Astor Court, 92–95
    Iris and B. Gerald Cantor Roof
        Garden, 95
M'Finda Kalunga Garden, 217–218
Michael Van Valkenburgh
        Associates, 190–191,
        194, 293. *See also* Van
        Valkenburgh, Michael
Milder, Avigail, 288
Miller, Lynden B., 42, 54, 61, 81,
        85, 87, 100, 150, 191, 201,
        256–257, 302
Minetta Green, 176
Minetta Triangle, 176
Miss, Mary, 200
Morris-Jumel Mansion, 44–46
Mother Carter Garden, 363–364
Mould, Jacob Wray, 215
Mount Vernon Hotel Museum and
        Garden, 106–107
M. Paul Friedberg & Associates,
        210. *See also* Friedberg,
        M. Paul

Murbach, Dave, 112
Museum of Modern Art, 116–117,
        120
    Abby Aldrich Rockefeller
        Sculpture Garden, *119*

Narrows Botanical Gardens,
        331–333
New York Botanical Garden, 137,
        252–265
    Benenson Ornamental Conifers,
        257, 260
    Collections, 264–265
    Enid A. Haupt Conservatory,
        254–256, *255*
    Everett Children's Adventure
        Garden, 265
    Home Gardening Center,
        260–261
    Jane Watson Irwin Perennial
        Garden, 256–257, *258*
    Nancy Bryan Luce Herb Garden,
        257
    Native Plant Garden, 262–263
    Peggy Rockefeller Rose Garden,
        263–264
    Rock Garden, 261–262
    Ross Conifer Arboretum, 257,
        260
New York Times Garden, 149
New York Vietnam Veterans Plaza,
        210
Nielsen, Signe, 182
9th Street Community Garden and
        Park, 228
91st Street Garden, 63–64

Noguchi, Isamu, 340–342
North Cove Harbor, 197–198

Oberlander, Cornelia Hahn, 149
Oehme, van Sweden and
    Associates, 194, 263
Olin, Laurie, 150, 201. *See also*
    Hanna/Olin
Olin Partners, 204
Olmsted, Frederick Law, 314, 317
Olmsted, Frederick Law, Jr., 40,
    103
100 United Nations Plaza, 129
Otterness, Tom, 194
Oudolf, Piet, 168, 204–205, 208

Pacific Street Garden, 309
Page, Russell, 101–103
Park Avenue Malls, *21*, 96–97,
    98, 100
Parque de Tranquilidad, 224–225
Parsons, Samuel, Jr., 180–182
Pelham Bay Park, 281
Perless, Robert, 137
Phillips, Roger, 100
Pier 41 Waterfront Garden, 301–
    302, *304*, *325*
Plaza Cultural de Armando Perez,
    227–228
Pleasant Village Community
    Garden, 49–51, *50*
Polshek Partnership Architects,
    71, 311
Price, Thomas Drees, 81
Price, Warrie, 204

Prospect Park, 317
Puryear, Martin, 170–171, 198

Queens Botanical Garden, 339,
    349–355, *350*, *353*
   Administration Building, 359
   Cherry Circle, 358
   Wedding Garden, 359
Queens County Farm Museum,
    356–357, 360
Quennell Rothschild and Partners,
    143
Quinn, Edmond T., 140

Rainforest Garden, Patterson
    Houses, 238–240
Rector Park, 199–200
Red Hook Community Farm,
    305–307
Red Hook Gardens, 300–307
   Erie Basin State Park, 303–305
   Pier 41 Waterfront Garden,
     301–302, *304*, *325*
   Red Hook Community Farm,
     305–307
Riverside-Inwood Neighborhood
    Garden (RING), 32
Riverside Valley Community
    Garden, 47–48
Roche, Kevin John Dinkeloo and
    Associates. *See* Kevin
    Roche John Dinkeloo and
    Associates
Rockefeller Center, 112–115, *118*
Rockefeller Park, 194

Rockwell Place Garden, 309–310
Rodale Pleasant Park Community
        Garden, 49–51
Rogers Marvel Architects, 209

Samuel Paley Plaza, *119*, 121–122
Saratoga Associates, 205
Sasaki, Hideo, 123
Sasaki Associates, 190
Schermerhorn, Richard, Jr., 87
Schwartz, Martha, 214
Second Cemetery of the Spanish
        and Portuguese Synagogue,
        Shearith Israel, 171
Serra, Richard, 214
Shakespeare Garden, *68*, *69*,
        73–75, *74*
Shaw, Ellen Eddy, 315
Sheridan Square Viewing Garden,
        175–177
Shiota, Takeo, 316
Shipman, Ellen Biddle, 257, 280
Silvetti, Jorge, 201
Simpson, Lusby, 148, 150
Sir Winston Churchill Park, 177
6BC Botanical Garden, 226–227
6th and B Garden, 226
Smith, Ken. *See* Ken Smith
        Landscape Architect
Smith, Mary Riley, 87
Snug Harbor Cultural Center and
        Botanical Garden, 376–387
    Connie Gretz's Secret Garden, 386
    Healing Garden, 386
    Heritage Rose Garden, 381
    Lions' Sensory Garden, 382–383

New York Chinese Scholar's
        Garden, *379*, 383–386, *391*
    Perennial Garden and Carl Grillo
        Glass House, 381–382
    Pond Garden, 380–381
    Richmond County Savings
        Foundation's Tuscan
        Garden, 386–387
    White Garden, 382
    World Trade Center Educational
        Tribute Center, *371*
Socrates Sculpture Park, 341
Sol Brillante, *223*
Sonfist, Alan, 230
South Cove, *185*, 200–201
Sprout, M. Betty, 81
Stephens-Prier House, Historic
        Richmond Town, 392–393
St. John the Divine. *See* Cathedral
        Church of St. John the
        Divine
St. Luke in the Fields. *See* Church
        of St. Luke in the Fields
Strawberry Fields, 75
Stufano, Marco Polo, 271, 274
Sullivan, Richard, 343
Summit Street, 296–297
Swindler Cove Park, 26–30
    Jonathan's Pond, 29

Taqwa Community Farm, 245–246
Teardrop Park, *185*, 194–196
Thomas Balsley Associates, 158,
        343, 345. *See also* Balsley,
        Thomas
Time Landscape, 230

Tolle, Brian, 197
Tremont Community Garden,
    247–249
Trump World Tower Garden, 129
Tudor City Greens, 132–134

United Nations Neighborhood
    Gardens, 83, 125–129
  Dag Hammarskjold Plaza &
    Katherine Hepburn Garden,
    126–127
  Japan Society, 127–128
  Mary's Garden, 128–129

Van Valkenburgh, Michael, 170.
    See also Michael Van
    Valkenburgh Associates
Varnell, David, 74
Vaux, Calvert, 180–182, 317
Vellonakis, George, 127, 177
Vera List Courtyard, 170–172, 172
Verity, Simon, 212–213
Veterans Memorial Garden, 361–362
Vollmer Associates, 199

Walcavage, Donna, 137
Wagner Park, 184, 201
Washington Market Park, 186–187
Wave Hill, 237, 269–277
  Flower Garden, 272, 274–275
  Monocot Garden, 273
  Wild Garden, 273, 275–277
Weintraub, Lee, 303, 305. See also
    Lee Weintraub Landscape
    Architecture
Weintraub and di Domenico, 186
Welch, Alexander McMillan, 32
West Side Community Garden, 57,
    65–67, 69
White, Hank, 149
Wittwer-Laird, Gail, 182, 197
Wright, John, 288

Yarkoni, Amir, 288
Yellin, Samuel, 102–103

Zimmerman, Elyn, 182
Zion, Robert, 117, 121, 128
Zopi, Mariella, 387